The
WHITE COLLAR WORKING CLASS

From Structure to Politics

Richard Sobel

Foreword by
Martin Oppenheimer

PRAEGER

New York
Westport, Connecticut
London

Library of Congress Cataloging-in-Publication Data

Sobel, Richard.
   The white collar working class : from structure to politics /
Richard Sobel.
        p.   cm.
   Bibliography: p.
   Includes index.
   ISBN 0-275-93026-2 (alk. paper)
   1. White collar workers — United States.   2. Social classes — United
States.   3. United States — Economic conditions — 1981-   4. United
States — Social conditions — 1980-   5. Proletariat.   I. Title.
HD8039.M4U575   1989
305.5'56'0973 — dc19   88-38720

Library of Congress Catalog Card Number: 88-38720
ISBN: 0-275-93026-2

First published in 1989

Praeger Publishers, One Madison Avenue, New York, NY 10010
A division of Greenwood Press, Inc.

Printed in the United States of America

The paper used in this book complies with the
Permanent Paper Standard issued by the National
Information Standards Organization (Z39.48-1984).

10 9 8 7 6 5 4 3 2 1

For Betty Debs and Walter Howard Sobel

At the anniversaries of their schools

Contents

Tables

Figures

Foreword

For a very long time, social scientists in the United States contributed little of either theoretical interest or empirical substance on the subject of the "middle classes." In marked contrast, by the end of the nineteenth century, major political figures in Western Europe, particularly Germany, generated intense discussion, buttressed by whatever social scientific data were available at the time. The central concerns were the current realities and potential trajectories of class structure and class politics. Particular attention focused on the rise of the "new middle class" of white collar employees.

The reason for this interest, which continues unabated in West Germany, France, Britain, Sweden, and Italy, has been the widely held view that appealing to the middle class is the key to political success in a parliamentary democracy. The main political question is still whether the masses of white collar employees are really working class, and hence susceptible to an appeal from the left. The contrary view is that their lot in life distinguishes white collar workers from the working class, and gives them a different set of interests. Consequently, any political approach to white collar workers must be distinctly different from the historical class appeals of the left.

In the United States both this discussion and substantiating research were absent. It was not until 1935 that two serious works on the subject appeared: Lewis Corey's Marxist analysis, *The Crisis of the Middle Class,* and Alfred M. Bingham's neglected political tract, *Insurgent America.* The works of several German exiles, highly empirical by the standards of that time, were virtually ignored, though some of Hans Speier's book was published in English translation by the W.P.A. After Corey, no major work on the subject appeared in the United States until C. Wright Mills' *White Collar* in 1951. Then a virtual social scientific vacuum existed until the movements of the 1960s generated new interest in the question of who shall be the agents of social change.

By the early 1970s, veterans of the student movement and the new left had entered academia. One of their tasks as critics of establishment social science was to dissect the prevailing theories of the embourgeoisement of the working class, and the theses of the "end of ideology." Although these initial discussions took place mainly in the pages of relatively unknown radical journals, a set of younger left-oriented scholars gradually began to make their weight felt in wider circles. Other young scholars coming from a left perspective were working in related fields, particularly on political topics such as theories of the State. These scholars began to constitute a "critical mass" (in both senses of critical) for increasingly serious and important work.

In recent years, the discussion of the class position and political trajectories of the middle classes has achieved a level of sophistication undreamed of by pioneers such as Corey and Mills. One has but to mention Braverman, Carchedi, Ehrenreich and Ehrenreich, Giddens, Poulantzas, and Erik Wright, and the debates around their work to recognize how far we have come theoretically and empirically in the past ten to fifteen years. (See, for example, the symposium in *Critical Sociology* vol. 15, no. 1, Spring, 1988). Positivist criticisms of such work--for instance, that Wright's *Classes* (1985) does not have "contact with the world" (that is, no numbers) until well into the work--misses the essence of such scholarship: a foundation of richly developed theoretical reflections on class and politics informed by empirical investigation.

This is the context in which to place Richard Sobel's work. The issues he ultimately addresses remain central for both scholars and political strategists: what are the connections between class and politics? Put in more empirically testable terms, what dimensions of class membership seem most relevant in developing class consciousness and class-based political behavior among workers in new occupations that diverge from the traditional blue collar working class? The general question has plagued serious thinkers for more than 200 years, and the more specific one for the hundred years since the "class" of white collar workers began to develop.

Sobel's quest follows the path taken by the pioneers in this field. It begins with an examination of the actual class situation of the white collar strata in an effort to separate speculation from real conditions. This approach contrasts with that which dismisses the notion of class altogether, or pretends that class is of decreasing significance. In the final analysis, the author comes down on the side of those who see the vast mass of white collar workers as members of the working class: wage-earners, mostly non-supervisory, with a sizeable minority completely proletarianized in deskilled jobs lacking any significant authority or decision making.

More importantly, the book puts together the evidence to support this thesis. The study therefore serves, first, as an important corrective to some of the more obscurantist discussions within Marxist circles that edge away from a definition of class that is based on objective structural conditions and relationships. And second it serves as a factually rooted answer to mainstream sociologists who pursue narrow studies of "stratification," avoiding the nasty conclusion that there are classes that stand objectively opposed to one another in the modern world of political and economic struggles.

The book provides a solid empirical basis for the argument that "'the new middle class' of white collar employees is not a separate class, . . . but part of the stratified working class." Here the notion of "proletarianization" enters the picture. Departing from writers whose general definitions are insufficiently helpful, Sobel breaks the term into various types, each of which he submits to rigorous empirical analysis. His conclusion is that at least on the dimension involving declining autonomy, proletarianization does not appear to be taking place. That leaves us with the gnarly issue of political behavior. What can history expect from these strata?

The "exceptionalism" of the American situation and the range of reasons for it (see Mike Davis, *Prisoners of the American Dream,* 1986; Reeve Vanneman and Lynn Weber Cannon, *The American Perception of Class,* 1987; and Chapter 2 of my *White Collar Politics,* 1985) make it impossible to make a definitive answer. Americans ought to know better than anyone that we cannot generalize. Union membership is higher virtually everywhere else in the Western world. So is participation in elections. So is class-based voting. The book rightly steers clear of promising final answers, choosing instead a parsimonious approach that gives particular strength to its conceptualizations and suggests paths for future inquiry.

The book also reminds us, however, of the considerable evidence that active involvement in work leads to more participation in wider politics. If some polarization in the dimension of working conditions tied to authority is now taking place, what does this imply for political participation? Here the final chapter points to a provocative path for future research, especially regarding the relationship between the world of white collar work and the political involvement of white collar workers. The book makes a contribution to the understanding of social class and political behavior in the United States. In doing so, it deserves the close attention of scholars everywhere concerned with the present and the future realities of class and politics.

Martin Oppenheimer
Rutgers University

Preface

Like "the white collar people" in C. Wright Mills's classic study, this book slips quietly into the modern literature on work and politics, aspiring to great accomplishments. In addressing central social and political debates about white collar labor, the work has undertaken four tasks. First, it identifies white collar class situation as largely working class. Second, it outlines a system of structural stratification within the white collar working class. Third, it clarifies the proletarianization questions for white collar labor. And fourth, it suggests the political consequences of structural class and white collar work.

In attempting to advance the recurrent debates about these issues, the book elaborates an economic model of class that is parsimonious in a theoretical sense. That simple structural model and a related model of complex within-class stratification also serve as bases for investigating proletarianization and in elucidating political outcomes. The work does not prove that economic class is the "correct" definition of class, but argues for this conception in its power, parsimony, and robustness in clarifying class analysis, structural change, and political action. To address theoretical issues and contribute to their empirical investigation, the book defines imprecise concepts like proletarian worker in structural terms and identifies proletarianization as a series of differentiated processes. The combination of traditional and marxian social and political analyses with empirical investigation seeks a provocative synthesis.

The structural identification and analysis of class both draw on various traditions and establish a basis for the "action" of the book. That action lies in demonstrating the motion of the white collar working class in terms of both proletarianization and political involvement. The structural forces underlying white collar politics also coincide with classic questions in democratic theory and political participation. Those skeptical of the economic approach to class analysis might take the structural definition as a point of departure and follow its developments sequentially in the theoretical and empirical explorations of class situation and political outcomes. Those sharing a more political bent might begin with the final chapter.

The book selectively addresses recent controversies. The theoretical discussions reflect Erik Olin Wright's earlier political formulation of contradictory class locations (1980) more than the recent crossnational focus (1985) on exploitation as the basis of class relations. The empirical investigation does, however, incorporate Wright's more current concerns about proletarianization in the U.S. (Wright and Singlemann, 1982; Wright and Martin, 1987). The study also briefly explores issues of gender stratification of white collar labor, and recognizes a centrally located role for women in social transformation. It does not, however, fully address feminist issues and research that, along with women in white collar work, have gained increasing prominence in the 1980s (cf. Crompton and Jones, 1984).

White collar authors write books but not under circumstances chosen by them. Originally this project envisioned two books, the first on white collar work and class, and the second on class and politics. Because the integration of the two topics seemed essential in a timely manner, and progress on another project required further attention, outlines of both volumes have been compressed into a single book concentrating on white collar work and suggesting its political ramifications. As in greater works, this may create an impression of rather abstract systematizing. But the book accomplishes its main purpose of clarifying the basic theory and class scheme, and investigating them currently, across time, and in relationship to political involvements.

Because reality and measurement have changed as this study proceeded, it has become more difficult to identify the important social phenomenon of white collar labor: White collar and blue collar are becoming more similar. White collar and blue collar are also no longer identifiable Census categories. Because fundamental change is sometime imperceptible, a half century hence the white collar/blue collar distinctions may have totally blurred. Recognition of white collar as a separate designation may slip from social consciousness just when white collar people become a political force.

The investigation of work and politics is also difficult because national surveys rarely include both topics. Though sociologists study work, and political scientists study politics, few social analysts investigate both empirically on a national scale. Yet investigations like the last chapter's exploration of a complex theory of congruent formality from work to politics require a large number of survey items in each sphere. While good fortune made it possible to include a series of questions on the 1985 Pilot to the American National Election Study, it was not possible to include a revised set on a larger survey. Even Erik Wright's important "Comparative Project on Class Structure and Class Consciousness" carefully measures the topics of its title but contains little on political participation.

As the modern standard for white collar analysis distinguishes between "liberal [and] marxian interpretations" (Mills, 1959, p. 167), this study draws upon the distinctions between traditional and marxian interpretations of work and politics, and between Marxist and marxian approaches. Marxist analysis suggests an adherence to more orthodox principles, while marxian analysis more currently draws from and critiques Marx's insights into structural class and politics. Uncapitalized "marxian," like "plain" marxist, suggests the drawing of appropriate insights without following a particular ideological approach. Traditional sociology and political science that understand class as socioeconomic status and consider white collar as middle class might well include structural features in their analyses. Marxian approaches that largely avoid multidimensional stratification within class might well incorporate structural differentiation within class analysis. Theorists of both the Marxist and traditional schools are sure to question both the theory and the attempt to address it empirically. The arguments here that draw from the insights of previous and contemporary scholars should generate further argument (cf. Katznelson, 1981) both by others and the author who hopes to to extend the analysis at an auspicious point.

This book could not have been completed without the help of friends and colleagues. Herbert Gintis contributed to the study in encouraging what he considered significant scholarship to reemerge as a book. Martin Oppenheimer's willingness to write a Foreword after critiquing the manuscript helped create perspective on the exploration. Oppenheimer's, Erik Wright's, and Kenneth Spenner's citation of earlier research in their provocative studies motivated the publication of the now revised source work for wider investigation. Dennis Breslin's research assistance and sometimes dissenting sociological insights helped sharpen the arguments and bring forth a revised presentation. Jameson Doig and Donald Stokes encouraged the investigation of the political consequences of work. The comments at various points by Nancy Andes, Samuel Bowles, Patrick Coby, Heinz Eulau, Gene Fisher, Michael Greenebaum, Steve Slaby, Steven Vallas, James Wright, and C. Ernesto Zirakzadeh helped in clarifying the arguments. The University of Connecticut, the Five College Partnership, the Picker Fellowship at Smith College, Princeton University, and the Woodrow Wilson School provided essential support for the research enterprise. Among those many who have my appreciation, Jon Biller, Keith Bradford, Alison Bricken, Zahid Bukhari, Lawrence Davis, Carol Evans, Kevin Hartzell, Sarah Hollister, Roxie Mack, Jimmy Nguyen, Lauren Pera, Steven Rosenstone, and Tom Smith made it possible to share this work with others. As scholarly, like social, progress is both an individual and cooperative enterprise, the propositions and omissions from this minor opus for which I am responsible will hopefully prod both scholars and white collars to extend the debates that inspired this work.

The
WHITE COLLAR
WORKING CLASS

1 White Collar and Class

INTRODUCTION

Because white collar looms large as a social phenomenon, it invites ever renewed attention to its character and significance. The prominence of white collar today derives in large part from both its magnitude in the labor force and its traditional aura of professionalism and independence. Since World War II, as white collar labor has expanded from a third to over half of the labor force, so has its portion working for wages and salaries grown from under 80 percent to over 90 percent. At the same time, white collar independence has declined as its self-employed fraction has dropped from more than one in five to less than one in ten. Still, white collar labor encompasses a diversity of professional, managerial, clerical, and sales occupations that have traditionally involved status distinctions from the rest of the labor force. Commonly considered the epitome of the "middle class," professionals and managers have long provided the image and allure for all white collar people. But today the white collar realities are more predominantly those of clerical and sales employees in what C. Wright Mills called the "enormous file" and "great salesroom." Many white collar employees today are in similar class and work situations to those of blue collar workers.

The heterogeneous nature of white collar labor becomes clearer through the intersection of occupation and class. Class in an economic sense, particularly allied with internal authority relations, provides a basis for the specification of the structure of white collar labor. The structural approach to class also provides a way to analyze changes both in white collar class situation and in within-class stratification over time. In addition, structural class analysis identifies consequences in the political realm that the structural aspects of class engender among white collar labor.

Crucial similarities between white collar and blue collar labor become apparent, moreover, when class and occupation are distinguished. Occupation embodies technical relations of work, the tasks done in the job, the part played in the technical division of labor. Class involves common relations to ownership of productive resources, machinery, and processes. Class crosscuts the occupational division of labor: each occupation may be divided into different classes. White collar is not the same as middle class. White collar labor may be part middle class and part working class. Certain white collar occupations such as lawyer are typically considered middle class because of the high concentration of self-employed, but lawyers who own and run large law firms differ significantly from lawyers employed in corporate legal departments. Similarly, blue collar is not the same as working class. Blue collar labor may be part working class and part middle class. Certain blue collar occupations such as laborers (or white collar occupations such as clericals) tend to be working class because they are so largely composed of employees. But those coincidences derive from the intersection of occupation and class, not from the definition of class by occupation. In essence, white collar and blue collar do not represent "horizontal" class differences; instead "vertical" class distinctions divide both white collar and blue collar occupations.

This analysis challenges the middle class image of white collar labor. The investigation draws upon both traditional and marxian perspectives on class, stratification, and politics. The approach combines the unidimensional economic definition of class with the multidimensional identification of within-class stratification based on the labor process, authority relations and conditions of work. The research demonstrates that most white collar labor is working class. It demonstrates that within the working class, there are patterns of stratification derived from the realities of the workplace. This analysis underscores the primacy of the economic realm for defining and explaining class. But it also brings multidimensional, within-class stratification to the marxian paradigm. The traditional sociological use of education, income, occupation, and prestige to define class, and the marxian use of political and ideological criteria for class definition (Poulantzas, 1973; Wright, 1977) both misidentify the basis for class. Each, however, suggests important foundations both for the analysis of stratification within economic class and for the generation of political activity among white collar employees.

CONCEPTIONS OF CLASS

In general, class involves common structural relations to ownership of productive resources. The variety of approaches to the idea of class, however, lead to the notion of class as an essentially contested concept (Calvert, 1982). The usefulness of the concept of class is undeniable, however, in analyzing how social and economic inequality are systematically produced and maintained. Even among marxian theorists, however, there are competing general conceptions of class: class as the states of consciousness among individuals (Poulantzas, 1975; Vallas, 1987), class as collective actors in contention (Thompson, 1963; Przeworski, 1977), and class as structural relationships and locations based on objective criteria (Poulantzas, 1973; Wright, 1978). This study adopts the approach that explicates class as economic and objective structural conditions and relationships within which social actors contend (see especially Wright, 1980; Burris, 1987; and Katznelson, 1981, for overlapping or alternative conceptions of class). These structural conditions are interrelated with the fundamental and enduring dependence of all social actors in capitalism on private property and the production of wealth, and the political and economic power that productive property affords (cf. Przeworski, 1985). Economic class is not the only conception of class, but it involves a powerful yet parsimonious definition. The logic of economic and structural class carries through in the social and political theoretical arguments and empirical analysis this study represents.

Without entering into a full discussion of economic class, a few points need to be explicated at the outset. First, the central power of the economic definition lies in its relational and structural qualities. Economic classes exist in relations with each other. Following from the relational definition are both the justification for economic class in the antagonism between classes over resources and power, and the outlines of the internal structure, and hence stratification, within classes. In essence, the differences between classes are mapped into the differentiations within classes. Ownership both defines and structures one's relationship to the means of production. The Marxist tradition defines "[c]apitalists [as] owners of the means of social production and employers of wage-labourers" (Marx, 1978, p. 473). Also the Weberian tradition recognizes that "[o]wnership . . . confers certain fundamental capacities of command" (Giddens, 1973, p. 108). Within the capitalist sphere, ownership implies domination while nonownership implies dependence. Ownership also implies exploitation while nonownership implies being exploited. Although class does not simply determine outcomes, the consequences of class encompass the range of likelihood of undertaking and experiencing domination and exploitation.

Neither domination nor exploitation, however, defines class in the ways Wright (1980) or Roemer's (1982) would propose. Domination and authority relations within the labor process, as the critique in Chapter 2 maintains, do not create different classes. They do not constitute the external bases for class; rather they establish the internal bases for stratification within the working class. Exploitation, moreover, is not an essential element for identifying class; it is a sufficient but not a necessary condition for being working class (cf. Bowles and Gintis, 1986, p. 23). If one is exploited, one is working class. But some unexploited and unproductive government employees and some only partially exploited and partially productive commercial employees are working class by virtue of nonownership.

Economic and structural class also establish interests that contribute to the antagonisms between classes. Ownership and its absence structure different interests over resources. Those interests are reinforced by the conflict over the control of resources that exploitation relations imply; interests are also reinforced by the conflict that authority relations generate. But interests do not themselves establish class. Interests are political consequences of class relations--class agents must formulate interests in collective action.

The economic nature of class in capitalism lies in the relations to ownership or nonownership of private productive property. "[A]ccording to the traditional interpretations of class structure, including those of Marx and Weber, 'class' is a phenomenon of production" (Giddens, 1973, p. 109). Capitalist production generates two distinct economic classes: owners and nonowners, capitalists and workers, bourgeoisie and proletariat. A capitalist class exists in a dominant and exploitative relationship with a subordinate class of workers. The working class depends for its livelihood on the production and material resources owned and controlled by capitalists. In these relations of production, capital is dominant and labor subordinate. A class of the self-employed who are simple commodity producers also exists, but it is outside the dominant mode of capitalist production. These petty producers or independents within the *petty bourgeoisie* are "self-employed producers who own their means of production and employ no labor of others" (Wright and Singlemann, 1982, p. S181); their existence is constantly threatened by the dynamics of capitalist development. Regarding capital ownership, both small employers and independents are petty bourgeoisie. Together they constitute a marxian "middle class" (distinct from the traditional sociological "middle class" based on occupation, income, or education, but overlapping somewhat in self-employment.)

Production relations as the basis of class involve a systemic conflict in the generation of wealth. "The analysis of the economic class structure, in terms of property relations," as Cottrell remarks, "serves to identify what is 'at stake' in political struggles in the long run (that is, the maintenance or transformation of the given pattern of possession of/separation from the means of production)" (1984, p. 4). Capitalists seek to maintain their monopoly of control over investment decisions, and to reduce labor costs, through technological rationalization or by dequalifying skilled labor. They also seek to appropriate surplus value and surplus labor in order to maintain their positions of privilege. Salaried or wage-earning employees, who depend on wage work, seek discretion and autonomy, and militate to bend the wage bargain to their advantage. Economic inequality produces differences in life chances and interests associated with the distribution of wealth, income, jobs, prestige, health, and knowledge. Fundamentally, class relations confer power: "social actors who dominate the prevailing material conditions are endowed with a corresponding power which is denied to those who do not" (Barbalet, 1986, p. 564). The reality that the even small owner "enjoys directive control of an enterprise, however minute, acts to distinguish him from those who are part of a hierarchy of authority in a larger organization" (Giddens, 1973, p. 110). Actors exist in relationships to structures of class relations, based on employment relationships. Those structures produce limitations and opportunities for the activities, preferences, and interests of individuals and groups. Class based on direct access to productive property and the means of production empowers the determination of "the nature and availability of jobs, the economic security of those employed in them, and the quality and prices of the means of life" (Barbalet, 1986, p. 565). This power determines who will suffer the dull compulsion to enter the labor market and who will purchase the labor of others. Identifying what is at stake in class differences in the power that property and capital afford illuminates the "gross processes of the dynamics of society and the changing bases of conditions out of which class differences arise" (p. 565).

Ownership of a significant amount of productive capital organizes possibilities that are qualitatively different from those available to the working class. Even small amounts of productive capital structure opportunities in distinctively different ways for owners than for the bulk of employees. Productive wealth establishes for owners actualities or potentials for advancement and action that are totally withheld from the vast majority of the labor force. Conversely, nonownership imposes basic constraints on the working class. A fundamental similarity among members of the working class is that, as nonowners, their lack of productive capital demonstrably structures and circumscribes their opportunities. A few exceptional cases among employees do not diminish the basic constraints that nonownership imposes on the working class. Nor does the differentiation within the working class obscure the fundamental similarity.

The unity of class also exists in the antagonisms between economically conflicting classes, not necessarily in homogeneity or shared interests within classes. The distinctions that have conventionally equated white collar to middle class and blue collar to working class are hardly greater than the divisions within blue collar labor. Labor "aristocrats" like craftworkers, for example, differ greatly from industrial laborers, yet both are in the working class. Asserting the primacy of economic class implies that the fundamental cleavage lies between employers and employees, not between the different strata within the working class.

Asserting a basic unity in nonownership, however, does not deny that significant differences do occur within the working class. As Freedman has argued, at the same time that the working class "has grown to include the overwhelming majority of . . . the population it has also been split into many divisions which have emerged from the material needs of capitalism as it has developed historically" (1975, p. 76). Among white collar labor, significant status distinctions based on educational credentials and organizational responsibilities reinforce the sense of privilege and superiority over manual, blue collar labor (cf. Derber, 1982). "The white-collar category . . . get[s] its occupational flavor from the engineers, managers, and professors at the top of the hierarchy, while its impressive numerical masses are supplied by the millions of clerical workers. . ." (Braverman, 1974, p. 350). Behind the badges of prestige that professionals are accorded, however, there are new forms of work organization, organizational and occupational hierarchies, external labor markets, a gender and race system, all of which restrict recruitment and advantage, most prominently for clerical workers, but also for professional and technical workers (Edwards, 1979; Hill, 1982). Labor market and work conditions, in particular, are structural divisions that create class fractions within the working class, and provide foundations for stratification. Basing class structure on ownership relations means that the "new middle class" of white collar employees is not a separate class, or in contradictory locations between classes, but part of the stratified working class. The economic definition of class is, then, both simple and powerful, and promotes the analysis of both divisions between and within classes. Division based on economic ownership creates differences of kind. Differences in degree produce stratification.

CLASS AS STRUCTURE

The structural definitions of class and subclass derive from Marx, but also draw regarding within-class stratification from the paradigms of modern social analysts. Identifying exactly what Marx meant by class is complex since virtually all his writings discuss class, but none undertakes a systematic review of the subject (cf. Dahrendorf, 1959, Ch. 1; Giddens, 1973, Ch. 1). While generally consistent, his definitions of class differ in various sources. The last chapter of

Capital III contains an unfinished discussion of class. Another section of *Capital III* approximates a basic definition of class.

> The specific economic form in which unpaid surplus labor is pumped out of the immediate producers determines the relation of domination and subjection as it grows directly out of and in turn determines production. On this is based the whole structure of the economic community as it comes forth from the relations of production, and thereby at the same time its political structure. It is always the immediate relations of the owners of the conditions of production to the immediate producers--a relation whose specific pattern of course always corresponds to a certain stage in the development of labor and its social forces of production--in which we find the final secret, the hidden basis of the whole construction of society, including the political patterns of sovereignty and dependence, in short, of a given specific form of government. (Marx in Dahrendorf, 1959, p. 13)

More simply put in *A Contribution to the Critique of Political Economy*, class refers to a "specific type of production, and of relations of production, which determines rank and influence of all other activities" (Marx in Dahrendorf, 1959, p. 15). Class is a relational and aggregate phenomenon. "[I]ndividuals are dealt with only in so far as they are the personifications of economic categories, embodiments of particular class-relations and class-interests" (Marx, 1967a, pp. 19-20). More precisely,

> classes are large groups of people which differ from each other by the place they occupy in a historically determined system of social production, by their relations (in most cases fixed and formulated by law) to the means of production, by their role in the social organization of labor, and, consequently, by the dimensions and methods of acquiring the share of social wealth of which they dispose. (Lenin, 1947, p. 492)

In the Marxist tradition, class is a structural and relational phenomenon. It refers to commonly held positions in the social structure of accumulation (Gordon, Edwards, and Reich, 1982), and a particular class exists only in relation to others. The main structuring principle behind class is economic. At the "highest level of abstraction," the pure capitalist mode of production, class involves only capital versus labor. From ownership relations and the structuring nature of production flow the class organizational structure of employers and workers. The economic level, or "base," is fundamental.

At a lower level of abstraction of "social formation," political and ideological factors come into play. They do not, however, fundamentally change economically determined class situation. The political and ideological levels of the superstructure are secondary. This does not mean, however, that the economic level causes all other aspects. "A more appropriate reading of the expression 'base' and 'superstructure' is that the base, like the foundation of a building, determines the limits of the variation of the superstructure, not that it defines all aspects of the superstructure" (Wright, 1976, p. 2).

> The economic level plays a determining role in shaping the political and ideological levels of social structure. . . . Within the economic level, social

relations of production play a determining role with respect to both exchange relations and technical relations. (p. 2)

The economic level outlines the limits of variation. That the economic level has a "determining role" in shaping both class and the other levels does not mean that the economic level causes the other levels. The process is not deterministic, it is dialectic; there is an interplay among factors: but one--production--is central. It energizes and also limits the others. "To say that the social relations of production play a determining role in shaping exchange relations . . . means that the social relations of production *determine* the limits within which the exchange relations can vary" (Wright, 1976, p. 17, emphasis in original). Within those limits, political and ideological relations may vary in relatively autonomous ways. This makes it possible for the other levels to have an impact on the social relations of production, to some degree, to overdetermine class. Yet the economic remains primary in defining class.

Significant variation, moreover, occurs within classes on the political and ideological planes. "Viewed historically, this means that the process of structural determination at the present is a consequence of the dialectical interaction of base and superstructure, production and exchange, social relations and technical relations in the past" (Wright, 1976, p. 18; cf. Carchedi, 1975a, pp. 7-9). The overall relations, which limit change, are set, and yet a continuing pattern of interaction emerges.

The base, or economic, level of production, moreover, has two parts: production and exchange. The production level refers to the relationships binding actors involved in producing goods, services, and other commodities. The social relations of production are thus the linkages among the people involved directly in production. Workers are in complex relations with capitalists, who control the process but are not directly involved in producing. Social relations of production are hierarchical; the group that controls production dominates how commodities are produced. Technical relations of production differ in that they refer to the division of labor among jobs (Wright, 1976, p. 3). Technical relations do not imply domination and supervision but specialization and coordination. The economic level of exchange involves the social relations in the exchange of goods and services already produced. One of these "goods" is labor power, the commodity form of human labor. Workers sell their labor power on the labor market prior to entering into the exploitative production relationship. Nonetheless, the structure of the production relationship is primary and implies control over the labor process. Just as Marx claimed that people make history but only under circumstances established for them, politics and ideology influence class but only within conditions constrained by economic relations (cf. Bowles and Gintis, 1989). In short, production relations set the limits and possibilities for the other superstructural levels.

The social relations of production are the independent variable because "the economic level plays a determining role in shaping the political and ideological levels and . . . the social relations of production play a determining role within economic relations" (Wright, 1976, p. 18). An analysis of classes should therefore be grounded in the social relations of production. Neither political nor ideological factors, the impact of industrialization or technology, nor the modernization of culture can be the fundamental starting point for understanding or changing society; they are aspects of the superstructure. Production relations generate the systemic antagonisms that create classes.

In essence, economic class is structural because it creates limits and possibilities. On the larger scale, economic class structures political and social consequences and outcomes. On the more specific level, the internal nature of economic classes are also structural. The organization of classes and subclasses within work establish likelihoods and possibilities for opportunities and activities on the job as well as off. The structural nature of class is similar in conception to Giddens's formulation of the "structuration of class relationships" (1973, pp. 107-8). Particularly pertinent is the concept of the "proximate" structuration of class relationships, "'localized' factors which condition or shape class formation" (p. 107). Proximate structuration is based on the division of labor in occupational tasks and in authority relations in the enterprise (as well as in the influence of distributive groupings in consumption). The division of labor involves the "allocation of occupational tasks within the productive organization" (p. 108). The "influence of differential authority is . . . basic as a reinforcing agent of the structure of class relationships . . . " (p. 108). Structural class in the internal sense establishes tendencies for certain results, though it does not determine outcomes.

Though creating class, the economic is neither unchanging nor unchangeable. As capitalism has developed, the basis of the economy has changed from agricultural to industrial to knowledge production. Ownership of productive resources determines class, but what constitutes productive resources changes with the economy. Though the economic sphere sets the limits of variation in class, the political and political-economic spheres can influence change in the economic sphere over time. Legal structures, collective action, and economic opportunities can influence the productivity of industries. In short, the political sphere may change the economic. But this does not change the definition of class that flows from the current economic foundation.

The economic and structural designations of class provide the bases for objectively specifying the organization of class structure, and empirically identifying working class membership and within-class stratification. The specification of class and class fractions also elucidates questions about proletarianization and deskilling. Decline in self-employment indicates class proletarianization. Even among doctors, the heart of the independent middle class, self-employment dropped between 1940 and 1980 from approximately three-quarters to roughly half. In classical Marxist theory, the process is inherent in the tendencies of capitalism to concentrate capital and to polarize society into antagonistic classes. Braverman's (1974) analysis of the degradation of work equates deskilling with proletarianization. However, though white collar labor has experienced class proletarianization in increasing wage employment, it has not become proletarian in the condition sense of being deskilled over time. Nor has white collar labor experienced an intermediate form of proletarianization over time in the decline of supervisory responsibility as intermediaries between capital and labor.

The conception of class discussed here contrasts, in particular, with the Weberian multidimensional approach. In traditional sociology, Weber's concept of class, while underscoring the importance of ownership and production, combines other factors with the predominance of the economic in Marxist conceptions. Rather than basing class solely on property or production relations, Weber considered market situation, the distribution of income, social status or prestige, social mobility, and power as foundations for social classes. Weber recognized that a central definition of class situation was economic, but developed a system of multidimensional stratification within class based on credential or skill qualifications, authority relations, and lifestyle differences. Hierarchies of skill or work control and those of prestige or mobility are, nonetheless, qualitatively different from ownership or lack of ownership of property.

Weber's later writings note the importance of property relations for class situations ([1922] 1968, p. 302).

> "Class" means all persons in the same class situation: (a) A *"property"* class is primarily determined by property differences, (b) a *"commercial"* class by the marketability of goods and services, (c) a *social* class makes up the totality of those class situations within which individual and generational mobility is easy and typical. (p. 302, emphasis in original)

Despite Weber's identification of property as one indicator of class situation, his more elaborate definition compared to the earlier stress on status groupings is tempered by a structural agnosticism. Weber did not develop an abstract treatment of capitalist development or capitalist dynamics sufficient to account for how class situations were structurally induced by relations of production (cf. Giddens, 1973, Ch. 2). Rather Weber stressed the "mode of governance" instead of the "mode of production." He emphasized how political leadership and political action were causal forces, often operating independently of forces and relations of economic production. In addition, Weber incorporated capitalist organization and capital-labor social relations into the larger rubric of rationalization and bureaucracy. His distinctive orientation led him to adopt a "pluralist conception of classes" (Giddens, 1973, p. 42). Although these multiple class situations were related--indeed social class is a unification of property and commercial class situations--Weber did not view any as more fundamental or determinant; rather he was uncommitted about the potentially greater consequences of one or another class situation and acknowledged the overlap among the three conceptions. Giddens and Wright share and extend these insights.

In *Class Structure in the Social Consciousness*, Stanislaw Ossowski (1963) recognized several historical types of classes. These include the Marxist approach, concentrating centrally on the relationship to the means of production and relations of dependence. They also include the more Weberian approaches to class using status stratification in which classes "are consequences of social statuses otherwise achieved" (p. 130). Neither approach is *per se* correct because "different conceptual categories correspond to different problems" (1963, p. 176). Classes are "basic groups" with internal cohesion in a social structure (1963, p. 141). The structure forms a system; there must be a systemic relationship in which each component has its position fixed by relationship to others (p. 148). Ossowski advocates the distillation and synthesis of dichotomous and continuous class definitions. The structural conception of class and the critique of various conceptions of white collar class here elaborate an approach to class analysis along these lines. The application of a synthesis of class and stratification advances the analysis of white collar labor and clarifies the white collar class situation at present and over time.

As Wright emphasizes,

> the analysis of class structure is intended not as the end point of an investigation, but as the starting point. The premise is that the structure of class relations establishes the basic context within which social struggle and change will take place. The purpose of studying class structure is to be able to understand the constraints on and possibilities of transformation. (1980, p. 365)

While the structural approach elucidates the basic distinctions between and within classes, other social factors influence divisions within classes. The relationship of gender to class structure is increasingly significant. As class refers to economic processes and the politics of production that bear on individuals regardless of gender, a woman who is also a capitalist would engage in class domination and exploitation. Although gender does not determine class, it is an important facet of differentiation within class. The gender bias of the working class is increasingly clear: 54 percent of women occupy working class positions as opposed to roughly 40 percent for men (Wright, et al., 1982, p. 722). Over half of all employed women (52.8 percent) are specifically classified by Wright as proletarian *workers,* and workers as a group are over 60 percent women (Wright, 1985, p. 197). Wright cautions that the "image which is still present in many Marxist accounts that the working class consists primarily of male factory workers simply does not hold true any longer" (1985, p. 198). This transformation implies not only differences within the working class but also different likelihoods of becoming involved in decisions both within the work sphere and in related outside politics.

The increasing proportion of women, in particular, in white collar work raises several other issues about class analysis. Is class determined at the level of the individual or at the level of the family (household)? With the wider participation of women in the labor force, a woman's economic class position is clearer if individuals are the unit of analysis. On the individual basis, class position is defined by one's own relation to ownership. When the individual is the basis for class, the family plays a role only in the sphere of reproduction of a class society (Wright, 1978).

However, when class is identified on the basis of the household or family the situation is more complex. If all members of a family are in the labor force in the same class position, the class situation of the household is clearly the same. Traditionally, for unmarried men and women not in the labor force, the father's position has defined class for the entire family. In cases of marriage, the male head of household has typically defined class for the spouse and children, too. These assumptions are increasingly recognized more as methodological conveniences than as fully explicated theoretical positions. The controversies and issues surrounding the class positions of women *qua* women, and those who are not in the labor force, extend beyond this study, but represent significant questions for further analysis (see Goldthorpe, 1983; Crompton and Jones, 1984; Garnsey, 1978).

OVERVIEW

This initial chapter suggests that simple, economically based class analysis, multidimensional structural stratification within class, and empirical investigation of white collar class situations begin to forge a new social analysis out of the traditional and Marxist perspectives. During a century of debate, competing theories have located white collar in various classes (see Oppenheimer, 1985). The economic and structural definitions of class and stratification intervene in the cycle of recurring theories of the "middle class" versus working class designations of white collar labor in order to clarify the question. Economic ownership defines class, while the authority relations and work conditions of the labor process define stratification within class. By critiquing the competing theories of white collar class, Chapter 2 clarifies the class situation of white collar labor as largely working class. Chapter 3 empirically demonstrates the working class situation of white collar labor, and elucidates the stratification by authority relations and work conditions within the working class. Together they challenge the "middle class" image of white collar labor.

After the introductory chapters clarify the working class nature of white collar labor, the study takes up the more complex proletarianization questions regarding class change. Following the review of theories of proletarianization in Chapter 4, Chapter 5 supports the thesis of class proletarianization as aggregate change in white collar class position, and questions the intermediary proletarianization thesis about changes in supervisory proportions among white collar labor. Chapter 6 also questions the condition proletarianization thesis that white (or blue) collar labor has become increasingly proletarian. In essence, the three proletarianization questions have conflicting answers. Class proletarianization has occurred in the growing proportion of employees among white collar, particularly upper white collar, labor. On the other hand, intermediary proletarianization of white collar labor has not occurred over the long term. There was no significant proportional decrease in supervisors or increase in employees from 1972 to 1988. Nor, apparently, has condition proletarianization occurred overall. Empowered employees increased slightly during the early 1970s, but those without authority changed little. There may have been slight intermediary and condition deproletarianization or polarization. Moreover, by the middle 1970s, the distinction between white collar and blue collar labor blurred as deproletarianization has also occurred among blue collar labor. In short, this research supports the thesis of simple proletarianization, challenges the thesis of intermediary proletarianization, and questions the thesis of condition proletarianization.

Both more general theories of white collar class and theories of the new working class suggest that both within and beyond structural analysis of class lie significant issues of politics. Political by their very nature, authority relations and work conditions should affect the wider political behavior of white collar labor both within and beyond the workplace. The empirical investigation in Chapter 7 indicates that there are political consequences both across congruent levels of formality and from being simultaneously white collar and working class, or white collar working class. There are also as yet unexplored political implications from change in white collar class structure. Proletarianization has consequences for working class formation, but deproletarianization may, in fact, generate more politically active outcomes. Proletarianization, moreover, need not produce "working class" politics, nor deproletarianization necessarily lead to "middle class" politics. In identifying a series of political issues, the concluding chapter suggests that white collar class structure, particularly in interaction with gender and consciousness, may well catalyze changes in politics in the political economy and the polity into the next century.

2 Theories of White Collar Class

INTRODUCTION

In the popular imagination, some traditional sociology, and much political analysis, white collar means middle class, and blue collar means working class. But occupation is not class, and white collar is not simply middle class. The economic conception provides the basis for a critique of designations of class that currently obscure the working class nature of most white collar labor. While some white collar labor is "old middle class" or *petty bourgeoisie* through small ownership or self-employment, most white collar labor is working class. Even what is often called "new middle class" of white collar employees is not mainly middle class. It is largely part of a stratified and diversified working class. The working class situation of white collar labor, while paradoxical, can be demonstrated both theoretically and empirically.

This chapter seeks to identify theoretically the class situation of white collar labor. First, it identifies the various theories of white collar class situation that analysts have proposed over the past century. This reveals the cyclical recurrence over time of similar conceptions of white collar class under different names. Second, based on the economic and structural approach to class, the chapter critiques the other conceptions of the class situation of white collar labor. In particular, it identifies how authority relations and structural conditions generate internal stratification within class rather than creating different classes. By synthesizing the structural approach and critique, the chapter cuts through the recurring conceptions of white collar class location and theoretically identifies the mainly working class situation of white collar labor.

Within both the traditional and marxian schools, there is a broad range of conceptions of class. While this study maintains an economic and structural definition of class, neither this approach to class nor this discussion of the class situation of white collar labor is definitive. Rather, both serve as points of reference for the analyses and critiques that this chapter and the theoretical critique of class change in Chapter 4 present. Moreover, the consistent application of structural class serves as a basis for the empirical investigation of white collar labor and politics in the chapters that follow.

THE CLASS SITUATION OF WHITE COLLAR LABOR

The debate over the class situation of white collar labor has been ongoing "without significant resolution" for almost a hundred years (Mills, 1951, p. 290; Coyner and Oppenheimer, 1976, p. 1). Since the late nineteenth century, various theories have essentially been repeated under different names without significant analytical advance or synthesis with empirical evidence. The overview and typology of the various theories of white collar class here attempts to move beyond the repetition of various approaches toward clarification. This chapter reviews several important theoretical statements in light of their understanding of the class position of white collar labor.

The literature approaches the class situation of white collar labor from essentially five major positions. The first position holds that white collar labor is middle class, or new middle class. The second position holds that white collar labor is part of an elite or managerial "new class." The third position holds alternatively that white collar labor is working class, or new working class. A fourth position holds that white collar labor is "in-between" the middle and working classes forming a "third force" (Coyner and Oppenheimer, 1976). A fifth position holds that white collar labor is divided between the capitalist class and the working class.

Middle Class Theories

Perhaps the most common view is that white collar labor is "middle class" defined in terms of income, lifestyle, culture, and affluence. Numerically large, this "class" encompasses over time more of the population as white collar employment grows. Often the basis of journalistic examinations of class in America, this view holds that the growing middle class is a stabilizing force in society. More scholarly approaches see the middle class "as a major force for stability in the general balance of the different classes" (Mills, 1951, p. 290). In essence, white collar forms a "buffer between labor and capital" (p. 290). This bridging-class takes over old middle class entrepreneurial and managerial functions in running society. Yet it has connections to wage workers. The middle class is the "balance wheel of class interests, the stabilizers, the social harmonizers" (pp. 290-91).

Virtually everyone, particularly white collar employees, constitute one great class--the middle class. This is similar to the theory that there are no classes in American society (cf. Meiksins, 1986). Related theory suggests that white collar is, in fact, synonymous with middle class; the "white-collar class" is the middle class (Bell, 1973, p. 13). These broad theories tie to the conceptions of a growing, homogenizing mass society of middle class members (p. 23). Here the white collar middle class consists of "mental" workers, while the blue collar working class is composed of manual workers. This constitutes the "end of ideology" approach to the end of classes (Bell, 1960).

A variant on the idea of a large, encompassing middle class is the theory of *embourgeoisement* (cf. Goldthorpe, et al., 1968). According to this view, a surge of upward mobility swells the ranks of the middle class, as blue collar workers who experience affluence adopt the lifestyle and values of the middle class. Embourgeoisement has especially affected craftsmen, the labor aristocracy of advanced industrial societies. "The absence of a revolutionary working class movement" derives from the fact that much of the British working class "merrily share the feast of England's monopoly of the colonies and the world market" (Lenin, 1939, p. 107). Sombart similarly suggests that "[o]n the reefs of roast beef and apple pie socialist Utopias of every sort are sent to their doom" (in Low-Beer, 1978, p. 3). Modern embourgeoisement theorists like Bell (1960) or Lipset (1981) see the end to the working class through assimilation to the middle class. Goldthorpe, et al. (1968, 1969) challenge the embourgeoisement thesis empirically and find little evidence that the industrial working class in Britain has taken on a middle class lifestyle.

New Middle Class Theories

A related set of theories holds that most white collar workers are members of a new middle class. The middle class in modern society can be divided into two parts, the old middle class of small property owners and the new middle class of white collar occupations (professionals, managers, clericals, and sales) (Mills, 1951, p. 65). Unlike the status of the old middle class that is conferred by property holdings, the status of the new middle class is gained by virtue of occupational skills, function, and prestige. Individuals in the new middle class have important "market capacities," based on training--educational, technical, or functional qualification and credentialing--that become salable commodities in the labor market (Giddens, 1973). Accordingly, the new middle class thesis argues that where property is no longer widely held and wage labor is widespread, occupational skills determine the standard of living one obtains from selling labor-power in the labor market.

Theories of the new middle class have a long history. Schmoller viewed the transformation of white collar strata into a new middle class as presaging significant cultural improvement and social contentment (1897 in Coyner and Oppenheimer, 1976, pp. 6-7). For Lederer, white collar workers were typically middle-class oriented in consciousness as identified by organizational tendencies and labor alliances (1912, p. 8, in Mills, 1951, p. 241). The *neue Middelstand* of salaried employees and civil servants appeared in the change for professionals and managers from self-employment to salaried employment for others (Lederer and Marshak, 1926). The essential shift came from a status based in property to one based in skills or function. The salaried (versus property-owning or wage-working) status represents the distinctive feature of white collar workers (Mills, 1951, p. 299). "The salary, as contrasted with the wage, has been the traditional mark of white collar employment" (p. 299). In fact, white collar employees are members of the "salariat" (p. 289; Bell, 1960, p. 222). Today, most professional and managerial personnel are salaried employees.

Another new middle class theory focuses on employees that do not work on production, who are, in other words, "unproductive labor" (Poulantzas, 1975). Such employees are the *new petty bourgeoisie*. This new middle class designation applies because of the proposed affinity of this "class" with the values, attitudes, and expertise of the old middle class of small owners, as well as similarities in managerial functions. Only manual, nonsupervisory employees, who produce surplus value, that is "productive workers," are members of the working class. Poulantzas includes in the new middle class upper white collar or professional and managerial labor that is unproductive. For ideological reasons, he assigns them to the new petty bourgeoisie. But lower white collar labor in clerical and sales work is also part of the new petty bourgeoisie, since their labor is mental and unproductive. Even if their conditions of employment closely parallel those of traditional, blue collar members of the working class, such white collar workers are new petty bourgeoisie.

The debate over the class position of "unproductive" commercial employees, or employees involved in the realization of surplus value, is also long standing. Here "function" or "functionality" defines class. Performance of unproductive labor puts employees in the new middle class (Poulantzas, 1975). Their absorption of surplus income also creates the new middle class designation when members are paid out of revenue drawn from surplus value (Nicolaus, 1967; Urry, 1973). In fact, Nicolaus (1967) holds that the function of the new middle class is to consume surplus. Since productive workers in the working class produce more than they and the capitalists can absorb, there must be a class that consumes more than it produces. The function of this "surplus class" is to consume surplus, and this determines its new middle class situation (O'Connor, 1973). While not designating them part of the middle class, O'Connor calls these unproductive workers "guard labor" for their control and reproduction functions.

Though Loren (1977) agrees that many white collar employees may share ideological (that is, conservative) affinity with the petty bourgeoisie, he does not thereby put them in a separate class. He also challenges the idea that a separate class is necessary to absorb surplus income. While Becker (1973, 1974) concurs that white collar labor has a function of consumption, he does not use this as a criterion for class.

Control of labor in production. Perhaps the most cogent arguments for the existence of a new middle class focus on the control functions performed in the primary sphere of production--the organization and control of production and the labor process. Supervisors and professionals are members of the new middle class because of their political dominance over other employees. In the early stages of capitalist development, the entrepreneurial capitalist performed this controlling role. Now those in managerial or supervisory positions, who control the labor of others, are not capitalist owners; they are new middle class. As the result of the "concentration of the enterprise brought about by modern technical methods," Lederer noted, "there emerges a class of technicians who, from a social point of view, cannot categorically be classified as either employers or workers" (1912, p. 3).

> The modern giant enterprises, however, have created an entire superstructure of technicians, an apparatus without which they would not be able to operate. . . . The functions of the technical employees are two-fold: either they are analogous to those of working men, only on a higher level (such as draftsmen or engineers) who prepare the production processes, or they are managers,

foremen, etc. plus the commercial employees of industry, who organize the production processes. (p. 6)

Those workers who, individually, perform the "function of capital" in organizing and controlling labor, or, collectively, perform the "global function of capital" are also new middle class (Carchedi, 1975a). Technicians in production, rather than performing an essential coordination function that expands the forces of production, are controllers of labor as part of a specific capitalist function in reproducing hierarchical relations of production (Gorz, 1972). Such technicians are in the new middle class (Gorz, 1972; Bridier, 1966). Certain essential coordination functions of technicians are, however, necessary to production (Il Manifesto, 1972). Moreover, technicians are being alienated and proletarianized like other employees (p. 78), including the "white collar proletariat" (p. 68). Eighty percent of employees in administration, for instance, "do nothing but repeat strictly predetermined tasks" (p. 69). "The specialization of activity of modern capitalism does not derive from the complexity of modern production alone but rather from the need to maintain capitalist hegemony amid this complexity" (p. 73). "Some degree of specialization is certainly required by the imperatives of large-scale technology, by criteria of productive efficiency" (p. 73n).

The capitalists' roles involve three types of class control (Wright, 1978; Carchedi, 1975a; Urry, 1973). Most important is the control of investments, financial or money capital (surplus value). In essence, this is ownership and financial control. Next is control of physical capital or machinery in production (constant capital). Last is the control of labor (or variable capital). Owners who do not control labor are in "contradictory locations within class relations" (Wright, 1978, p. 63). In Wright's analysis, such employees are neither in one class, nor another, yet they share certain characteristics with members of each, since "the three processes that constitute capitalist social relations of production do not always perfectly coincide" (1978, p. 74). The place of supervisors is ambiguous because of their combination of capitalist function and wage status (Urry, 1973, p. 186). Nominal supervisors essentially belong to the working class (Wright, 1978, p. 77).

Such analysis involves class, not at the highest, economic level of abstraction, but at the level of the social formation (Wright, 1978, pp. 73-74). No clear line or criterion exists for determining when people in "contradictory class locations" can be assigned to a specific class. The combination of the functions of collective worker and the global function of capital creates contradictory positions (Carchedi, 1975a). Supervisory functions are, however, in the productive sector and hence connected to the economic basis for class.

Control in reproducing hierarchies. Some white collar employees are new middle class based on their role in reproducing or preserving hierarchic capitalist social relations. The Professional/Managerial Class (PMC) of white collar employees fulfills important functions of social control and reproduction of the conditions of capitalism (Ehrenreich and Ehrenreich, 1977). The PMC's role is a particular development of the monopoly stage of capitalism. Its members include teachers, social and health workers, psychologists, lawyers and others who are involved in social control through professional service functions (1977).

Analogous to supervision in production, persons involved in social control in the reproduction of society and, in particular, in reproducing or maintaining the hierarchical social relations of capitalist society, are new middle class. The "middle class, new managerial strata" have similar roles of social control in social organization (Oppenheimer, 1972, pp. 30, 32).

A related new middle class approach lies in the theory of delegation (Croner, 1954 in Dahrendorf, 1959, pp. 91-92). "According to Croner the function of white collar employees corresponds essentially to the dismemberment of the activity of the leader," which "necessarily entails 'delegation'" (Crozier, 1971, p. 31). "The explanation of the special social position of salaried employees can be found in the fact that their work tasks have once been entrepreneurial tasks" (Dahrendorf, 1959, p. 53).[1] "Historically, most clerical occupations were differentiated out of the leading positions in industry, commerce and the state" (p. 53), and hence retain some authority to delegate. There is a "new social class: white collar" (Croner in Dahrendorf, 1959, p. 9). It is a "subdivision of the entrepreneurial function in industry and of leading positions in the state" (p. 91). The idea of delegation appears in many new middle class theories, and identifies white collar occupations as elite positions because of supposedly similar functions. Through the process of delegation, clerks are like managers. Bureaucrats in private industry and businesses are like state officials.

Political and ideological determinants of class. Related designations of new middle class situations involve theories in which political, including conflict, and ideological factors determine class situation. One conception is the idea that class situation is determined not by the relation to production but by relationship to authority in any "imperatively coordinated association" (Dahrendorf, 1959, pp. 136-38). Also related to the political theory of class, but also to conceptions of structurally indeterminate class positions, is the idea that only in struggle does class situation emerge (Przeworski, 1977). Class exists not in the abstract but only in concrete situations. Alignment in revolutionary or prerevolutionary conflict determines class situation. A weak version of this theory holds that class and class conflict are intimately intertwined with authority relations (Dahrendorf, 1959, p. 136). A stronger version argues that classes are only phenomena in history and cannot be structurally or categorically defined (Thompson, 1963, p. 9). Class cannot be determined outside of class struggle.

Moreover, Poulantzas (1975), Wright (1978), Carchedi (1975a, b), and Przeworski (1977) maintain that ideological factors can codetermine class. Certain white collar workers supposedly share an ideological affinity with the traditional petty bourgeoisie (Mills, 1951, p. 296). The new petty bourgeoisie is ideologically similar to the traditional petty bourgeoisie (Poulantzas, 1975). Ideological considerations are two-fold. First, the expertise of mental workers and, second, the values shared with the petty bourgeoisie place white collar workers in the middle class (Poulantzas, 1975; Pannekoek in Mills, 1951, p. 296; Bridier, 1966).

"New Class" Theories

The "new class" theories include the conception that the middle class is an elite that runs the business and governance of society. It is related to middle class theories, in particular, those emphasizing the managerial functions of the middle class. This is often tied to the idea of white collar or professionals as the new social rulers, whose training and expertise give them the abilities to manage technological society. In other formulations these rulers are modern-day philosopher kings, educated technocrats, the brain trust (Bazelon, 1963), the "new mandarins" (Chomsky, 1969), or the "best and the brightest" (Halberstam, 1972). Although the technological elite is only a small segment of the white collar labor force, it gives the entire sector a particular connotation. Here is a social synecdoche, describing the whole for the part: as some white collar people rule society, all white collar people share in the ruling function, or, as some white collar people run business and government, all white collar people are part of an elite (Braverman, 1974, pp. 349-50; Mills, 1951, p. 292). The managerial character of the white collar elite gives a favorable image to the white collar sector. Since some in the white collar sector run the key institutions of society, all white collar employees have some managerial prestige and power. The nonclass character of the "new class" emerges when it is conceived as a "new elite" (cf. Birnbaum, 1969). But these technical elites are better seen as a separate new class.

The new class theory is not a theory of the middle class, which implies a class above and a class below, but a theory of a new ruling class. "It seems obvious that so long as the middle class is a middle class there must be a class above it, and once it is a ruling class it is no longer the middle class" (Dahrendorf, 1959, p. 54). The nineteenth century Marxist term "middle class" describes a group between the ruling class and the working class. In the last century in Europe, the emergent class was the capitalist, the "middle class" between the landed aristocracy and peasantry. In the United States, without a hereditary aristocracy, the capitalist class is the ruling class. In new class theories, the new class is the new ruling class.

A premiere formulation of the new class idea described a "general staff of the industrial system" consisting of "technicians, engineers and industrial experts," that could run the production system more efficiently than profit-motivated businessmen (Veblen, 1965, pp. 440-41; cf. Stabile, 1984). Similar ideas lie in the conception of technocracy, popular in the depression decade of the 1930s and the idea of a "managerial revolution" (Burnham, 1941). Other members of the new class include scientists in leadership roles in postindustrial society, "scientists and engineers within the technostructure" and the "educators and research scientists of the educational/scientific estate" (Galbraith, 1967, p. 291; Touraine, 1971; cf. Bell, 1973). More generally, the new class consists of intellectuals and technical intelligentsia tied to cultural capital and opposed to the traditional capitalist bourgeoisie. This new class concentrates in the social and state spheres and shares an education-related "culture of critical discourse." (Gouldner, 1979). The identification of new (ruling) classes in eastern Europe and deproletarianized of their ruling circles suggest that new classes are developing in both capitalist and communist societies (Djilas, 1957; Parkin, 1971). Variants of the theory propose that technocrats are only agents of the rulers, rather than the rulers themselves.

Both the left and the right have contributed to renewed debate over new class theories. Recent criticisms from the left extend the idea of the new class as a new ruling class in eastern Europe (Szelenyi and Martin, 1988). The right sees the new class as essentially comprising white collar employees in their "functions" as bureaucrats, information manipulators, and social managers, particularly in governmental spheres (cf. Bruce-Briggs, 1979, p. 17). While those on the left typically see the new class as a potential new working (or universal) class, those on the right see it as a new ruling class.

Working Class Theories

Another major set of theories views white collar labor as members of the working class like blue collar workers (Kautsky, 1971). Often presented in a marxian framework, this theory gives the term white collar employee "a proletarian cast" (Mills, 1951, p. 292). Nonowners, wage-paid, hierarchically controlled, and performing fragmented labor, with little say in decision making, the bulk of white collar employees are working class. Changes in the situation and organizational tendencies of white collar employees constituted a "proletarianization of the middle class strata" during the years surrounding World War I in Germany (Lederer and Marshak, 1926, p. 25). Contrary to an earlier nonworking class formulation (Lederer, 1912, p. 44), for these "new middle class" groups "the fact of being employed in a dependent capacity triumphs over all class and traditional constraints" (Lederer and Marshak, 1926, p. 25). Their identity and social interests had become tied with labor. There are also "nonsocialist" working class views of the class situation of white collar labor (Speier, 1934, p. 125n; Coyle, 1928, p. 25). Many working class analyses extend theoretical statements with data-based investigations of working conditions.

While neither a Marxist nor subscribing solely to a working class theory, in his classic work on white collar, Mills held that "objectively . . . the structural position of the white-collar mass" was becoming "more similar to that of wage workers" than to that of the self-employed old middle class in terms of working conditions and social situation (1951, p. 297). Though not holding to a strict working class view about salaried employees in Germany during the Depression, Speier considered salaried employees as the "youngest stratum in the working classes" (1934, p. 111). His discussion of the "rise of the unskilled and semi-skilled salaried workers" noted the "assimilation of the processes of work in the office to that in the factory" (1934, p. 118). In essence, like the craftsmen during the revolution, the clerk had become proletarian rather than independent as an entrepreneur (Speier, 1939, pp. 10, 17). Clerical work itself became fully dependent, both in employment situation and conditions. Three signs of the sinking level of white collar workers included the mechanization of their work based on specialization, the insecurity regarding unemployment, and the increasing recruitment from strata "considered inferior in social esteem" (Speier, 1934, p. 122). Closely tied to these factors was the transformation in the gender composition of white collar labor. The number of women was increasing as the remaining men tended to retain the authority previously associated with the "confidential" clerk (cf. Speier, 1939, p. 122).

Other working class theories hold that the "classification of white collar workers as a separate middle class has no foundation in fact" (Budish, 1962, p. 18). All white collar employees, except top management, are working class (Becker, 1973; Freedman, 1975; Loren, 1977; Edwards, 1979), or all except managers, officials, and proprietors are in the "white collar working class" (Mandel, 1970, p. 54). The designations of "new white collar mass" (Oppenheimer, 1972, p. 30) and "an emerging white collar proletariat" (Bowles and Gintis, 1976, p. 201) suggest the working class nature of white collar labor. The latter designation is tied to changes in the educational system. Both the system of higher education and the people schooled there are being integrated into the system of wage labor (Bowles and Gintis, 1976). This is similar to class proletarianization and is an impetus for a political response.

The degradation, deskilling, and fragmentation of the labor process continue as capitalism develops (Braverman, 1974). This includes the "mechanization of the office" (p. 326) and the "office as manual labor" (p. 319) in factory-like conditions. The "growing working class occupations" (p. 291) include clerical, sales, and service work. The designation of white collar workers as unskilled and semiskilled underscores both the divisions within and similarities between white collar and blue collar labor (Speier, 1934). Keypunching, for example, is actually a semi-blue collar job (Braverman, 1974, pp. 332, 347). This designation highlights the routinization of office work into a factory-like process. Aspects of working class conditions occur at each level of white collar work. In terms of income and skills required on the job, there is little difference between most white collar and blue collar jobs (Braverman, 1974, p. 297).

Most lower white collar employees in clerical and sales jobs are in the working class (Wright, 1980). In fact, the proportion of lower white collar employees who are nonsupervisory members of the working class (54.5 percent) is greater than the proportion of upper blue collar workers in the same position (32.1 percent) (Wright, 1980, p. 205). "Crafts occupations are . . . much less proletarianized . . . than clerical white collar occupations," a result tied to the inclusion of foremen in the crafts category (Wright, 1977, p. 12).

In general, Marxists consider lower white collar employees to be working class because they are wage labor. But also their labor market and work situations closely approach those in the blue collar sector (Edwards, 1979; Zimbalist, 1979). White collar employees are nonowners and are as alienated as the rest of the working class since they do not have control over production or the labor process. The labor of white collar workers, particularly in the circulation and distribution sectors, is partially exploited (D. Smith, 1974). These workers produce surplus labor and help realize surplus value by turning products into profits for whose value they are not fully paid (Smith, 1974, p. 207; Budish, 1962, p. 14; Hodges, 1971). Commercial employees are partially exploited and hence partially productive. Thus they are in the working class. Similarly, government workers are in the working class for their assistance in reducing the social costs of production (Smith, 1974; Freedman, 1975; Loren, 1977).

The working class encompasses ever more clerical and sales workers. The labor force has developed as Marx foresaw (Szymanski, 1972, p. 103).

Of all Karl Marx's predictions about the trends of Western capitalism, the one that has most clearly been verified is that the proletariat--workers who do not themselves own their own tools, but rather are forced to sell their labor to someone else who then appropriates their labor, would be an ever increasing percentage of the total population. (p. 103)

Most lower white collar employees (white collar proletariat) and most technical and professional upper white collar employees are increasingly in the working class (1972, pp. 114-15).

"The feminization of office jobs is certainly one of the fundamental phenomena in the evolution of the occupational structure" (Crozier, 1971, p. 15), and one associated with an increasingly working class position for women. "To the old white collar group which had pretty much retained its social status . . . was added a new group consisting in part of females with distinctly inferior social status" (p. 16). In the mid 1960s, "[e]ighty percent of the fantastic increase in the numbers of American white collar employees during the last twenty years is due to the massive recruitment of females" (p. 16). Moreover, "this rapid rise in number of white collar jobs results almost entirely from the shift in female occupations and the rising percentages of the work force that is female" (Szymanski, 1972, p. 111).

> In terms of the social class composition of the population, there has been no significant tendency for the white collar proletariat to grow relative to, or at the expense of the blue collar proletariat. What has happened is that the women from blue collar families whose husbands work in factories or at similar jobs have left home and taken jobs . . . as saleswomen or office workers. (p. 111)

The joint working class nature of white collar/blue collar families reinforces the notions both of the working class situation for white collar workers and of the proletarian situation of women in particular.

New Working Class Theories

Several theories consider white collar labor as part of a "new working class" (cf. Hyman and Price, 1983). Some of the theories focus on the upper white collar, professional, and technical occupations in strategic positions in the political economy. Others focus on "the white collar mass," particularly lower white collar labor, as part of the the new working class (Oppenheimer, 1972, p. 30). The "new" working class is either replacing the old working class or the old working class has become less central.

Technicians in advanced industries are located in the working class, because, like the traditional industrial working class, they hold strategic positions, central to the modern, automated production process, and thereby potentially able to paralyze industry. Mallet (1963), Belleville (1963), and Gorz (1964) developed the approach in case study analyses of technologically based French industries. Akin to Veblen, Mallet (1963, 1975), Belleville (1963), and Gorz (1965) emphasize that the technically skilled members of the white and blue collar sectors are in the new working class. Technicians, scientists, and skilled workers in the advanced sectors of industry are tied to the transformation of the productive process of society (cf. Gorz, 1965; Blauner, 1964). The technicians in technologically advanced industries such as aeronautics and electronics are new working class because of their skills and centrality in production; at the same time they are experiencing increasingly peripheral roles in decision making (Mallet, 1975). The new working class includes strategic professionals central to both production and reproduction of modern society (Davidson, 1967). The kinds of demands of this group are also new in that they focus on control of the production process rather than on wages or physical working conditions.

Veblen anticipated the ideas in the conception of technicians as "indispensable to productive industry" (1965, p. 442), and the "soviet of technicians" controlling the production process as part of a "self-directing General Staff of the country's industry" (p. 443). Similar to the historic role ascribed to the industrial proletariat, these technicians could "incapacitate the country's productive industry" through a general strike (p. 463). This new working class formulation is thus close to that of engineers as technocrats in new class theories.

The American statements of the new working class theory include in the class the upper stratum of highly skilled workers as well as blue collar technicians (Gottlieb, Gilbert, and Tenney, 1967; Gottlieb and Piercy, 1967; Hodges, 1971). Professional and technical employees, including both blue collar technicians in advanced industries, and service workers like teachers and researchers who perform important social reproduction functions, comprise the class. Other American expositions of this theory explore the class situations of upper white collar professional and technical jobs or of the emerging white collar proletariat (Davidson, 1967; Calvert, 1968; Calvert and Neiman, 1971; Smith, 1974). A focus on higher education, particularly community colleges, and the ties of professionals and managers to university education characterize one variant of new working class analysis (cf. Bowles and Gintis, 1976). Because of the advantaged position, the new working class is sometimes considered to be new middle class (cf. Miles, 1971; Low-Beer, 1978).

The new working class theories are working class theories, and, in particular, new theories of the working class. More specifically they are theories of a *new* working class. Since self-employment has traditionally been connected with the white collar sector, particularly professional and managerial jobs, some white collar professionals and managers have been "proletarianized" by virtue of their status as employees. This is proletarianization in the original sense of the word as movement from independent employment to dependent employee status (Roslender, 1981).

More proletarianization oriented theories see the new working class as emerging from the declining position, status, and conditions of white collar employees whose labor process is being fragmented and whose jobs are being "deskilled." These changes are associated with loss of decision making, declining conditions of work, and the degradation of the labor process in general (Braverman, 1974). This general process occurs specifically in the white collar sector (Glenn and Feldberg, 1979; Kraft, 1979; Crompton and Reid, 1982; Crompton and Jones, 1984; Shaw, 1987). Since the conditions of white collar work were once more autonomous and skilled, the lowered status is a new situation. The conditions of employment have declined so that white collar employees are experiencing proletarian conditions at work. On the other hand, technicians in automated industries are in newly strategic positions in the political economy.

In sum, the theory that technical employees and professionals are new working class has three bases: their changing class positions, their changing labor process and work conditions, and their new centrality in the automated workplace. But the theories have both working, middle, and new class elements (cf. Sobel, 1984).

"Third Force" Theories

"Third force" theories hypothesize that white collar labor occupies a third position, neither middle class nor working class (Coyner and Oppenheimer, 1976). In optimistic expositions tied to societal reform, white collar workers are considered a distinctive *in-between* group (Bernstein, 1899 in Coyner and Oppenheimer, 1976). This independent group has the potential, in alliance with other strata, for moving society accretionally in a reform direction (Coyner and Oppenheimer, 1976, p. 1). In Germany during the 1930s, union officials maintained that white collar employees were distinguished in having separate interests from workers; hence they needed a separate organizational vehicle. "Commercial employees are different from all other gainfully occupied groups . . . [N]otwithstanding rationalization in the large-scale enterprise, the skilled commercial employees cannot be dispensed with" (quoted in Dreyfuss, 1938, vol. 2, p. 134).

In the pessimistic version of this theory, the white collar sector is an "occupational salad," with no organizing principle (Mills, 1951, p. 291). In this sense, white collar *class* is negatively defined. There is no principle binding the stratum other than its lack of connection with either the capitalists or workers. It is in "limbo" between the other two classes (Coyner and Oppenheimer, 1976, p. 10). "The 'middle position' of white-collar people between independent employers and wage workers, 'a negative characteristic--rather than definite technical functions,' is the social mark of the salaried employees and establishes their social character in their own consciousness and in the estimation of the community" (Lederer, 1912 in Mills, 1951, pp. 241-42).

There are several hallmarks of the third force schools. The optimistic strains like Bernstein's consider white collar to be independent and positively distinct. The pessimistic strains like Mills's negatively distinguish white collar as not owners and not workers, though still dependent employees. Third force studies tend to combine discussions of factors such as ideology, class identification, or stratification, which distinguish this group from the traditional working class, with reviews of relevant data about the conditions of clerical employees. The theoretical analyses indicate the criteria that distinguish white collar labor as a separate class, group or stratum from either capitalists or workers. The data analyses resemble those of the investigations associated with working class theories in the focus on objective, deskilled conditions.

White collar employees constitute a third force due to a combination of contrasting factors (Mills, 1951; Klingender, 1935). On the one hand, white collar tend to be in the same economic position as blue collar employees: Most white and blue collar are dependent employees, working for wages and salaries, and share, at least at the lower levels, pay and work conditions. On the other hand, white collar employees tend to identify with the middle class, see themselves as middle class, and aspire to upward mobility. In short, the combination of essentially working class conditions but middle class identification puts white collar labor in a third position. A Marxist third force theory views the white collar sector as composed of "semi-working class sections" or "bordergroups" (Klingender, 1935, p. xii). Once a quasi-managerial position, by the mid 1930s clerks had taken on a subordinate role. Clerks still worked in close contact with managerial personnel, however, and continued to assume a middle class ideology.

Another third force analysis places white collar labor in a separate class because the conditions under which its members live and work distinguish them from other propertyless employees. Prior to World War I, white collar consisted of the "gainfully employed who are neither employers nor workers" (Lederer, 1912, p. 3). While not owners, white collar employees could not be placed in the working class with manual workers. Socially, the group fell in a middle position; it was a different and distinct group. Even at that time there was a merging of the "lower strata of salaried employees with the proletariat and the higher stratum of salaried employees overlap with the class of employers, managers, immediately above them" (p. 8). Each of the other classes tended to absorb the salaried employees, who, however, might still maintain the possibility of independence and higher status (p. 9). Though no "uniform technical function" distinguished the white collar sector, it was distinct from either owners or workers based on "social appraisal" (p. 9). At the turn of the century, Marx's prediction of a growing "homogeneous proletariat mass" did not "conform altogether to reality" (p. 10).

An additional third force view locates the new middle class between the classes; it is independent, *sui generis* (Lederer and Marshak, 1926, pp. 3-4). "The fact that the position of the 'new middle class' is an intermediate one between the classes makes the criterion rather a negative one" (p. 5). Since its class situation was not based on technical or economic functions but on common social position, the group could "be comprehended as an entity only in contradistinction to the other classes" (p. 6).[2]

In a study of blackcoated workers or clerks in England, Lockwood (1958) recognized that class was defined by economic position (Marx) or secondary economic and work conditions (Weber). Beyond class distinctions there was a third level of stratification in status. The material factors were offset by white collar employees' higher status position; this might be contradictory to economic class. Similarly, to the extent that the situations of white collar employees have been proletarianized they are similar to blue collar labor (Speier, 1934, 1939; Geiger, 1949). Yet these factors generate stratification within the propertyless. The theories distinguish the white collar employees from the capitalist class above and the manual workers below based on skills, esteem, and attitudes. In Speier's earlier work on white collar labor in Germany, social valuation, or esteem, separated the salaried employee from the manual worker; these were "differences in rank within a class" (Speier, 1934, p. 129). Though not created by the nature of white collar work itself, social estimation is both claimed by the white collar worker and acknowledged by the blue (1934, p. 128). The sociological investigation of white collar work should note the objective differences between white and blue collar labor and determine their importance (Speier, 1939, p. 15). The white collar situation is proletarian yet the social position of white collar employees does not only depend on their objective situation.   Since white collars "stand in a certain relationship to other social strata, their 'being' is not theirs alone" (p. 15).

Stratification within white collar groupings elucidates white collar social structure and its changes (Speier, 1934, p. 133).   The "restructuration of the proletariat" essentially involved within-class stratification of the white collar groups.   It is based along technical and hierarchic lines, particularly in terms of conditions of employment, complexity of jobs, and responsibility levels (Speier, 1939, p. 113).   The white collar sector is essentially "between" the capitalists and the working class of industrial workers.   It constitutes a separate class of white collar employees.   This class, moreover, is neither a new middle class, nor a new (ruling) class.

Division Between Middle and Working Classes

Another formulation divides the white collar sector between two classes: the capitalist class and the working class (Lederer and Marshak, 1926; Corey, 1935; Dahrendorf, 1959; Aronowitz, 1971; Becker, 1973, 1974; and Freedman, 1975).   The major owners of capital themselves and those high level, owning executives and managers who partake in the economic prerogatives and privileges of the owners are themselves part of capital.   The bulk of white collar employees, including lower level supervisors, employed professionals, and administrative labor, are part of the working class.   Simply, they do not own; they lack power in decision making; their conditions of employment have declined.   They are working class.   By this definition, most of both the new middle and new working classes are in the working class.

The larger part of white collar labor is in the working class.   Only those top white collar members functioning as capitalists are outside of the proletariat (cf. Corey, 1935; Loren, 1977, pp. 151-55).   The new middle class is not a class, but instead consists of two strata (Corey, 1935, p. 147).   The aggregation of salaried employees is divided between an "upper layer of managerial, supervisory and technical employees in corporate industry" who are "wholly identified with monopoly capitalism" and "the masses of lower salaried employees" (Coyner and Oppenheimer, 1976, p. 16).   In true class terms, the middle class, or new middle class, includes only small independent enterprisers and upper managerial employees.   The latter perform the more decisive functions of supervision and control that independent enterprisers once performed.   Managerial members of the new middle class are "institutional capitalists" despite their dependent employee status.   The mass of white collar employees, nominally members of the new middle class broadly defined, are, in fact, members of the "new proletariat" and closely allied to other wage workers (Corey, 1935, p. 259).   The new proletariat emerges out of changes in the (old) new middle class (Corey, 1935, p. 261n).   Some white collar workers are in the (new) middle class and some in the working class (Corey, 1935).

A similar two class approach develops from the distinction between technicians and technocrats.   Technicians in industry and the service sector lack significant power; the technically and scientifically trained technocrats serving in managerial positions run production (Aronowitz, 1971, pp. 195, 201).   Those white collar members who are in bureaucratic hierarchies are connected to the middle class; those not in bureaucratic hierarchies are in the working class

(Dahrendorf, 1959, p. 55). "The ruling class theory applies without exception to the social position of bureaucrats, and the working-class theory equally generally [sic] to the social position of white collar workers" (p. 55). The approach clears up the confusion between a ruling class, some of whose members may be placed in a social "middle class," and a "new middle class," most of whose members are in the working class. There is stratification within both classes, but the classes are distinct. The fundamental working class unity among most white collar employees lies in nonownership and the wage relation, though functions may put them into different class strata or fractions. In essence, the white collar new middle class is divided between two classes, with the large majority in the working class, and a small fraction in the capitalist class.

The distinctions between the middle class and the working class do not imply that there are no differences within the two broad classes. There are, for example, differences between supervisory employees and nonsupervisory employees, and differences in mobility patterns and cleavages along the white-collar/blue-collar line. But these are not class divisions. They constitute class fractions and strata within the working class (Freedman, 1975). The different groups within classes are bound by common relations to production. Political and ideological factors influence class fraction and are bases for stratification within the working class. Just as there is multidimensional stratification in traditional sociological theory, so too can there be multidimensional stratification in marxian class analysis; the distinctions are based on use values and functions among superstructural factors. Like Ossowski (1963), Mallet calls for development "toward a Marxist sociology of work" to explore more fully these patterns of "differentiations within the working class" (Howard, 1975, pp. 68-75).

CRITIQUE OF THE CLASS SITUATION OF WHITE COLLAR LABOR

The Basis of the Class and Structural Critique

The structural definition at the level of the modes of production holds, as Chapter 1 argues, that class is an economic phenomenon defined by relationship to ownership of the means of production. The fundamental, structuring basis is the economic level of production. Economic class is the focus here. This structural basis provides the foundation for the critique of theories of the class situation of white collar labor. Class as defined on the economic based level involves structural characteristics that delimit the dimensions and interests of the class. Economic class is not simply definitional or deterministic, but conduces and inhibits the possibilities for class members both absolutely and in relation to each other. There is, in particular, a basic working class unity in nonownership and wage or salary paid labor. Nonownership and wage labor status structurally unify the working class on both real and conceptual levels. The class situation of white collar labor rests on the relationship to ownership or nonownership. All white collar employees who are nonowners, and hence wage-laborers, are members of the working class. Within the white collar sector, only owners, including owning managers, are in the capitalist class. Simply put, white collar employees are split along class lines created by the division between owners and nonowners of the productive means. In sum, most white collar labor is in the working class, though a small part at the top is in the capitalist class.

There are, of course, differences within the working class, white and blue collar, as there are differences within the capitalist class. But these are not class differences. The arguments that maintain that factors besides ownership create class distinctions are on a lower level of abstraction. The secondary level of social structure or social formation involves factors such as politics and ideology. In essence, these involve discussions of more traditional social class, not economic class.

The question of what factors should constitute the definition of class is, of course, the subject of major controversy in class analysis. In traditional sociology the debate involves the unidimensional versus multidimensional view of stratification. In marxian terms, it involves the question of whether political and ideological factors can determine class. "The political level refers to the social relations of domination and subordination involving the use of power" (Wright, 1976, p. 3), especially in relationship to the state, but also within production. The ideological level "refers to social relations of domination and subordination involving ideas" (p. 3). It involves the relationship within status hierarchies--the way people are viewed in an unequal structure. The ideological level involves not just ideas, values and consciousness, but the social relations of domination and subordination to which ideas contribute. "Ideas become part of the social structure at the level of ideology only when they are embodied in real social relationships" and have consequences for people (p. 4).

The differentiations within the working class require sociological analysis also from a Marxist perspective (Howard, 1975, pp. 68-75). Social stratification is at the level of class fraction or strata within the working class, not at the level of separate classes (Freedman, 1975). Based on these principles, this critique identifies most distinctions as occurring within the working class, not between the working class and capitalist class. While not determining class differences, secondary economic factors, like labor market position, as well as political and ideological factors, contribute to differences in class fraction. They also contribute as well to the differential affinities for participation in class action. In short, this critique applies a unidimensional theory of economic class and a multidimensional theory of within class stratification based on secondary economic, political, and condition criteria to the analysis of white collar labor.

Critique of New Middle Class Theories

Both traditional and marxian analysts who consider white collar labor to be part of the new middle class challenge the conclusion that most white collar personnel are in the working class. Those new middle class theses of white collar work are the central focus of the analytical critique. The position taken here is that the "new middle class" itself, like the white collar sector as a whole, is divided between the working class and the capitalists. In other words, most members of the new middle class are actually in the working class; the new middle class is, for the most part, a fraction of the working class. The new middle class should not generally be understood as a separate class but as largely a stratified constituent part of the diversified working class of modern capitalism. The major part of the new middle class is in the working class, but some is in the old middle class of bourgeoisie and petty bourgeoisie. This is not to deny differences within the working class but to assert an essential unity based on nonownership of the means of production.

Theorists then identify white collar labor as new middle class for three sets of reasons--secondary economic, political, and ideological. Important challenges to the working class designation of white collar labor assign white collar labor to the new petty bourgeoisie, or new middle class, because such workers perform functions or have interests that are distinctive and theoretically antagonistic to the working class (Poulantzas, 1975; Carchedi, 1975a, 1975b; Nicolaus, 1967; Wright, 1978). This critique challenges those nonworking class designations of white collar labor which base class on secondary economic, political, and ideological criteria.

Secondary Economic Criteria for Class

While Poulantzas (1975) holds that the economic sphere determines class position, he does not consider that relationship to ownership alone determines class: Only labor that is productive (produces surplus value) is working class. Since most white collar labor is unproductive labor, it is "new middle class." This assignment is questionable on several levels. First, class designation on the basis of ownership considers the complicating overdetermination of class by other criteria, such as the unproductive nature of certain labor, only as the bases for within-class stratification. Second, Poulantzas includes as unproductive some who are properly productive. "We shall say that productive labour, in the capitalist mode of production, is labour that produces surplus-value while directly reproducing the material elements that serve as the substratum of the relation of exploitation: labour that is directly involved in material production by producing use-values that increase material wealth" (1975, p. 216). This is unsatisfactory because to be productive one must simply produce use-values, which can be either physical commodities or services. *Capital I* defines the "worker who is productive" as "one who produces surplus-value for the capitalist or, in other words, contributes towards the self-valorization of capital" (Marx, 1976, p. 644). A productive worker need not produce material goods. Service workers that produce more value than they are paid are also productive. When someone works for an employer who makes a profit from the employee's services, that capitalist profits from selling the services, and hence the worker is productive. In Marx's classic example, even teachers whose students pay more for education than the teacher earns in salary are productive and exploited.

> If we may take an example from outside the sphere of material production, a schoolmaster is a productive worker when, in addition to belabouring the heads of his pupils, he works himself into the ground to enrich the owners of the school. That the latter has laid out his capital in a teaching factory, instead of a sausage factory, makes no difference to the relation. (Marx, 1976, p. 644)

Third, it is a mistake to designate certain occupations, such as commercial clerks, as completely productive or unproductive since their activities may often have a dual character. There is, as Wright notes, a "dual quality of social positions as both productive and unproductive" (1978, p. 47). "A good example is grocery-store clerks. To the extent that clerks place commodities on shelves (and thus perform the last stage of the transportation of commodities), they are productive; but to the extent that they operate cash registers, they are unproductive" (p. 47).[3]

Finally, while some commercial employees are unproductive, they are not unexploited. Exploitation is sufficient, though not necessary, for working class designation. Most white collar employees are indirectly exploited of surplus value; they are more directly exploited of surplus labor in realizing more value than they receive in pay. Commercial employees are partially exploited. Though they do not directly produce surplus value, they do help realize value in commercial activities like selling and record keeping (Poulantzas, 1975). In making the sale, employees turn commodities into money as part of a process of partial exploitation.

> The commercial worker produces no surplus value directly. . . . His wage is not necessarily proportionate to the mass of profit that he helps the capitalist to realize. What he costs the capitalist and what he brings in for him are two different things. (Marx, 1967b, p. 300)

The commercial employee's partial exploitation exists in that no matter how high the pay, "as a wage laborer he works part of his time for nothing" (Marx, 1976, pp. 132-33). The commercial employee does not directly create surplus value, "but adds to the capitalist's income by helping him to reduce the cost of realizing surplus value, inasmuch as he performs partly unpaid labor" (1967b, p. 300).[4] The "unpaid labor of these clerks, while it does not create surplus value, enables [the merchant] to appropriate surplus value, that, in effect, amounts to the same thing with respect to his capital" (Marx, 1967b, p. 294).[5] In short, commercial employees are at least partially exploited members of the working class.

Political Criteria for Class

Theories that assign a new middle class situation because political and ideological factors are considered to be coequal are also deficient when the economic is the basis for class. In this regard, Wright (1978) stands between Poulantzas (1975) and Carchedi (1975) and constructs a complex class map.[6] Although capitalists and workers remain theoretically identifiable in Wright's scheme, many of the diverse work and market situations cannot be unambiguously reduced to a simple class situation. What makes these class locations contradictory is the theoretical assumption that different class locations give rise to fundamentally different (and potentially antagonistic) experiences and interests. What Wright considers the *fundamental* character of these interests impels him to place white collar labor into various in-between categories. Small employers are located between capitalist and petty bourgeoisie, managers between capitalist and worker, and semi-autonomous employees between petty bourgeoisie and worker. Wright, however, misplaces equal emphasis on divisions between and within classes. Rather than creating ambiguous class locations, typical authority features of work, such as hierarchical structures, in fact, create within a single class patterns of stratification defined by structural subordination.

Supervision as Necessary Coordination

Functional theories of the new middle class, based in the "global function of capital" (Carchedi, 1975a) or on control functions of, for instance, the "Professional-Managerial Class" (Ehrenreich and Ehrenreich, 1977), are also open to question when class derives from ownership. Supervision is "connected with power to give orders" (Speier, 1939, p. 51). Such power or control creates class fraction. Supervision is necessary in the coordination of production (Marx, 1967b; Becker, 1974; Gorelick, 1977). Performance of the global function of capital, like other function or use-value, identifies fractions within a class, not a separate class (Freedman, 1975, p. 43). Supervisors are erroneously located in a new middle class because they perform the function of capital (Carchedi, 1975a, pp. 24-25) or they dominate employees in the production hierarchy (Poulantzas, 1975, p. 15; Wright, 1978). Placements on the basis of function or use value contribute instead to fractions in the working class.

Locating supervisors in the new middle class implies that supervision is a capitalistic function. While managers and some supervisors perform what was once part of the capitalist's role, it is not an inherently capitalist activity. Supervision is necessary in any production process to ensure smooth operation; it constitutes the performance of productive labor (Freedman, 1975). Supervision is a socially necessary use of labor-power (Becker, 1974; see also Oppenheimer, 1985, pp. 16-17). Administrative labor, including supervisors and technicians, is also a socially necessary use of labor power. All "work of social administration," coordination of social activity, "aids in the reproduction of social labor through its contribution either to production or to the coordination of production" (Becker, 1974, p. 444). Such coordination would be "technically useful and reproductively necessary outside the confines of the capitalist mode" (p. 444). The socially necessary, noncapitalist character of this work underscores its working class nature.

Supervision is part of the increasingly collective process of production. By necessity it becomes socially organized. *Capital I* notes that

> no longer the individual laborer but rather the socially combined labor power becomes the actual agent of the collective work process. . . . One individual works with his hands, another with his head, one as manager, engineer, technologist, et cetera, the other as overseer, a third as direct manual laborer or mere helper. Thus more and more functions of labor power are being subsumed under the immediate concept of productive labor and the workers under the concept of productive workers.[7] (Marx in Marcuse, 1972, p. 12)

These workers are "directly exploited by capital," and are members of the "collective laborer." This is so whether their work is "more remote or close to immediate manual labor" (Marx, 1967b, p. 300). *Capital III* summarizes the point more succinctly.

The labor of supervision and management is naturally required whenever the direct process of production assumes the form of a combined social process. . . . All labor in which many individuals cooperate necessarily requires a commanding will to coordinate and unify the process. . . . This is a productive job, that must be performed in every combined mode of production. (Marx, 1967b, p. 383)

In short, supervisors are working class, since

most technical administrators are steeped in the immediate work of production, functioning just over the heads of the scientists and technicians from whose ranks they are drawn. Their labor is *alienated* since they lack control over the purposes and results of production and they are *exploited* as a part of the "aggregate" technical mass producing either surplus value for a capitalist or reductions in the social costs of production for the capitalist class as a whole. In brief, they are workers. (D. Smith, 1974, p. 215, emphasis in original)

Supervisory functions have two aspects, coordination and control. Coordination of the labor process, the "function of the collective worker," is not antagonistic to working class membership (Carchedi, 1975a, p. 24). Coordination, or administrative labor is essential in the creation of value in production (Becker, 1973). There can be no production of scale without coordination. While coordination is a function of supervision, it is not a capitalist function *per se*. Nominal supervisors who perform coordination alone in production, without significant hierarchic control, clearly are working class as nonowners.
Supervision is social, productive, and a socially necessary use of labor power (Freedman, 1975, p. 64).

The growth of the managerial function within capitalism confirms . . . the concentration and centralization of capital. This process develops *pari passu* with the increasing social division of labor, and hence creates a body of managers to coordinate the different operations of the firm. This constitutes no change in the property relations of capitalism, no creation of a new class. Rather, property relations become less personalized, more abstract, and achieve the *appearance* of independence from human relations. (p. 64, emphasis in original)

"Marx clearly includes these 'supervisory' workers in the ranks of wage labor, assigning them the position of skilled workers, whose wages, 'like any other wage, find a definite market price'" (1975, p. 65). *Capital III* holds that

the labor of supervision and management, arising as it does out of the supremacy of capital over labor . . . is directly and inseparably connected . . . under the capitalist system, with productive functions that all combined social labor assigns to individuals as their special tasks. . . . (Marx, 1967b, p. 386)

"It must be re-emphasized," Freedman insists, "that *middle-level management* is part of the working class" (1975, p. 65, emphasis in original). Though highly paid, such managers do not own sufficient capital to join the capitalist class.

The class situation of top management is somewhat more complex. When managers are actually employees of the firms for which they work, they are working class. When they are "employees" of their own corporation, they are actually self-employed owners. Managers are capitalists only if they own significant capital in productive enterprises, either the firm in which they are employed or in other firms. But it is ownership that makes them capitalists, not their managerial occupation or function.

A distinction, though not a class distinction, does, however, exist between the managerial work involved in the extraction of surplus, and the socially necessary work of supervision. Authority relations distinguish the higher "command class" from the lower command class (Robinson and Kelley, 1979, after Dahrendorf, 1959). The higher command class of managers exercises authority, including supervision, over the lower command class of supervisors (cf. Bowles and Gintis, 1989, p. 54). The elite end of the managerial/supervisory spectrum performs functions of capital, but little coordination. Such managerial work involves mainly hierarchic control of labor for exploitation. To the extent that managers have power over subordinates and over decision making in the firms, as members of the higher command class, they are in a higher fraction of the working class. In this sense, they are closer to the capitalist class than nonmanagers. Empirical evidence on ownership by managers and on the proportion of managerial work in control versus coordination would help to frame and clarify the class and subclass situations of high level managers, particularly those who control labor in the assistance of exploitation.

The distinction between managers and other supervisors is important both for the analysis of stratification within the working class and for the investigation of structural change over time. Those supervisory employees with real power over subordinates are managers (distinct but overlapping with managerial employees) in a higher fraction of the working class. Those without such power are considered to be nominal supervisors. Managers are in a higher fraction of the working class that is more similar in supervisory function and authority to owners than to nominal supervisors. Nominal supervisors are similar to other working class members, except for greater authority and skill levels.

There are, however, distinctions and conflicts between supervisors and other members of the working class. "The requirements for foremen and supervisors arise out of the hierarchization of the job structure: this structure must have its specific social agents whose job is the supervision and maintenance of fractions within the working class" (Freedman, 1975, p. 74). Locating supervisors outside the working class "is a confusion of class *role* with class *membership*" (p. 74, emphasis in original). As wage laborers, supervisors are working class, though they may have antagonistic functions. Because they control labor, supervisors are in a higher fraction of the stratified working class.

Locating supervisors in the new middle class involves a misleading focus on the hierarchy in production (Gorelick, 1977). Explorations of changes in labor process organization overemphasize the techniques of hierarchy and control and underplay the significance of class (Marglin, 1974; Stone, 1974; Bowles and Gintis, 1976). "Hierarchy is not class" (Gorelick, 1977, p. 28). The emphasis on hierarchy as such distorts class analysis. The economic realm of ownership and exploitation is the basis for class. "Alienation is simultaneously a process of creation of wealth by workers and robbery by owners" (p. 31). The autonomous treatment of hierarchy outside its economic context "results in the uprooting and embourgeoisement of the concept of alienation" (p. 30). Focusing on hierarchy turns a qualitative concept of class into a quantitative one like stratification (p. 32). "Magnifying hierarchy" reifies it and turns it from a "form and mechanism of class rule into a metaphor for class itself" (p. 30). "Coordination, 'directing authority,' and the division of labor were for Marx *general* social processes, which, under capitalism, took *particular* oppressive forms" (p. 30, emphasis in original).[8] The distorting emphasis on hierarchy makes class a continuous rather than a dichotomous concept (p. 32, after Ossowski, 1963), though properly applied, the analysis of hierarchy lays the basis for a marxian analysis of within class stratification. From its economic foundation, the central fact of class is the creation of capital, "the process of production or the production of surplus value" (p. 31).

Even Carchedi, a central theorist of the functional new middle class, acknowledges indirectly that supervisors or technicians are not necessarily new middle class. Over time all labor experiences two forms of proletarianization. The first is the movement of skilled labor to average labor; the second is "devaluation through dequalification" in which administrative labor loses the global function of capital and joins the working class (1975b, p. 392). The processes comprise the "proletarianization of the new middle class," moving from employee to worker (Carchedi, 1975a, p. 65). This is almost completed among clerical employees. "In short, proletarianization is the limit of the process of devaluation of the new middle class's labour power, that is, the reduction of this labour-power to an average, unskilled level coupled with the elimination of the global function of capital" (p. 65). In these two processes, the new middle class loses the global function of capital, and the labor power is devalued to a working class situation.[9]

The class situation of those who exercise social control or assist in social reproduction is in a higher fraction of the working class. Analogously to supervisors in production, social workers, teachers, ministers, and psychologists assist in the socialization and reproduction of the future labor force. By socializing future employees, agents of social control contribute to reproduction of hierarchical capitalist social relations outside the sphere of production. In this way, the agents indirectly assist exploitation within production. By contributing to socialization for hierarchically organized capitalist society, they aid in social control; this contributes to the exploitation of labor. However, they are employees who perform necessary coordination functions for any society, although in this specific case the society is capitalist.

Moreover, reproduction is not production. Reproduction is not an economic function in production and does not determine class. Socialization, like coordination, is a function of any social system. Distinguishing the proportion of coordination versus control in socialization is harder than in production, but ultimately affects stratification, not class. Teachers, social workers, and social services providers as employees are not middle or capitalist class since they are not self-employed. They are typically nonsupervisory employees, who neither own capital nor control labor in production, though they perform coordination. They are in a skilled fraction of the working class.

The class situation of relatively high level administrators in social service bureaucracies including schools is, due to their authority and managerial responsibilities, in a higher fraction of the working class. The class situation of highest-level government official, including executive officers in the federal government, is more complex (Sweezy, 1942, p. 232). Most important in determining their class situation is that they control the state apparatus of investment and production. Much state activity directly or indirectly produces surplus value. The state in capitalism is both a producer and an executive coordinator. As *de facto* owners of the state's productive capacities, high officials of government are *de facto* capitalists.

The political formulations that imply that there is no "class-in-itself" discovered by careful research and analysis but only "class-for-itself" in class struggle, imply, on the one hand, that white collar labor has an indeterminate class position, and, on the other hand, that white collar labor will not join other workers in class struggle, and hence are middle class. Such Marxist analyses help defeat their own goal. These theories neglect the structural imperatives that predispose certain actions in class struggle. Without an adequate analysis of the structural determinants of class-in-itself, on which class-for-itself is based, it is unlikely that a class-in-itself will become a class-for-itself in struggle. Class-for-itself implies a synthesis of theory and practice, praxis--a mixture of class consciousness and class struggle. Class struggle without class consciousness involves activism, not revolution. And revolution is an ultimate, not a normal, state of society. When clear class analysis abets class consciousness, class struggle and revolutions may result (see Marx in Bendix and Lipset, 1966, p. 9).

Ideological Criteria

Marxists and traditional analysts also locate white collar labor in the new middle class because of the employees' ideologies. Traditional sociologists place white collar employees in the new middle class because they supposedly think of themselves as middle class, or because more prestige attaches to white collar work. White collar labor is "new petty bourgeoisie" because its members supposedly have "know-how" or "secrecy of knowledge" (Poulantzas, 1975, pp. 238, 240). Or a distinction between mental and manual labor distinguishes class: White collar employees are in an ideologically dominant position in relation to manual workers; they share the values of individualism and reformism of the old petty bourgeoisie (Poulantzas, 1975, p. 237).

But ideology is not ownership. There is no economic or structural basis for the claim that ideology dominates the economic sphere (Freedman, 1975). Ideology or prestige are ideas that cannot structurally affect class. Nor do values and attitudes alone remove the structural and economic constraints of class location. Class identification cannot change class position. Moreover, deskilled white collar workers in clerical and sales jobs, in particular, have no more "secret knowledge" than comparable blue collar workers. Many white collar jobs lack significant skill and knowledge. They are similar to what Marx called homogeneous, abstract labor (Braverman, 1974; Carchedi, 1975a). Skilled craftworkers have much greater expertise than most clerical workers. Blue collar craftworkers constitute an aristocracy of labor, yet they remain working class.

New middle class theories based on ideology actually support the working class situation of white collar labor (Lederer, 1912). In relationship to nonownership, white collar and blue collar employees are in similar class positions. That white collar employees are nonowners in similar conditions to manual workers--but thinking differently--actually argues for assigning white collar to the working class. In both ownership and physical conditions the objective situations of white and blue collar labor are similar, so their class situations are similar. Ideological distinctions do not involve class.[10] Poulantzas' designation of those who hold different ideologies or have certain expertise as new petty bourgeoisie similarly represents an idealist fallacy (Freedman, 1975). Ideological domination may separate workers from each other in consciousness but not on the structural, economic basis. Prestige and class identification have no material basis. And while they may contribute to stratification, they do not affect class situation.

CONCLUSION: WHITE COLLAR AS WORKING CLASS

Among the five major theories of the class situation of white collar labor, though the new middle class formulation is most prominent, the working class formulation is most persuasive. Since a fraction of white collar labor is middle class, white collar labor is divided between the middle and working classes. But the predominant portion is working class. In critiquing a century of recurrent debate, the application of an economic definition of class clarifies the working class nature of most white collar labor. The critique is based on economic class and multidimensional within-class stratification. Differences in kind--ownership versus nonownership--determine class, while structural differences along a spectrum determine stratification. Although the ends of the propertyless spectrum are distant, they are not different in the same way that owners differ from nonowners. Capitalists derive their wealth and standard of living from their ownership of productive resources and from exploitation of workers. Though not all owners prosper, to the extent that they remain owners, they retain the possibility of producing wealth. Their ownership also provides for considerable independence and autonomy. Workers cannot maintain an acceptable standard of living unless they earn wages from employment. Even salaried employees may lose their jobs in a tight labor market and have few resources to fall back upon. Within the working class of both white and blue collar labor, different labor processes, authority relations, and work conditions are objective bases of stratification. Secondary economic, political, and social factors define fractions or strata within classes. But they do not constitute class distinctions.

In sum, the popular and social images of white collar as middle class are not sustained by the theoretical analysis. Since economic relations to productive ownership define class, the vast majority of white collar labor is working class. A small white collar section is part of the middle class of self-employed, but few are large capitalists. The empirical investigation in the next chapter illustrates the class situation of white collar personnel, and further develops the working class image and reality of white collar labor.

NOTES

1. In prewar Germany, Deutschnationaler Handlungsgehilfen-Verband (DHV), the German-National Federation of Business Employees considered white collar employees to be essentially entrepreneurial in character (Speier, 1939, p. 12), separate from blue collar labor, and hence middle class (see Dreyfuss, 1938, vol. 2, p. 134).

2. In essence, this view implies that white collar employees, or the white collar stratum, either do not have a class position, because class could only be capitalist or proletarian, or is a separate class. In the former case, white collar is *declassé*; in the latter, it is tied to both other classes at the margins.

3. An additional example in which a position may be solely productive in one case and solely unproductive in another is a janitor (Wright, 1978). "By every definition of unproductive labor, a janitor in a bank is unproductive. No surplus-value is produced in a bank and thus the labor of all bank employees is unproductive. A janitor in a factory, however, is productive, since cleaning up a work area is part of the socially necessary labour time in the actual production of commodities." Do the janitors have different class positions or interests? That productive and unproductive employees share the same interests clarifies their similar situations (Wright, 1976, p. 17). "The fundamental fact 'is' that all workers, by virtue of their position within the social relations of production, have a basic interest in socialism" (p. 17). Arguments on the level of interests are political, however, and do not determine class.

4. Carchedi calls this indirect exploitation "economic oppression" (1975a, p. 18). The distinction between surplus value exploitation and surplus labor exploitation lies in the differences between appropriation of economic value, which is directly translatable into wealth, and appropriation of labor which only indirectly assists in this translation.

5. Nicolaus (1967) suggests that commercial employees are unproductive because they do not produce surplus value, but actually consume it: Their function is to consume surplus value. This mistakes position in consumption (which defines class fraction) for position in production (which defines class). The focus on consumption is similar to the income or lifestyle approaches to class. Nicolaus uses function to define class, but function can only affect class fraction. He mistakes consumption of an increasing flow of produced commodities (that all classes consume) for the consumption of surplus value extracted from workers in production. Capitalists extract surplus value by obtaining goods and services whose total value exceeds that paid to labor. Profit is realized when products are consumed, but surplus value is not consumed by the buyer, middle class or not. Loren (1977) challenges both Nicolaus and Malthus on this point. Consumption is not a new middle class function but a characteristic of all societies that produce goods. Consumption or receipt of surplus income does not determined class. Tying income, and its consequences such as lifestyle, to class mistakes effects for causes. A class's income, however, is related to ownership.

6. More recently, Wright (1985) has changed his formulation of contradictory class locations and reconsidered Marxist class theory. He has moved away from the stress on domination and control in defining class relations

toward a conception of capital ownership and economic exploitation based on skill, credential, and organizational assets in a rational choice model (cf. Roemer, 1982). "Domination-centered concepts of class" are deficient because they "tend to slide into the 'multiple oppressions' approach to understanding society," with no particular centrality for class (p. 57). The basis of class relations now becomes exploitation, the unequal distribution of "productive assets." Exploitation depends on whether a group would be better off if it withdrew its "per capita share of productive assets." The working class is exploited because it would be better off withdrawing its share of assets, but capital prevents this. Wright abandons the labor theory of value as a basis for establishing exploitation, and invokes individual choice to establish interest. The role of the working class thereby diminishes. "It was always problematic whether workers will be formed into a class," since the class structure does not determine the outcomes of those attempts (p. 123).

Skills, credentials, and organizational assets become the new bases for contradictory class locations in a class structure of 12 positions (8 generally middle class). The "new" middle class in marxian class theory are those "non-working class wage earners" (1985, p. 187) that are neither exploiters nor exploited (p. 86). In this formulation they are in contradictory locations within exploitation relations (p. 285). Some of the classes, however, are no longer relational since they are identified by attributes or skills; for example, experts by professional occupations, rather than structural features (1985, p. 153). These locations are more accurately identified as class fractions. Moreover, Wright's turning away from the Weberian path emphasizing effective control and domination based on property relations toward assets exploitation, in fact, leads Wright closer to Weberian multifactoral theories of class and stratification linking structure and agency.

The question of whether, in an exploitation based analysis of class, knowledge, skills, or credentials constitute productive forces that create wealth is an essential one. In a marxian sense, labor power can be considered as the minimal capital of the worker, and skilled labor power as greater capital. To the extent that technical knowledge and skills are productive and the owner of the knowledge can capture the returns, they constitute forms of wealth, and the producer is a small owner. In order to exploit this, however, the producer would typically have to be or become self-employed. The issue is not the skill per se but the opportunity to exploit it in a capitalist sense. Perhaps the 3.4 percent of the labor force (1980), concentrated among professionals and skilled craftworkers that are as "expert non-managers" (Wright, 1985, p. 195) might constitute a core of knowledge capitalists. An additional 12.2 percent of "semi-credentialed employees" would not have enough knowledge capital to be creators of productive wealth. While theories of exploitation and knowledge based class are provocative because they are connected to production, the theory of appropriation of productive assets as a form of exploitation is similar to the consumption theories of class criticized in Note 5. (See Bowles and Gintis, 1989, p. 54 for a similar critique.)

In attempting to create a point of departure for the neo-Marxist analyses of class structure, Wright (1986, p. 115), in fact, contributes to a new recurrence of new middle class theories of white collar class, and to extending marxian classes, now akin to class as income, along a continuous spectrum (cf. Loren,

1977 in Note 2 to Chapter 3). The title of Szelenyi and Martin (1988) suggests the cyclical nature of debates over new middle class and new class formulations.

7. This is taken from an early version of Chapter 6 in *Capital I*, published as *Resultate des unmittelbaren Produktionsprozesses*, (Frankfurt: Neue Kritik, 1969). See Marx, 1976.

8. The "twofold" nature of supervision in capitalist production (coordination versus control), parallels the twofold nature of technology (technical advancement versus reducing wages by intensifying the labor process), and the twofold character of the commodity (use value and exchange value) (Clawson, 1980, p. 192). The commodity's twofold nature derives from labor's twofold nature.

9. There is an empirical basis for examining Carchedi's distinctions between forms of proletarianization (Wright, 1978). The Panel Study of Income Dynamics (1975-77) asks supervisors about their authority to affect the pay or promotion of supervisees; such powers would establish them as managers rather than nominal supervisors. In the Panel Study (1975) only half of all supervisors had such powers; this significantly reduces the size of the managerial/supervisory group in real terms. Wright (1976) suggests that many nominal supervisors are in similar situations to those of nonsupervisory members in the working class.

10. On the level of conditions of work and their "semiskilled" nature, lower white collar jobs are similar to lower blue collar jobs. Moreover, skilled white collar technicians blur with skilled blue collar technicians. While conditions themselves do not determine class, a large proportion of white collar employees are in conditions similar to blue collar workers. The situations of white collar and blue collar have been merging at comparable levels: Upper and lower white collar respectively become more similar in characteristics to their counterparts in upper and lower blue collar labor. See Chapter 6 here for a more extended discussion of the blurring of the white collar/blue collar line.

3 The Extent of the White Collar Working Class

INTRODUCTION

If theory contradicts white collar's middle class image and assigns most white collar personnel to the working class, what does the evidence reveal about the class realities of white collar labor? The first of three extended presentations of empirical investigations, Chapter 3 tests the theory of the previous chapter by illuminating the current class situation of white collar labor. Identifying the class and subclass situations of white collar, respectively, with unidimensional economic class and multidimensional within-class stratification, and using government data and national sample surveys, Chapter 3 accomplishes three tasks. First, it shows that most white collar labor is, in fact, working class. Second, it identifies divisions or fractions within the white collar working class, particularly between supervisory and nonsupervisory labor. Third, it demonstrates that significant segments of white collar labor are in proletarian conditions. The cross-sectional, structural analysis of current class situation in this chapter lays the basis for the analysis of proletarianization in the following chapters.

Most white collar labor is in the working class, and hence the working class within white collar comprises the largest portion of white collar labor. Most white collar labor is also nonsupervisory, and some is in proletarian conditions. Most white collar labor is working class because its members are nonowners. As employees, more than three-quarters of white collar labor are wage- or salary-paid. While relationship to ownership defines class, supervisory responsibility identifies class-category. Roughly two-fifths of white collar labor is supervisory, and three-fifths is nonsupervisory, though there are subdivisions within both groups. The labor process, including authority relations and conditions of work, defines subclass within the working class. About a tenth of white collar labor are proletarian *workers* in working class conditions, nonsupervisory employees who lack significant authority and decision making power at work.

DEFINITIONS AND OPERATIONALIZATIONS

White collar generally means the nonmanual occupations and work involved with people or information in office and business settings. The main white collar occupations of professional (and technical), managerial, clerical, and sales (U.S. Census, 1970) are divided into two major groups. Upper white collar includes the professional and managerial occupations. Lower white collar includes the clerical and sales occupations (Packard, 1959, p. 37; Wright 1977, p. 26). White collar labor here generally means all personnel in white collar occupations (cf. the white collar labor force). Particularly when analyzing the proletarianization process, labor also refers to the work in occupations (cf. labor process). There are three formal classes: capitalists, petty producers, and working class. The capitalist class consists of owners who employ (employers), self-employed who employ others. The petty producers consist of the self-employed (independents) who do not employ others. The working class consists of nonowners, the not self-employed who work for others for wages and salaries.

Large capitalists are major owners of means of production who employ a significant labor force producing goods and services. Small capitalists are minor owners who employ a few goods or services producing employees. Capitalist owners possess resources at least potentially capable of producing revenues adequate to employ others and produce a profit. Petty producers (independents) produce goods and services for fees, but do not employ others, though they may rely on the help of unpaid family members. Although united by ownership and self-employment, employers and independents are different classes (capitalist versus petty producers) (Loren, 1977, p. 44, 50). Petty producers are involved in simple commodity production on their own rather than in capitalist production and relations with employees. The petty (petite) bourgeoisie (old middle class), or "lower strata of the middle class" (Marx, [1848] 1978, p. 479-80), typically encompasses both small employers[1] and independents. The marxian (old) middle class of owners overlaps but is distinct from the sociologically identified "middle class," generally defined by income, education, and occupation. Yet both middle classes typically enjoy the independence and affluence that constitute important parts of the more familiar definition and provide the aura and image to white collar labor.

Roughly a tenth of the labor force is self-employed. A small additional proportion (e.g., 2.0 percent, PSID, 1977) are employees who have second, self-employed jobs, which do not affect the employees' basic class situation. There are generally more employers than independents among the self-employed. The highest proportion of nonfarm self-employment occurs among managerial employees, which include owners and proprietors. Some professional occupations still have large proportions of self-employment. For instance, as recently as 1970, about 60 percent of doctors, 55 percent of lawyers, and 35 percent of architects were self-employed (U.S. Census, 1970). Nevertheless, the increasing proportions of even these professions in the working class confirms Marx and Engels' observation in the *Manifesto* that capitalist development "has stripped of its halo every occupation hitherto honored" and "converted the physician, the lawyer, the priest, the poet, the man of science, into its paid wage-labourers" ([1848] 1978, p. 476; see Loren, 1977, p. 41).

Large capitalists constitute less than 1 percent of the labor force (cf. Lundberg, 1968, p. 22).[2] Large owners, heads of firms with over 50 employees, constitute only 4 percent of all employers (7.6 percent), or 0.3 percent of the labor force (Wright, 1985, pp. 197, 209). At most a quarter of adults (New York Stock Exchange for 1985) and a fifth of households own even one share of stock (U.S. Census, 1984, p. 8). Only one in ten households has over $5000 in stock. In other words, there are few owners, but ownership creates a major distinction between the capitalist and the working class (though minimal holdings do not make an owner except in a nominal sense). Thus at least three-quarters of adults are nonowners. Because such a small proportion of the population are truly major owners and employers in the capitalist class, this study uses the more general terms, "owners" or "employers," or Wright's (1979) term, "small employers" for all employers. Among owners, employers and independents encompass large capitalists, small capitalists, and petty producers.

Modifying Wright's conceptualization of a three class structure--the bourgeoisie, petty bourgeoisie, and proletariat--the main classes here are employers, independents, and working class. Wright also identifies three *contradictory locations* among these classes (small employers, managers/supervisors, and semi-autonomous employees) (1978, p. 63). But this study considers small employers to be a subdivision of employers, and both managers/supervisors and semi-autonomous employees to be part of the working class. For Wright (1976), supervisory power suggests a quasi-class distinction from nonsupervisory employees. Supervisory and nonsupervisory employees are the two major subdivisions or class-categories within the working class. (The term "class-categories" is also used as the general term for the subdivisions within classes.) As employees, supervisors are members of the working class, but their relation to authority makes them less central to the working class than are nonsupervisory employees. Supervisors are further divided into managers,[3] with significant authority, and nominal supervisors, with limited authority.

The basic typology of classes and class-categories in this study then includes employers, independents, supervisors, and (nonsupervisory) employees. The more detailed typology distinguishes employers and independents in the owning middle class, divides the supervisory working class into managers and nominal supervisors, and divides the rest of the working class into the subclasses (or subclass categories) of authorized employees, normal employees, and workers. Nonsupervisory employees as the characteristic segment of the working class constitute the central working class; their combination with closely related nominal supervisors constitutes the expanded central working class. Within the central working class, authorized employees, normal employees, and workers, as defined more fully later, are distinguished by relatively more empowered versus more proletarian work situations and compose the central sector of the working class. Figure 1 schematically outlines the basic class structure and demonstrates rough equivalences among parallel terms.

Because the focus of this analysis is on white collar occupations and class, and the investigation uses labor force data, conclusions here apply mainly to personnel employed for pay or temporarily unemployed. The results based on labor force data are a proxy for the class composition of the entire population. Those not in the labor force (e.g., the permanently unemployed, homemakers,

Figure 1.   Class Scheme and Equivalents

Bourgeoisie	Capitalist	large owner/employers	
petty bourgeoisie	"old middle class" Petty producers	small owner/employers Independents	
Proletariat	Working class	Working class	
	"new middle class" (expanded central working class)	supervisors	managers nominals
	(central working class)	employees (general employee)	authors normals workers

Note: Vertical dimension indicates class scheme. Horizontal dimension indicates equivalent categories. Indented names indicate subcategories within class. Capitalization means class; small letters mean class-category or subclass. Parentheses indicate general categories encompassing those below in similar class. Nominals are nominal supervisors; normals are normal employees. (Middle class designations for points of reference.)

or students) are not directly represented in the analysis. A few nonemployed are capitalist class members living off investment income, but most of the nonemployed are in working class position due to their lack of ownership. Because most people outside of the labor force are not owners, excluding the nonemployed introduces an upward class bias into the results. Since this study emphasizes white collar and the working class, it does not focus on distinctions among owners within the capitalist class, though it provides some attention to white collar labor near the capitalist class, such as top level managers.

DATA SOURCES FOR THE ANALYSIS

Chapter 3 analyzes the recent class and subclass situations of white collar labor. Two major sources of data illuminate those situations. The first are government reports including the Census of Population and Current Population Surveys (CPS), which identify work status and occupation. The Census and CPS use the term "class of worker" to distinguish self-employed from employees (U.S. Census, 1970, Report PC-2-7A). Class of worker data indicate the percentages of self-employed and wage earners in various occupations. Unfortunately, the data only provide information on this most basic class-related distinction between self-employment and wage employment.

Recent Censuses (1970-80) and Current Population Surveys (1967-89) have classified self-employed in incorporated businesses as "employees of [their] own corporations." This obscures the position of employing self-employed as owners, and raises the reported proportion of "employees" in the labor force. Until the 1960 Census, employees of their own corporations were included among the self-employed, and excluded from wage and salary employees. In 1970, they were included among employees but enumerated separately. Their inclusion only increases the total proportion of employees by 1.6 percentage points (1970 Census), and 2.4 points for overall white collar. However, among managerial occupations the inclusion of employees of one's corporation noticeably increases the size of the employee category (8.2 points), though excluding them leaves almost three-quarters as true employees (73.4 percent) (U.S. Census, 1970). For data after the 1970 Census, however, it is impossible to remove employees of their own corporations from the employee figures.

The second major data source consists of a series of recent national sample surveys of the population that include the appropriate variables for analyzing white collar class and subclass situations. The Survey of Working Conditions, 1969-70 (SWC), the Quality of Employment Survey, 1972-73 (QES), Americans View Their Mental Health, 1976 (AVMH), the American National Election Study, 1980 (ANES), and the General Social Survey, 1972-88 (GSS) include variables on labor force status, occupation, self-employment versus wage employment, and supervisory versus nonsupervisory responsibility. These variables permit identification of the basic class-categories of employers, independents, supervisors, and employees. The first three surveys, particularly the Survey of Working Conditions and Quality of Employment Survey, include variables on the conditions of work that provide the bases for estimating the proportions in the three subclasses within the white collar working class.

Class Position: Census of Population Data

Based on the 1970 data that permit the inclusion of employees of their own corporation among owners, self-employment is slightly higher among white collar labor (9.9 percent in 1970) than in the overall labor force (9.3 percent) (Table 1). Upper white collar is 15.1 percent self-employed. Professionals are only 9.0 percent self-employed, but fully a quarter (26.1 percent) of managerial personnel, whose Census category includes owners and proprietors, is self-employed. Lower white collar is only 5.1 percent self-employed, largely because self-employment among clericals is almost nil (1.9 percent). There is, however, continuing self-employment among sales representatives (13.1 percent). The proportions of self-employment are slightly smaller for 1980. This reflects generally decreasing relative self-employment (though the absolute numbers have increased in the Current Population Survey) as well as the inclusion of employees of their own corporations in the employee category.

Conversely, from 1970 to 1980, about 90 percent of all white collar labor has been in the working class. Thus, the vast majority of white collar labor have been nonowners working for wages and salaries (or piece-rate and commissions). Moreover, differential patterns of class distributions exist between upper and lower white collar occupations. The upper white collar occupations tend to be less working class, while lower white collar tend to be more working class.

Upper white collar labor is roughly 85 percent working class. There is, however, a fairly wide difference between the percentages of professionals and

Table 1. Classes as Percentages of White Collar Occupation Groups, Government Surveys, 1970-80

	1970 Owner	1970 Employee	1975 Owner	1975 Employee	1980 Owner	1980 Employee
White Collar	9.9	89.5	8.2	90.9	8.2	91.2
Upper White Collar	15.1	84.6	12.6	87.3	11.6	88.2
Professional	9.0	90.9	7.8	92.2	7.7	92.2
Managerial	26.1	73.4	19.4	80.2	17.2	82.5
Lower White Collar	5.1	94.1	3.7	94.8	4.5	94.4
Clerical	1.9	97.2	0.9	97.5	1.4	97.3
Sales	13.1	86.0	11.2	87.4	13.3	86.0
Total Labor Force	9.3	90.1	9.8	90.3	9.8	90.6

Note: Employees of own corporation included in self-employed for 1970; in employees in 1975 and 1980. Total Labor Force, abbreviated after as Total, includes all occupational groups: white collar, blue collar, service, and farm. Percentages are proportions of white collar occupational groups that are, respectively, self-employed (owners) and employees (i.e, not self-employed).
Sources: Census, 1970; unpublished CPS, 1975 and 1980.

managers in the working class. Although over 90 percent of professionals are working class, only about 75 to 80 percent of managerial personnel are so situated since the category includes owners. On the other hand, the high proportion of professionals who are working class members challenges the image of professionals as largely self-employed.

Among lower white collar labor, the working class proportion is even higher. Overall, 95 percent of lower white collar labor is wage or salary paid. Clericals are almost completely working class since approximately 97 percent are employees. In the 1970s, however, only about 86 percent of salespersons were in the working class. This lower figure reflects continuing self-employment among sales representatives. For the most part, however, the large majority of white collar labor has been in the working class in the 1970s and 1980s.

By 1980, white collar labor has become a majority in the labor force (52.2 percent). With 91.2 percent of white collar labor as employees, the white collar working class encompasses 47.6 percent of the labor force. By 1982, with white collar growing to 53.3 percent of the labor force, though white collar employees remain the same proportion, the white collar working class grows to 49 percent of the labor force. In short, by the beginning of the 1980s, close to a majority of the labor force is in the white collar working class.

Census data do not distinguish between employers and independents, or between supervisors and nonsupervisors. Nor do they provide information on work conditions. Moreover, due to a change in occupational coding, the Census and Current Population Survey data do not include codes that identify white collar occupations after, respectively, 1970 and 1982, so exact comparisons beyond those points are not possible. The series of national sample surveys, however, do contain data that distinguish supervisors from employees and identify conditions at work.

Working Class Situations: National Sample Surveys

The four national surveys between 1970 and 1980 (SWC, QES, AVMH, ANES) indicate whether owners and employees supervise others or not. These distinctions form the bases for distinguishing, on the one hand, between employers and independents, and, on the other hand, between supervisors and other employees in the working class. The three national surveys conducted in the 1970s (SWC, QES, AVMH) identify the conditions under which employees work. Those work conditions form the bases for distinguishing within the nonsupervisory working class between authorized employees, normal employees, and workers. Because the emphasis here is on divisions within the working class, and the self-employed comprise only roughly a sixth of the labor force, there is no specific analysis of independents (about 5 percent) and employers (about 10 percent) among white collar (see Table 27 in Chapter 5). The initial analysis of the data provides estimates of the proportions of supervisory and nonsupervisory employees within white collar occupations. Further analysis indicates the proportions in the central working class and in working class conditions among nonsupervisory white collar employees.

BASIC DIVISIONS WITHIN THE WORKING CLASS

From 1970 to 1980, about forty percent (39.0 to 43.4 percent) of white collar labor are supervisors (see Table 2). Between two-fifths and one-half of white collar labor (41.3 to 50.0 percent) are nonsupervisory employees (Table 3). In upper white collar, supervisors comprise about half (46.5 to 57.6 percent) of all employees. Only one-fifth to one-third of upper white collar labor (19.5 to 31.8 percent) is nonsupervisory. Since upper white collar includes managerial employees, it is again not surprising that there is a higher proportion of supervisors and a lower proportion of employees among that group.

The relationship reverses in the lower white collar sector. About two-thirds to three-quarters of lower white collar (65.0 to 71.2 percent) is nonsupervisory. On the other hand, less than a third (32.1 to 24.8 percent) of lower white collar is supervisory. As in the Census data, the proportion of self-employment in the lower white collar sector is small: supervisors and employees constitute almost the entire group (data not shown).

Supervisory responsibility varies among the four main white collar occupations. From 38.2 to 62.9 percent of professionals are supervisors (Table 2). Between 30.3 and 50.9 percent are nonsupervisory (Table 3). The proportion of managers who supervise, at 42.2 to 55.6 percent, is roughly the same as professionals. Only 4.8 to 11.1 percent of managers are nonsupervisory employees. On the other hand, clerical employees are about two-thirds (65.8 to 72.5 percent) nonsupervisory; about a third to a quarter are supervisors (34.0 to 26.8 percent). The sales sector is approximately two-thirds nonsupervisory (62.5

Table 2. Supervisors as Percentages of White Collar Occupations, National Surveys, 1970-80

	1970	1973	1976	1980
White Collar	43.4	41.4	39.9	39.0
Upper White Collar	53.9	57.6	49.4	46.5
Professional	62.9	62.2	45.8	38.2
Managerial	42.2	51.3	54.6	55.6
Lower White Collar	32.1	24.8	30.1	25.8
Clerical	33.4	26.9	31.3	26.8
Sales	28.5	19.1	25.5	20.7
Total	36.1	34.1	31.4	31.2

Sources: Survey of Working Conditions, 1969-70; Quality of Employment Survey, 1972-73; Americans View Their Mental Health, 1976; and American National Election Study, 1980.

Table 3. Nonsupervisory Employees as Percentages of White Collar Occupations, National Surveys, 1970-80

	1970	1973	1976	1980
White Collar	41.3	46.4	48.0	46.4
Upper White Collar	19.5	22.1	30.3	31.8
Professional	30.3	31.5	47.8	50.9
Managerial	5.4	9.4	4.8	11.1
Lower White Collar	65.0	71.2	66.5	72.0
Clerical	65.8	72.5	66.3	72.5
Sales	62.5	67.7	66.8	69.0
Total	52.2	54.9	57.3	56.7

Sources: Survey of Working Conditions, 1969-70; Quality of Employment Survey, 1972-73; Americans View Their Mental Health, 1976; and American National Election Study, 1980.

to 69.0 percent); the proportion of supervisors in sales is far smaller (19.1 to 28.5 percent). The lower proportion of supervisors among sales comes from high working class membership and fairly high self-employment.

Unit of Class Analysis: Individual versus Household

This study concentrates on class analysis at the level of the individual, and relies predominantly on surveys in which respondents are individuals without reference to household position. Such individuals are the respondents in, for example, the Survey of Working Conditions and the General Social Survey (GSS). In the individual approach, aggregating class for individual survey respondents produces the class composition for the entire labor force. In an analysis of class as a household construct, the head's position establishes class for the entire group, in particular, the spouse and children.[4] In cases of married households, the husband has traditionally been considered to be the head. In households of unmarried people, the gender and class position of the head depends on the actual situation of that individual. The Panel Study of Income Dynamics (PSID), 1975 to 1977 provides the basis for identifying class in terms of household by asking questions of (or about) the head of the household unit. In the PSID for 1977, men headed 75.3 percent of households and women headed 24.7 percent.[5] Table 4 presents white collar class situations based on households from the 1977 PSID, while Table 5 presents comparable figures for individuals from the 1977 GSS.[6] Because the PSID contains data on household heads, the results are not fully comparable with the figures developed from the SWC or GSS based on individuals. Nonetheless, the PSID household figures for 1977 (the latest Panel Study wave to include questions about supervision) provide a useful comparison to the GSS figures for 1977 based on individuals.

At virtually every level, a higher proportion of individuals (GSS) than of households (PSID) are nonsupervisory employees. For instance, in the GSS nearly half (48.9 percent) of white collar labor are employees, while in the PSID only a third (33.1 percent) are employees. Similarly, upper white collar labor in the GSS (35.5 percent) consists of more employees than in the PSID (20.8 percent). An exception to the higher employee proportions in the GSS is lower white collar labor where the employee percentages are virtually the same in the GSS and PSID (64.9 versus 65.4 percent, respectively). This is largely because there are relatively more clerical employees (71.5 percent) in the PSID than in the GSS (62.8 percent). In addition, higher proportions of supervisors than employees appear in the PSID than in the GSS. For the white collar sector as a whole, there are 47.3 percent supervisors in the PSID and only 39.2 percent supervisors in the GSS. More than half of upper white collar labor are supervisors in the PSID (55.1 percent), but less than half are supervisors in the GSS (48.2 percent). A slightly smaller percentage of lower white collar are supervisors in the PSID (27.3 percent) than are supervisors in the GSS (28.4 percent), again because of clericals. In fact, the PSID results show higher percentages of supervisors for the total labor force (41.5 percent) than do comparable GSS figures (30.6 percent).

Table 4. Class-categories Based on Household Heads as Percentages of White Collar Occupations, Panel Study of Income Dynamics, 1977

	Independents	Employers	Supervisors	Employees
White Collar	4.0	15.5	47.3	33.1
Upper White Collar	4.7	19.4	55.1	20.8
Professional	2.0	10.6	51.0	36.4
Managerial	7.1	27.1	58.6	7.2
Lower White Collar	2.2	5.1	27.3	65.4
Clerical	0.0	0.0	28.5	71.5
Sales	6.2	14.7	25.1	54.0
Total	4.3	10.9	41.5	43.3

Note: Weighted N = 79,750. Because PSID results are not representative of the entire labor force, occupational categories are not weighted to CPS percentages. Here and in other tables of class-categories, percentages sum horizontally to 100 with rounding.

Table 5. Class-categories Based on Individuals as Percentages of White Collar Occupations, General Social Survey, 1977

	Independents	Employers	Supervisors	Employees
White Collar	2.2	9.7	39.2	48.9
Upper White Collar	2.0	14.3	48.2	35.5
Professional	4.3	4.9	42.6	44.1
Managerial	2.2	27.0	55.1	15.7
Lower White Collar	2.4	4.3	28.4	64.9
Clerical	0.6	2.6	34.0	62.8
Sales	9.1	7.3	12.7	70.9
Total	4.0	6.9	30.6	58.5

Note: N = 907. Occupations not weighted to CPS percentages in order to be comparable to the unweighted occupations based on PSID in Table 4.

Gender and Class Analysis

Because class in the Panel Study of Income Dynamics is based on the position of typically better situated and largely male heads of household, the PSID results show higher class or subclass positions overall than individual based surveys like the GSS. Of the approximately three-quarters of household heads who are men, for instance, 11.2 percent in the PSID for 1977 are employers and 42.1 percent supervisors, while only 1.0 percent of women household heads are employers and 30.6 percent supervisors. A class distribution based on household heads that are disproportionately men tends to be skewed higher than class based on individuals, men or women, without reference to household position. The one example of lesser situated employees in the PSIDs--clericals--also suggests gender disparities. Women who head households tend to concentrate in nonsupervisory clerical jobs while the supervisory responsibility remains in male hands (cf. Crozier, 1971).

The analysis of occupations as a whole masks disproportions between men and women. In 1975, white collar labor is exactly 50 percent male and 50 percent female (CPS, 1975). But the upper and lower white collar divisions have unequal gender compositions. The upper white collar sector is two-thirds male (67.7 percent), while the lower white collar sector is almost the same proportion female (68.8 percent). By 1980, white collar has become 53.2 percent female. Upper white collar is slightly less male (63.2 percent), but lower white collar is even more dominantly female (71.2 percent). Women continue to move into the low level clerical jobs that are currently 80.1 percent female.

Percentages for the white collar sector as a whole give a summary impression because upper and lower white collar, men and women, balance out. Yet the class situation of upper white collar labor translates into that of better situated men, and the class situation of lower white collar labor translates into that of lesser situated women.[7] In short, a proxy for gender situation is to consider upper white collar to represent males, and lower white collar to represent females. Moreover, the exact male/female split in the white collar sector is not a neutral statistic. While in 1980, women constitute a majority (53.3 percent) in white collar jobs, women make up only a minority (42.4 percent) of the entire labor force. Thus, though the concentration of women in white collar jobs might appear to be a sign of high status, most of those jobs involve lower white collar work in clerical and sales as well as service jobs. Similar patterns occur by race, where blacks, particularly black women, tend to fill lower white collar and service jobs (see Wright, 1985, pp. 197-202). The realities of white collar work for most women are very different from those for most men.

Distinctions between the Working Class and Central Working Class

Just as among owners whether one employs others or not distinguishes employers from independents, among nonowners, whether one supervises or not distinguishes supervisors from nonsupervisory employees. One may further distinguish within the working class between supervisory employees with power (that is, managers) and those without power (nominal supervisors). (The class-category, manager, differs from the occupational category, managerial jobs, though there is considerable empirical overlap). Managers have real power over their subordinates, while nominal supervisors have little say over theirs.

Supervisory responsibility implies the power to give orders (Speier, 1939, p. 51). Managers correspond roughly to nonowners in the higher command class (Robinson and Kelley, 1979) who exercise authority, including supervision, over the lower command class; the lower command class supervises only nonsupervisory employees. Managers are typically not owners, but have similar levels of authority over employees. Nominal supervisors are employees, but have lesser levels of authority and skill. A Panel Study (1975-77) question (see Figure 4 in Chapter 5) on whether supervisors have a say in their subordinates' pay or promotion suggests a distinction along a power dimension between managers and (nominal) supervisors (cf. Wright, 1976). The PSID (1975-77) also asks the number of people a supervisor oversees. In order to be a manager one ought to have certain authority and oversee at least a limited number of persons; here managers are supervisors who have a say in pay or promotion over at least three employees. Nominal supervisors are nonempowered supervisory employees. Table 6 divides supervisors as a whole into managers and nominal supervisors. It also identifies the proportion of total supervisors that each division comprises. Roughly half (52.4 percent proportionally) of white collar supervisors are managers and half (47.6 percent) are nominal supervisors.

Table 6.   Managers versus Nominal Supervisors as Percentages of White Collar Occupations, Panel Study of Income Dynamics, 1977

	Managers	Nominal Supervisors
White Collar	24.8	22.5
	(0.524)	(0.476)
Upper White Collar	31.7	23.4
	(0.575)	(0.425)
Professional	17.8	33.2
	(0.349)	(0.651)
Managerial	43.8	14.8
	(0.747)	(0.253)
Lower White Collar	6.9	20.4
	(0.251)	(0.749)
Clerical	5.0	23.5
	(0.175)	(0.825)
Sales	10.6	14.5
	(0.422)	(0.578)
Total	17.9	23.6
	(0.431)	(0.569)

Note: Figures in parentheses (e.g., 0.428) represent proportions out of the total supervisors (i.e., out of the sum of managers plus nominal supervisors).

Based on the Survey of Working Conditions, Wright shows that white collar labor includes 38.3 percent supervisors and 44.2 percent employees (1977, p. 27), while the analysis of the SWC here shows that white collar includes 43.3 percent supervisors and 41.5 percent employees. This difference derives largely from the different classifications of teachers. Wright excludes teachers from the supervisory category (that is, he classifies all teachers as nonsupervisory employees) on the basis that those answering "yes" to the question about supervising are referring to students, not to other employees (1977, p. 8). Wright finds that more than half the teachers in the SWC indicate that they supervise; but in the PSID only about a quarter indicate that they supervise *employees* (1976, p. 140). In the QES (1973), 60 percent of teachers supervise; in the PSID (1977), about 25 percent of teachers supervise. The higher QES proportion suggests that many of the SWC/QES teachers include students as people they supervise.[8] (Even nonadministrative teachers may also supervise student teachers and paraprofessionals.) Including all teachers in the working class decreases the number of supervisors and increases the number of nonsupervisory employees. In this study, supervisors are members of the working class, and supervision either of other employees or of students assigns teachers as (largely nominal) supervisors.

The clearest working class situations are those of the nonsupervisory employees since they are dependent and without significant authority. Because of their unambiguous working class situation, nonsupervisory employees are considered central members of the working class, or central working class (CWC). Because nominal supervisors are similar in authority levels to nonsupervisory members of the working class, they are considered part of the expanded central working class (ECWC) along with (nonsupervisory) employees (CWC). By including nominal supervisors with other employees as expanded central working class, Table 7 identifies the proportions of white collar labor who are owners, managers, and ECWC.

As Table 7 shows, roughly three-fifths (55.6 percent) of white collar labor are in the expanded central working class. In the upper white collar occupations, nearly half (44.2 percent) are in the extended central working class. About 86 percent of lower white collar are in the extended central working class. Thus including nominal supervisors extends the central working class by over 20 percentage points by incorporating that half of all supervisors (47.6 percent) who are only nominally supervisory into the expanded central working class. Only among managerial employees are the majority of supervisors actually managers (43.8 percent, or 74.7 percent proportionally). The proportion of professionals in the expanded central working class is relatively high (69.6 percent), but most professionals in the expanded central working class are relatively advantaged nominal supervisors or authorized employees. In sum, most supervisors are not managers and, as nominal supervisors, belong more closely with other working class members in the expanded central working class. The distinction between managers and nominal supervisors becomes particularly meaningful when investigating the changes in the structure of the white collar working class over time (see Chapter 5).

Table 7.   Class-categories with Nominal Supervisors in Expanded Central
Working Class as Percentages of White Collar Occupations, PSID,
1977

	Owners	Managers	ECWC
White Collar	19.5	24.8	55.6
Upper White Collar	24.1	31.7	44.2
Professional	12.6	17.8	69.6
Managerial	32.1	43.8	22.0
Lower White Collar	7.3	6.9	85.9
Clerical	0.0	5.0	95.0
Sales	20.9	10.6	68.5
Total	15.2	17.9	66.9

Note: Expanded central working class (ECWC) includes nonsupervisory
employees (Table 4, column 4) plus nominal supervisors (Table 6, column 2).
Managers are empowered supervisors (Table 6, column 1). Owners include
independents plus employers (Table 4, column 1 plus column 2). Percentages
sum horizontally to 100 with rounding.

The General Social Survey also provides a basis for distinguishing between
managers and nominal supervisors (see Table 36 and 37 Appendix to Chapter 5).
In this case, managers are simply supervisors who have subordinates, a definition
that does not necessarily identify real authority relationships. While compared
to the PSID in 1977, the proportions of nominal supervisors in white collar
occupations (overall, upper, and lower white collar) are approximately the same
in the GSS for 1977 (23.5, 27.2, and 19.1 percent, respectively), the proportions
of managers in the GSS are significantly smaller (16.4, 21.7, and 19.1 percent,
respectively). The greater proportions of PSID managers is surprising in terms
of the stricter PSID definition of manager. The difference may result from the
higher likelihood that as household heads PSID respondents would have greater
authority than corresponding general respondents in the GSS.   Including
nominal supervisors, the expanded central working class contains almost
three-quarters (72.4 percent) of overall white collar labor.

Distinctions within the Central Working Class

A significant part of white collar labor is not only in the central working
class but also is in specific working class conditions.   This means that a
significant portion of white collar labor not only belongs to the working class,
but is in conditions on the job like those of workers on the assembly line.
Wright uses the term managers here to designate all supervisors.   Wright
distinguished among nonsupervisory (nonmanager) employees between
semi-autonomous employees and *workers* (1977, p. 9; 1980, pp. 182-85).

Semi-autonomous employees feel that they have "a lot" of both freedom and decision making on their jobs. Nonsupervisory employees who are not semi-autonomous are workers. Roughly one-tenth of white collar labor are semi-autonomous. Roughly one-sixth (16.5 percent) of upper white collar and half (54.5 percent) of lower white collar labor are workers (see Table 8).

Wright's formulation of semi-autonomous employee is weak both in conceptualization and in what the results suggest. While worker is the category of most concern, Wright operationalized semi-autonomous employee based on only two variables, freedom and decision making. Although these variables suggest what a worker may be, Wright proposed little theoretical or empirical validation for their selection. Also, the results for nonsupervisory labor in upper white collar jobs indicate a problem with defining worker using these two variables. A majority of upper white collar labor (57.7 percent), where relatively free conditions might be expected to prevail, are workers and only a minority (42.3 percent) are semi-autonomous. The relative proportions of workers and semi-autonomous employees in lower white collar jobs, where conditions would typically be more restricted, appear to be more reasonable (83.6 and 16.4 percent, respectively).

Table 8.   Class Locations According to Wright as Percentages of White Collar Occupations, SWC, 1969-70

	Petty Bourgeoisie	Employers	Managers	Semi-Autonomous Employees	Workers
White Collar	5.8	11.6	38.3	11.5 (0.260)	32.7 (0.740)
Upper White Collar	8.6	19.7	43.2	12.1 (0.423)	16.5 (0.577)
Lower White Collar	2.2	0.9	31.7	10.7 (0.164)	54.5 (0.836)
Total	6.0	7.3	34.2	11.0 (0.209)	41.6 (0.791)

Note: Managers here include all supervisors. Figures in parentheses (e.g., 0.260) are the respective proportions of nonmanagerial employees that semi-autonomous employees and workers represent.
Source: Wright (1977, p. 27) based on unweighted data from the Survey of Working Conditions, 1969-70 and calculations for white collar overall. Totals based on weighted average of upper and lower white collar proportions. Percentages sum horizontally to 100 with rounding.

DEFINING WORKING CLASS CONDITION

This study provides a definition of proletarian working class conditions and their opposite based on a detailed evaluation of the factors that structure work. *Workers* are employees in working class conditions. Because autonomy (freedom on the job) turned out not be a significant predictor in the empirical analysis that follows, Wright's term for independent employees, semi-autonomous employee, was abandoned. It was replaced by "authorized employee," tied to a significant predictor, authority on the job. The term *author* (cf. Hobbes, 1985, pp. 218-20), suggesting both the authority and creative dimensions serves as a shortened designation for authorized employee.[9]

Although all nonowners are working class, not all members of the working class are *workers*. This is because there are significant differences within the working class. On the most general level, the working class consists of two class-categories: supervisory employees and (nonsupervisory) employees, or the central working class. Among nonsupervisory employees (CWC), those employees most similar to supervisors in terms of authority over their own actions are authorized employees, or authors. Nonsupervisory employees, without authority, are "general employees." Those general employees in proletarian work situations are workers. General employees who are not workers are *normal* employees; normals are the residual employees between authors and workers in conditions around the norm for members of the central working class. In sum, the working class consists of supervisors and employees divided, on the one hand, into managers, nominal supervisors, and on the other, into authorized employees, normal employees, and workers.

Within the working class, it is particularly important to identify workers since they are the most proletarian members. While the image of the classic proletarian worker on the assembly line may be distinctive, exactly what makes such a person a worker is not immediately apparent. Nor is it obvious that other people throughout the occupational structure, for example, in white collar work, might also be proletarian. Certain characteristics in the literature suggest the description of a worker.

Operationalizing "Worker"

Although the term *worker* in this exact sense does not appear in the *Manifesto* or *Capital,* the concept of proletarian worker derives from Marx, who used the words "workmen," "labourers," "proletariat," and "workers" similarly. In the nineteenth century, conditions of most industrial working class jobs were close to those suggested by *worker*. Most members of the working class performed "alienated, externalized labor" (Marx, 1977, p. 84).[10] Such workers were "completely shut off from all self-activity" (p. 508). *Capital I,* does, however, differentiate between "detail labourers" in manufacture (p. 321), who repeatedly perform "the same simple operation" (p. 372), and a "superior class of workmen," some of whom were scientifically trained (Marx, 1967a). This suggests the distinction between authors and workers.

Identifying various occupational dimensions that might define worker or author, Blauner (1960, 1964) discusses both powerlessness in work (1960), and the complementary factor, control. Powerlessness has four major social dimensions and subdivisions. The first is separation from ownership of the means and products of production. The second is the inability to influence managerial policies. The third is the lack of control over opportunity for employment, and the fourth is lack of control over the labor process.[11] Though Blauner did not develop scales based on his concepts, based on his conception, workers would have little voice in policy and decision making, both on what is produced and how it is produced. They would also lack control over the opportunity to work and over the labor process itself.

Oppenheimer identifies the "proletarian type worker" along several dimensions (1973, p. 213). First, the primary source of income is wages (the sale of labor time in advance of the creation of a commodity), determined by large-scale market conditions and bargaining. Second, within an extensive division of labor, a worker performs only a small number of tasks in a total process, and works on only part of a product. Third, the pace of work, the character of the workplace (typically bureaucratic with a hierarchic command structure), the nature of the product, and the uses to which it is put are not determined by the worker but by superiors. Fourth, like wages, the fate of the product is determined by market conditions. Fifth, the worker lacks discretion and judgment, and work is standardized. Sixth, the specter of unemployment and pressures to increase productivity hang over workers. Finally, to defend their situation from deterioration in living or workplace standards, workers move toward collective organization or bargaining. The "white collar proletarian type of worker," represented by lower-white collar employees, contrasts with the "professional," artisan-like employee.

Kohn (1977) identifies "occupational self-direction" as a key causal variable for inculcating values. He measures it on a single scale composed of three dimensions: closeness of supervision, substantive complexity of work, and routinization of work. Closeness of supervision includes dimensions of autonomy, decision making power, and ability to plan ahead. Substantive complexity involves the relative complexity and amount of time spent on work with people, data, and things. Routinization of work (complexity of organization of work) involves the definition of a complete (as opposed to fragmented) job and the level of repetitiveness of work tasks. While Kohn's metrics for each of the three main subdimensions and an overall, single-factor scale of occupational self-direction do not designate the scores that might indicate a worker, such an employee would be closely supervised and perform simple and routinized jobs.

Guttman's (1965) "Facets of Job Evaluation" scale rates job features independently of line of work or prestige rating using a 12-level Guttman scale based on 5 factors related to supervision or autonomy. These include specificity of guidelines (involving a policy dimension), subordination of supervision, time of supervision, and freedom to change tasks received. A fifth dimension, "level of the receiver," is optional and ambiguous. A worker would labor under specific supervisory guidance and have little opportunity to change tasks.

Jenkins, et al. (1975) standardizes objective measures of job characteristics using observation by trained examiners rather than relying on the subjective responses of survey respondents. Examination of 500 employees throughout the labor force identified 18 major job factors such as autonomy and pace control that distinguish among employees. A worker would be low on variety, skills, certainty, autonomy, pace control and cooperation.

Based on Blauner, Kohn, Guttman, Jenkins and Wright, the dimensions that describe employee situations include decision making power, supervision level, complexity of work, physical conditions and movement, pace and press of work, and job security. (Distributive factors like consumption or income were excluded *a priori* from the potential subclass designating variables because they do not structure patterned relationships in the ways that ownership or authority relations do.) The Survey of Working Conditions, 1969-70, and Quality of Employment Survey, 1972-73, contain appropriate questions about occupational dimensions by which to distinguish workers from other employees. The process involved (1) identification of the factors that constitute workers and nonworker employees; (2) development of a subclass metric based on those factors; (3) development of criteria for cutoff points for worker and nonworker categories; (4) incorporating the cutoff points into operational definitions of class-categories, and (5) crosstabulating the class-categories by the appropriate occupational groups in the white collar sector.

Development of a Metric and Identification of Discriminating Factors

In brief, the procedures for determining which factors actually identify worker and nonworker are as follows. The four basic class-categories were recoded into a dummy variable distinguished by levels of authority. Independents, employers and supervisors became "authorities" (1) and nonsupervisory employees remained by themselves as "subordinates" (0). Variables in the Survey of Working Conditions that identified the structural dimensions connected in theory to the definition of worker were selected for further analysis. Those variables that correlated at least at .10 with the class variable were then run in a stepwise, linear regression against the recoded dummy variable.[12] This identified the 15 most significant predictors at p less than .05. Stepwise discriminant analysis determined the final variables that best discriminated between the groups of authorities and employees. The stepwise feature gave the order, from best to worst, among the discriminators. In running the discriminant analysis on the Survey of Working Conditions, seven variables turned out to be the best predictors. A similar group was developed from the Quality of Employment Survey. Each indicates a significant dimension that defines worker or its opposite. Figure 2 lists the variables in order of their discriminating power.[13]

The variables selected generally describe workers and authors .[14] For example, a worker would be someone who is supervised, is not required or allowed to plan ahead or make decisions, is neither given enough authority over others to do one's best work nor allowed to be creative on the job, and experiences very repetitious work. Most workers have short job tenure and belong to unions. Conversely, authors would experience loose supervision, be allowed to plan and make decisions, have enough authority, and creativity, and experience diverse work. They would have considerable job tenure without belonging to a union.[15]

Figure 2.   Statistically Significant Variables for Worker Metric, Survey of Working Conditions, 1969-70, and Quality of Employment Survey, 1972-73

1. Is there one person you think of as your immediate superior or boss--someone who is directly over you?

2. How much is this like your job? A job that allows you to make a lot of decisions on your own.

3. How much is this like your job? A job that requires you to be creative.

4. How many years and months have your worked for your present employer?

5. Are you being given enough or not enough . . . for you to work your best? The authority to tell certain people what to do.

6. How much is this like your job? A job that requires you do things that are very repetitious.

7. As part of your present job do you belong to a union or an employees' association?

These dimensions structure class and subclass in different ways. The empirical evidence corresponds to Giddens' two types of class structuration, mediate and proximate (1973, p. 107-8). Most of the discriminators correspond to proximate structuration in the division of labor (e.g., repetition, creativity) or authority (e.g., authority, decision making). Other variables correspond to mediate structuration regarding defense against the vagaries of limited market position (e.g., tenure and unionization). The subclasses of authors, normals, and workers also roughly correspond to the labor market segments of independent primary, subordinate primary, and secondary markets (Edwards, 1979, Ch. 9).[16]

The discriminant coefficients (c's) from the classification analysis produced scores for all the employees. The distribution of scores for supervisory versus nonsupervisory employees provided the basis for distinguishing the subclasses within the central working class. Nonsupervisory employees were divided to distinguish authors from workers. The residual respondents were designated normal employees. The basis for the distinctions were relationships to the central tendencies and dispersions of supervisors versus nonsupervisory employees. Authors were statistically closer to the supervisors than were other employees.

The equation for distinguishing authors from other nonsupervisory employees was developed based on the relationship between the means for supervisors and employees. The cutoff point (K), an equal number (N) of standard deviations (S) from the respective means (X), represents a location of "equal" distance (NxS) from the central tendency of each distribution. Scores

Figure 3.   Equations for Cutoff (K) Between Authors and General Employees

$$K(s) = \overline{X}(s) - N \times S(s)$$

$$K(e) = \overline{X}(e) + N \times S(e)$$

$$N(s) = N(e) = N$$

$$K(s) = K(e) = K$$

$$N = \frac{\overline{X}(s) - \overline{X}(e)}{S(s) + S(e)}$$

$$K = \frac{\overline{X}(s) * S(e) - \overline{X}(e) * S(s)}{S(e) - S(s)}$$

Note: K = cutoff, N = number of standard deviations (S), (s) = supervisor, (e) = employee.

above this cutoff (K) are "closer" to the central-distributional tendency of supervisory employees and identify employees as authors, because they are more similar to supervisors than to general employees.   Scores below the cutoff point identify general employees.   Figure 3 contains the equations for determining the cutoff between authors and general employees.   Scores between the cutoff and the mean for general employees identify normal employees whose location on the scale are around the norm.   Scores below the mean for general employees identified workers whose location on the scale are below the norm.[17]

The cutoff point and mean among general employees then were used to divide nonsupervisory employees for each white collar occupation into (1) authors, (2) normal employees, and (3) workers.   Crosstabulation established the subclass distributions within the white collar occupations.   Table 9 shows the divisions of white collar occupations into central working class membership and subclasses using the Quality of Employment Survey, 1972-73. (Tables 50 and 51 in Chapter 5 provide full class-category distributions for the SWC and QES.)

About one-fifth of all white collar labor are authors, one-sixth are normal employees, and one-tenth are workers.   As might be expected for white collar as a whole, proportions of authors (e.g., 0.431) in white collar labor exceeds the proportion of workers (e.g., 0.226).   As might also expected from the better situation of upper versus lower white collar labor, the proportion of authors is higher for upper white collar labor (0.520) than both the proportion of workers in upper white collar (0.226) and the proportion of authors in lower white collar labor (0.403).   Conversely, the proportion of workers is higher for lower white collar labor (0.235) than for upper white collar labor (0.204).   The less advantaged the white collar occupation generally, the higher the proportion of workers and the lower the proportion of authors.   This relationship should also apply for blue collar labor.

Table 9. **White Collar Subclasses as Percentages and Proportions of the Central Working Class, Quality of Employment Survey, 1972-73**

	Central Working Class	Authorized Employees	Normal Employees	Workers
White Collar	46.4	20.0 (0.431)	15.9 (0.343)	10.5 (0.226)
Upper White Collar	22.1	11.5 (0.520)	6.2 (0.281)	4.5 (0.204)
Professional	31.5	15.6 (0.495)	8.6 (0.273)	7.3 (0.232)
Managerial	9.4	5.9 (0.628)	2.9 (0.309)	0.6 (0.064)
Lower White Collar	71.2	28.7 (0.403)	28.3 (0.362)	16.7 (0.235)
Clerical	72.5	26.6 (0.367)	29.2 (0.403)	16.6 (0.229)
Sales	67.7	34.5 (0.510)	16.3 (0.240)	16.9 (0.250)
Total	54.9	22.2 (0.404)	19.7 (0.359)	12.9 (0.235)

Note: Percentages for central working class equal total of all nonsupervisory employees, and represent the sum of the percentage for authors, normal, and workers with rounding. Figures in parentheses (e.g., 0.431) are proportions out of total nonsupervisory employees for each subclass.

Workers and the Class Structure

In contrast to the aura that white collar still possesses, about one-tenth (10.5 percent) of white collar labor in 1973 is in conditions analogous to classic proletarian workers in industry. These white collar workers represent about a quarter (0.226) of nonsupervisory white collar employees. Thus, a significant proportion of white collar labor are workers. Not surprisingly, among upper white collar, professional and managerial jobs, the percentages of workers are smaller. Only 4.5 percent of upper white collar labor are workers, in relative proportion about one in five (0.204) employees. In the lower white collar sector, on the other hand, about one in six is a worker (16.7 percent), a quarter of lower white collar employees (0.235). Clerical employees are, in fact, the most proletarian in white collar labor; almost one in six are workers. This is nearly a quarter (0.229) of nonsupervisory clerical employees. In sum, workers make up a small but noticeable proportion of the labor force even in white collar jobs. Almost one quarter of nonsupervisory white collar employees (0.226) are in working class conditions.

CONCLUSION: WHITE COLLAR IN THE WORKING CLASS

In short, the evidence about the working class realities of white collar labor also supports the theoretical challenge to the image of white collar as "middle class." As nonowning, wage- and salary-paid employees, the large majority of white collar labor is in the working class. In fact, over 90 percent of white collar as a whole is working class. Upper white collar labor, including managers and professionals, is just less than 90 percent working class. Lower white collar labor, including clericals and sales, is about 95 percent working class. Structural class based on individuals or household produces similar results. Table 10 summarizes the class situation and subclass realities of white collar labor in the recent period.

Table 10. Summary Table: Working Class Situations as Percentages of Major White Collar Occupational Groups

	Working Class (Position)	ECWC (NME)	CWC (NSE)	Workers (Condition)
White Collar				
Individual	91.2	72.4	48.9	10.5 (0.226)
Household	81.2	55.6	33.1	---
Upper White Collar				
Individual	88.2	62.9	35.7	4.5 (0.204)
Household	76.6	44.2	20.8	---
Lower White Collar				
Individual	94.4	83.3	64.2	16.7 (0.235)
Household	92.4	85.9	65.4	---

Note: ECWC means expanded central working class; CWC means central working class; NME means nonmanagerial employees; NSE means nonsupervisory employees. Figures in parentheses (e.g., 0.226) are the proportions of nonsupervisory employees that are workers. --- means no data available.

Sources: For working class position, Current Population Survey, 1977; for expanded central working class (ECWC) (individual), unweighted GSS, 1977; for ECWC (households), PSID, 1977; for central working class (CWC) (individuals), unweighted GSS, 1977; for CWC (household), PSID, 1977; for workers, QES, 1972-73.

Although most white collar labor is working class, there are also significant differences within the white collar working class. Differential patterns of class and of subclass stratification appear across white collar occupations. Some white collar employees are managers; more are supervisors; most are nonsupervisory employees in the central working class. Including nominal supervisors along with nonsupervisory employees creates an expanded central working class roughly half again as large as the white collar central working class. From half (55.6 percent on a household basis) to three-quarters (72.4 percent on an individual basis) of white collar labor are expanded central working class. From a third (33.3 percent, household) to half (48.9 percent, individual) of white collar labor are central working class. Moreover, some white collar employees are even in similar conditions to proletarians in industry. Though not large in absolute terms, the one-in-ten (10.5 percent) white collar worker constitutes nearly one-quarter (0.226) of the white collar central working class. In short, there are clear ties between white collar labor and the various dimensions of the working class. The cross-sectional analysis of current realities of white collar class challenges the middle class image of white collar and sets the stage for the longitudinal examination of the theories and realities of white collar proletarianization.

NOTES

1. Marxists consider the nonemploying self-employed (petty producers) to be involved in simple commodity production in that they produce commodities (goods and services) through their own work, without the assistance of employees. These self-employed are owners "of their own means of production" (Wright and Singlemann, 1982, p. S181), and hence self-employment and ownership are both indicators of class. Wright (1980, p. 181) calls the self-employed, both employers and nonemployers, *petty bourgeoisie*. Referring to nonemployers, Loren uses the term *petty producers* (1977, p. 10), and Centers *independents* (1949, p. 50), the identification typically used in this study.

2. Loren includes in the capitalist class people earning more than $25,000 a year on the assumption that high incomes represent the fruits of exploitation in surplus value (1977, Chapters 4 and 6). His figures for the class division of the labor force as a whole are close to the Census-based estimates based on class of worker (see pp. 257-60). There are also three government-collected statistical studies of industry that can be used with Census data to explore class position, supervision, and nonsupervisory employment. See Appendix in Sobel (1982a) and Chapter 5, Note 1 in this study.

3. In some cases, Wright (e.g., 1977) uses *manager* as the general term for all supervisors; in others (e.g., 1976), he distinguishes managers from nominal supervisors on the basis of power. Here manager has the second meaning.

4. In many studies of social standing, the class situation of the husband or father provides the class designations for all members of a family. A current debate revolves around whether the class position of employed, married women should be evaluated on the basis of the women's individual situations, in relationship to the husbands' positions, or on the basis of the family unit as a whole (cf. Loren, 1977, p. 32). This is particularly complex in families where

working spouses represent different class positions, though inter-class marriages are relatively infrequent (Packard, 1959, p. 153). "Paul Sweezy has argued that the basic test of whether two families belong to the same class or not is the freedom to intermarry" (Ehrenreich and Ehrenreich, 1977; Sweezy, 1953, p. 123). Rossi (1974) and Coleman and Rainwater (1978) have attempted to define social status on a basis that includes both spouses. See also Goldthorpe, 1983; Erikson, 1984; and Mann, 1986. I would like to thank Nancy Andes for recent information on this issue.

5. The PSID (1975 to 1977) includes self-employment and supervisory variables, and interviews both household heads (usually male) and some spouses; the GSS also asks about spouses' self-employment and supervisory status. These data make it possible to operationalize class based on the work situation of both partners, and to explore household, family, and interactive operationalizations of class (cf. Note 4 above).

6. Figures from the Panel Study are not fully comparable with those from surveys like the SWC because PSID respondents are household heads. Because the types of respondents are different, PSID results are not included in the longer time series in Chapter 5.

7. Clerical work is the largest major occupational category (in 1980, 18.6 percent overall, 35.1 percent for women) and four-fifths (80.1 percent) of the people employed there are women. In 1980, on the other hand, sales included more men (54.7 percent) than women (45.2 percent). The same sort of differential exists for black versus white members of the labor force. For instance, while blacks made up 11.2 percent of the labor force in 1980, only 5.1 percent of managers and sales workers were black. On the other hand, 11.1 percent of clerical workers were black. Black women in particular tend to be concentrated in lower white collar and working class positions. (See Wright, 1985, pp. 198-201.)

8. See Wright, et al., 1982, pp. 719, 721, and Sobel, 1982a, Ch. 5 for more detailed analyses of the class situation of teachers.

9. In *Leviathan,* Hobbes also uses the term *author* in a sense connected to authority. An author is a "natural" person who "owns" the actions of himself and possibly those of another (artificial) person, or "actor," acting by the author's authority. Hobbes captures the sense of authority unto oneself which constitutes author as authorized employee. Yet, by virtue of his being an authorized employee, at least indirectly subordinate to an employer or supervisor, the author here is also an actor in a Hobbesian sense. I thank Timothy Kaufman-Osborn for bringing this to my attention. See Bowles and Gintis (1986, pp. 26, 209) for a somewhat similar conception of author.

10. In the *Enquête Ouvrière* of 1880, Marx attempted to discover the exact working conditions among the proletariat of France (see Marx, 1964, pp. 203ff). This early example of survey research was detailed and exhaustive, but too complicated for more than a few workers to return the questionnaires.

11. The Roper Study (1947), *The American Factory Worker,* on which Blauner (1964) based his analysis, also asks a number of questions about conditions of work. The focus of Blauner's *Alienation and Freedom: The Factory Worker and His Industry* is on blue collar workers. Among factory workers, Blauner includes those working in automated chemical plants. In new working

class studies, technicians in continuous process industries have been typically seen as white collar workers.

12. Linear regression was employed only as a data reduction technique since its use with a dichotomous dependent variable violated the assumption of normality. For the final selections of variables, discriminant analysis was used because it is more robust and appropriate for categorical data (cf. Klecka, 1980, p. 61). See Sobel (1982a, Chapter 3) for details.

13. The best discriminators for both SWC and QES are: (1) having a boss (V81/V134); (2) being allowed to make decisions (V627/V103); (3) having the opportunity to be creative (V631/V104); (4) years on the job (tenure: V611/V76-V77); (5) having enough authority to tell people what to do (V622/V118); (6) having repetitious work (V624/V106); and (7) belonging to a union (V319/V489).

The discriminant (classification) equations for SWC and QES were, respectively:

$$SWC = -11.437 - 0.153*V81 + 1.117*V627 + 1.514*V611 + 1.201*V622 + 0.798*V624 + 0.327*V631 + 1.203*V319.$$

$$QES = -23.806 + 2.160*V103 + 1.553*V104 + 5.970*V106 - 0.177*V134 + 1.497*V489 + 1.074*V118 + 1.677*TENURE.$$

14. An eighth variable, having the opportunity to develop one's abilities, also turned out to be significant for 1970. It was not included in the metric or class operationalizations for that year because it was not significant for comparable 1973 data (QES). In order to compare figures for 1970 and 1973 in Chapter 6, the respective results had to be based on exactly the same variables and procedures.

15. In the Survey of Working Conditions, for women alone, autonomy was a significant discriminator. Since autonomy discriminates between "authorities" and "subordinates," this suggests that only when women are in positions of authority do they have significant autonomy. In the discriminant analysis for the QES, neither autonomy nor opportunity to develop abilities was a significant predictor.

16. Edwards (1979, Ch. 9) describes segmentation into independent primary, subordinate primary, and secondary labor markets. Independent primary workers have job security and stability, career progressions based on skills, and typically self-pacing jobs. They include professionals, supervisors, long term white collar clerical, sales, and technical workers (p. 174), as well as blue collar craftworkers. Subordinate primary workers have some job security and possibilities for advancement in relatively well defined jobs, which, though typically unionized, are repetitive and involve little personal control. They include traditional blue collar working class production jobs and lower level unionized clericals (p. 173). Secondary workers have casual, dead end jobs, with little job security, typically in service sectors but including lowest level, nonunionized clerical workers (p. 167). In sum, the independent primary labor market includes most upper white collar workers, while the subordinate primary and secondary labor markets include different parts of lower white collar labor. The market segments are generally characterized by a related type of control (pp. 179, 182-83). "Technical control leads to subordinate primary employment . . . bureaucratic control to an independent primary market, [and] simple control results in secondary-type jobs" (p. 183). "The different systems of control are not the

only force pushing toward labor segmentation, but they surely are one of the most important" (p. 183).

17. Comparing histograms of the actual distribution of scores (based on regression), identifying a "hypothetical worker," and examining distributions for "representative" occupations (e.g., assembly line workers) suggested the range of percentages of employees in the various subclasses (that is, authors, normals, workers); this also helped to develop the cutoff points. Using the regression co-efficients from the SWC to develop a metric, preliminary estimates indicated that 44 percent of assemblers, and 33 percent of assemblers in the auto industry--classic examples of proletarians on the assembly line--were workers. Crosstabu-lations of class-categories with the variables (e.g., decision making) that define workers and authors showed that on each positive characteristic workers scored lower than authors.

4   The Proletarianization Questions and White Collar Labor

INTRODUCTION

The theoretical analysis in Chapter 2 and the empirical investigation in Chapter 3 challenge both the middle class image and theories of white collar labor, and clearly identify most white collar as working class. But the question remains whether, as white collar labor has grown over time, it has become more or less working class, and, if so, in what ways? In essence, this raises the proletarianization questions, or the theories of white collar proletarianization. Does the white collar working class loom larger or smaller over time?

This issue is complex because both the traditional and marxian theories of structural change are much less well developed and precise when applied to white collar labor. "The meaning of the term 'proletarianized' around which the major theories have revolved, is by no means clear. . . . Only by keeping objective position and ideological consciousness separate in analysis can the problem be stated with precision and without unjustifiable assumptions" (Mills, 1951, pp. 295-96). Moreover, the empirical investigation involves examination of changes over time in three types of structural class situations, one between classes and two within the working class. The three types of proletarianization--class, intermediary, and condition--roughly parallel the divisions between and within classes. Class proletarianization comprises the change from ownership to nonownership of productive resources. It involves moving from the capitalist class to the working class, or more simply, from ownership and self-employment into nonownership and wage or salary employment. Condition proletarianization is the relative decline versus improvement in the labor process within the working class. It involves a more complex process that encompasses the decline of authority relations and working conditions toward those of proletarian workers. Condition proletarianization refers both to the overall condition of labor and the structural work conditions that employees experience.

Between class and condition proletarianization lies intermediary proletarianization. This involves the decline in supervisory responsibility. It is identified by a decrease in the proportion of those employees with supervisory responsibility and an increase in the proportion of those without supervisory responsibility. The term *intermediary* proletarianization indicates both that the process is intermediate between class proletarianization and condition proletarianization and that it affects supervisors, who are intermediaries between capital and labor. Because supervisory status is a proxy for work with significant authority and decision-making, and nonsupervisory employment for being proletarian, intermediary proletarianization is a proxy for condition proletarianization. Changes in the proportions of managers represent a more complex form of intermediary proletarianization, though changes in nominal supervisors also represent changes within the white collar working class.

In the theoretical development in Chapter 2, white collar labor was basically proletarian if, in general, it was working class and, in particular, was in working class condition. In Chapter 4 the direction of motion of working class situation is central. On the one hand, an occupation that is less than half working class, but whose proportion in the working class is increasing, is being proletarianized. On the other hand, an occupation more than half in the working class, whose working class proportion is declining, is experiencing deproletarianization. An occupation simultaneously experiencing relative increases or decreases in the respective working class situations is experiencing polarization.

Chapter 4 examines four questions regarding proletarianization of white collar labor. First, it develops the theories of class proletarianization, the movement from ownership to nonownership. Second, it develops the theories of intermediary proletarianization, or the loss of supervisory responsibility. Third, it develops the theories of condition proletarianization, or degradation of the labor process, in the growth of workers. Paralleling the discussions of supervisors and workers in the last chapter, Chapter 4 focuses on intermediary and condition proletarianization. The chapter also recognizes the contradictory theoretical specifications that make the analysis of proletarianization particularly complex. Finally, Chapter 4 develops a number of hypotheses regarding the different forms of proletarianization of white collar labor. The empirical investigations in Chapters 5 and 6 help to clarify the questions that are contradictory in theory.

TYPES OF PROLETARIANIZATION

Class Proletarianization

In the middle of the nineteenth century, Marx and Engels proclaimed the class proletarianization of the middle class of small owners (Marx, 1977, p. 222). "Society as a whole is more and more splitting up into two great . . . classes directly facing each other: Bourgeoisie and Proletariat." Capitalist industrial development increased the size of the working class because "the lower strata of the middle class--small tradespeople, shopkeepers, and retired tradesmen generally, the handicraftsmen and peasants--all s[a]nk gradually into the proletariat." The working class increased in magnitude, "recruited from all classes of the populations" (p. 227), including "entire sections of the ruling classes" that were either "precipitated into the proletariat" or at least so threatened by the advance of industry (p. 229).

Class proletarianization derives from the centralization and concentration of capital over time. "The accumulation of capital *spreads wage labor* as the prevalent system of production [and] draws a larger proportion of the population into wage-labor status . . . " (Gordon, Edwards, and Reich, 1982, p. 19, emphasis in original). It is part of the centralization and "collectivism" of capital and decline in the market possibilities for small enterprisers in monopoly capitalism (Corey, 1935, p. 180). The first transformation, or "crisis," affecting the middle class was the proletarianization crisis that took place during the upswing of capitalist development and resulted in the loss of ownership of property for most of the "middle class." This crisis of property, the loss of self-employed status, was an accomplished fact for most of the middle class by World War I (Mills, 1951, p. xiv).[1] By 1930, 75 percent of the middle class were dependent employees--middle class only for the occupational tasks they performed (Corey, 1935, p. 275). The concentration of capital brought about "centralization and proletarianization" that created a "new petty bourgeoisie" of officials and clerical employees, "semi-working class sections" or "bordergroups" (Klingender, 1935, pp. xxii, xvii).

Class proletarianization of the petty bourgeoisie--the disappearance of independents and small employers--has continued to affect the class structure into the last quarter of the twentieth century (Singlemann and Wright, 1978, p. 17; Gordon, Edwards, and Reich, 1982, p. 228). The destruction of self-employed locations among the petty bourgeoisie and small employers is an ongoing process. This is particularly clear in the case of professionals, once in "free professions," now mainly employed in large organizations and associations (see Larson, 1977, p. 234).

The penetration of capital results in the separation from ownership for various groups, but there is no accompanying increase in the creation of places of productive workers. In other words, "the rate at which capitalism destroys small production is greater than the rate at which it generates places of productive capitalist employment" (Przeworski, 1977, p. 360). Instead a group appears whose class relations are indeterminate and who are separated from the socially organized process of production.[2]

Intermediary Proletarianization

As Chapters 2 and 3 indicate, most supervisors are in the working class because they are nonowners. The loss of the function of capital for supervisors constitutes intermediary proletarianization between class and condition proletarianization. As modern industry developed, the middle class of small enterprisers declined "as an independent section of modern society" and was largely replaced "in manufacturing, agriculture and commerce by managers, supervisors and foremen" (Corey, 1935, p. 140n after Marx). By the middle 1930s, there had been a decline in the technical component of work and in real authority among foremen and supervisors (Speier, 1934, p. 116; 1939, pp. 29-38). As rationalization and hierarchy increased, "technical personnel," including foremen, engineers, and technicians in giant enterprises experienced a general decline in objective situations and authority (Speier, 1939, pp. 28-29).

For Carchedi (1975a), the "work of control and surveillance" is tied to capital. Supervisors in monopoly capitalism perform the "global function of capital" in organizing and controlling labor, as well as the "function of the collective worker," and the "work of coordination and unity of the labour process." These functions assign supervisors to new middle class (1975a, pp. 24-25). The loss of the supervisory functions of capital constitutes part of proletarianization. In intermediary proletarianization, new middle class members, essentially supervisory labor and administrative personnel, lose their control function over (collective) labor.

The proletarianization of the new middle class of supervisory and administrative personnel lies in two interrelated processes (Carchedi, 1975b, pp. 384-86). First, "devaluation through dequalification," or the technical devaluation of labor power, involves a fragmentation of the work of the new middle class from skilled to average labor (p. 384). Second, the loss of the "global function of capital" is a structural development that affects both supervisory labor and (white collar) employees as a consequence of technical devaluation (pp. 385-86).

The theoretical arguments regarding intermediary proletarianization predict deproletarianization (or "debureaucratization," Low-Beer, 1978, p. 12), but the reasons are very different both within and between marxian and traditional approaches. Marxists suggest that the concentration and centralization of capital produces a greater need for an administrative apparatus for continuing appropriation of skills from and control over workers; this produces an expansion of the agents of social control (Wright and Singlemann, 1982, p. S188; cf. Braverman, 1974). As supervision involves the social relations of control and discipline over the labor process, or the control over variable capital (labor), intermediary deproletarianization involves the gain in autonomy and control among supervisors; as a consequence, it produces related loss of autonomy and control in the labor process for employees who are supervised (cf. Singlemann and Wright, 1978, p. i). The higher proportions of managers and supervisors lead to closer oversight of employees and thereby more proletarian conditions. More practically, Wright suggests that U.S. labor laws that restrict supervisory personnel from unionization contribute to larger supervisory proportions in the United States than in other nations (1985, pp. 223-25). Since supervisors are not eligible for unionization, the larger supervisory force reduces potential union membership. "The extension of supervisory functions to segments of the working class may be one facet of the general efforts by capital to weaken the union movement in the United States" (p. 224).

Postindustrial theorists like Bell (1973) suggest that more sophisticated technologies require greater involvement in control and decision making among a greater proportion of the labor force. In general, technological change requires a greater supervisory labor force. Complex developments such as automation require larger investment in managerial and supervisory expansion, or more supervision of machines, not of employees. The substitution of capital for labor may increase the proportions of supervisors and decrease the proportions of nonsupervisory employees. Technological developments then imply that more supervisors are involved in the oversight of automated processes and machines rather than in the oversight of employees' work activities. In comparing the much larger supervisory force in American versus German steel factories (cf.

Wright, 1985, p. 223), Harbison, et al. concluded that "the greater mechanization of operations the greater is the need for close supervision and the less is the dependence on the skilled craftsman" (1955, p. 37). Because there are more educated people in the United States, more are eligible to be supervisors (p. 35). New working class theories describe nonsupervisory skilled technicians overseeing automated processes in advanced industries (cf. Mallet, 1975).

The increase in managers over time would constitute a "managerial demiurge" (Mills, 1951, Ch. 5), and complex intermediary deproletarianization. The distinction between managers and nominal supervisors is important not only for the analysis of stratification within the working class but also for the related investigation of structural change over time. Supervisory employees with real power over subordinates are managers in a higher fraction of the working class. Those without such power are nominal supervisors who are still generally more skilled than members of the central working class. In the analysis of intermediary proletarianization, the growth of managers indicates complex upgrading and deproletarianization. However, because managers are in a higher fraction of the working class that is more similar in supervisory function and power to owners than to nominal supervisors, the growth in managers is not *per se* a revealing indication of changes in the overall working class. Because nominal supervisors are more similar to other working class members than managers, the growth of nominal supervisors is a more telling indication of the upgrading of the working class as a whole since their skills and responsibility levels are similar but higher than most nonsupervisory employees.

Despite the emphasis on proletarianization in Marxist analyses, marxian theorists as well as postindustrial analysts expect that there will be an increase in the proportion of supervisory labor over time, or intermediary deproletarianization. Marxians see this as an increase in control of labor through greater supervisory oversight. The postindustrialists see this as an aspect of the upgrading of skills. Wright and Singlemann indicate that both intermediary proletarianization and deproletarianization occurred during the 1960s (1982, pp. S194-95), while Wright and Martin (1987) find even clearer evidence of intermediary deproletarianization during the 1970s.

Condition Proletarianization

The most prominent theories of proletarianization concern the degradation of the labor process under monopoly capitalism, or what constitutes condition proletarianization (see especially Braverman, 1974). "Capitalist accumulation continually *changes the labor process,* both through employers' introduction of improved technologies and new machines and through the imposition of increasingly intensive labor-management systems upon workers" (Gordon, Edwards, and Reich, 1982, p. 20; emphasis in original). Work conditions decline as jobs are "deskilled" and the labor process is fragmented. These changes occur both in the loss of decision making authority and in the decline of conditions of work, in particular, among white collar labor.

Condition proletarianization, or *emiseration*, is inherent in the "general law of capitalist accumulation."

> Within the capitalist system . . . all means for the development of production
> transform themselves into means of domination over, and exploitation of, the
> producers; they mutilate the labourer into a fragment of a man, degrade him
> to the level of an appendage of a machine, . . . estrange from him the intellectual
> potentialities of the labour-process. . . . [A]s capital accumulates, the lot of the
> labourer, be his payment high or low, must grow worse. (Marx, 1967a, p. 604)

The final result of condition proletarianization is similar to what Marx
called "simple labor in the abstract" or "labor in general" in *Capital I* (Marx,
1967a, p. 51). The process of condition proletarianization (being proletarianized)
brings labor to the state of condition proletarianization (having been
proletarianized).   The final result would be a predominance of *workers*.
Capitalism tends to reduce all labor to simple labor, though at different and
sometimes contradictory rates (Bowles and Gintis, 1977).

The degradation of the labor process that results from the need to
expropriate greater amounts of surplus value lies at the center of of the capitalist
production process.   Marx traces the decline in the conditions of work as the
progression from the formal subordination of labor to the real subordination of
labor to capitalist control (Marx, 1976, pp. 1019-38).   The formal subordination
of labor emerged from a period of simple cooperation, when the division of labor
was only generally differentiated.   Workers combined their efforts in productive
activity in order to increase the collective output or to distribute the burden of
production.   Marx (1976) saw the actual beginnings of the subordination of
workers in the intensification of cooperation among the guilds that produced a
distinctive division of labor within the workplace.   In the detailed division of
labor, a fundamentally new type of work and a new form of exploitation
appeared.   In manufacturing, skilled tradesmen, formerly apprenticed in their
craftwork, confronted a new collective production process.   Here work was
subdivided and routinized; skills were fragmented and further specialized; tools
were adapted to exceedingly narrow operations.   The progressive differentiation
of tasks in the factory required intervention of the capitalist.   The capitalist was
to do for the collective worker what previously the worker had done for himself:
determine the purpose, pace, and method of production (Marglin, 1974).   The
private ownership of the tools and raw materials by the capitalist and workers'
increasing dependence on capitalists for wages were preconditions for the actual
capitalist labor process.

The real subordination of labor to capital occurred when the factory form
and machine technology combined to produce both the intensification of the
labor process (increased deskilling) and the valorization process (the shift to
relative surplus value).   Under real subordination, changes in the organization
of work made real in production what had previously been only a potential:

> In handicrafts and manufacture, the worker makes use of a tool; in the factory,
> the machine makes use of him. . . .   In manufacture the workers are the parts
> of a living mechanism.   In the factory we have a lifeless mechanism which is
> independent of the workers who are incorporated into it as its living
> appendages. (Marx, 1976, p. 548)

The change from formal to real subordination that accompanies technological
advances in production means that capital uses labor in a much more impersonal

way. "It is not the worker who employs the conditions of his work, but rather the reverse, the conditions of work employ the worker" (Marx, 1976, p. 548). These new forces of production, brought into being by the social relations of production under manufacture, have disastrous consequences for the conditions of work.

> The special skill of each individual machine-operator, who has now been deprived of all significance, vanishes as an infinitesimal quantity in the face of science, the gigantic natural forces, and the mass of social labour embodied in the system of machinery. . . . (Marx, 1976, p. 549)

The real subordination of labor under factory and mechanized production describes the final state of condition proletarianization. Labor's reduction to wage-labor is a token of the turning of human labor power into a commodity. As a commodity, labor power takes on a lifeless quality as merely one of the abstract factors of production. Decision making authority and skills are divorced from workers, and become instead part of the rationalized power of management. Although the changes in the labor process identified by Marx referred largely to industrial labor, white collar labor has not been exempt from such effects (Klingender, 1935; Mills, 1951; Braverman, 1974).

One of the recurring examples of proletarianization surrounds the movement of the clerk of the nineteenth century from a respected quasi-managerial occupation to a reduced position in the twentieth century. Like the craftsman during the industrial revolution, the clerk experienced condition proletarianization (Corey, 1935, pp. 249-51; Klingender, 1935, p. 2; Speier, 1939, pp. 10, 17; Braverman, 1974, pp. 350-51). At one point the clerk was destined for entrepreneurial independence; a dependent situation was only an interim position. The typical career ran "apprentice-assistant-boss." The occupation of clerk had taken on a subordinate role by the middle 1930s (Klingender, 1935); the shift, however, was not obvious since clerks still worked in close contact with managers and continued to assume a "middle class ideology." By the end of World War II, clerical work was fully dependent both in employment situation and conditions (Speier, 1939). In the 1930s, the second crisis of capitalism, the crisis of employment, brought accompanying degradation of the positions and conditions of salaried employees in general to those approaching workers'. Braverman's contention that "clerical employees of the early nineteenth-century enterprise" were the "ancestors of modern professional management" rather than of "the present classification of clerical workers" underscores the significance of the change (1974, p. 293) and the importance of the loss of authority as aspects of condition proletarianization.

During the Depression-created employment crisis of the middle class, the "new" middle class, was no longer a true class but became an aggregation of salaried employees (Corey, 1935, p. 140n). The Depression brought the "proletarianizing tendency" for managerial employees (Corey, 1935, p. 250). By the middle 1930s large offices could be considered "white collar factories." In 1935, if a "broadly defined" middle class included "all salaried employees and professionals" (p. 274), only a quarter of the labor force was middle class. Three-fifths were wage workers, an almost 15 percent increase in the working class from 1870 to 1935.

Three significant indications of the reduced level of white collar workers appear, first, in the mechanization of work based on specialization, second, in the insecurity about unemployment, and, third, in the fact that a larger proportion was being drawn from strata "considered inferior in social esteem" (Speier, 1934, p. 122). Closely related were changes in the sexual composition of white collar labor. Accompanying the general proletarianizing of salaried work was the shift quantitatively in favor of women, but qualitatively in favor of men (p. 122). While the number of women increased, particularly in the clerical occupations, men tended to retain the authority and high level positions in the white collar sphere associated with the male "confidential clerk" (1934, p. 122). Men in high clerical positions retained the more distinctive and managerial aspects of the clerks of old, though they too have tended to lose real authority.[3] Even among foremen and supervisors, there was a decrease in real authority (Speier, 1934, p. 116).

The theme that the filling of white collar jobs by women is an indication of the proletarianization of previously high-level clerical and sales position is a persistent one in the literature. The "feminization" of office work is a "fundamental phenomen[on]" of the evolving occupational structure (Crozier, 1971, p. 15). But, according to Crozier, the impact on men and women is different. "The proletarianization of white-collar employees does not have the same meaning at all for women, and not heads of family, who comprise the majority of the group" (Crozier, 1971, p. 15). Since many working women come from outside the labor force or from jobs in domestic service, their movement to lower white collar work should be seen as upward mobility for the individuals and downward valuation for the clerical positions. But the proletarianization process, *mirabile dictu,* does not seriously affect either men or women; the arrival of women in white collar jobs "was superimposed on a process of mechanization and automation." The effect on men was limited (Crozier, 1971, p. 16).

> Men were pushed toward more skilled occupations and toward executive positions so that the general proletarianization of the white collar group . . . was not experienced as such by those directly involved. To the old white collar group which had pretty much retained its social status--when it had not improved it by technical and hierarchical promotion--was added a new group consisting in part of females with distinctly inferior social status. (p. 16)

For two decades through the middle 1960s, 80 percent of the "fantastic increase" in American white collar employees was because of the "massive recruitment of females" (p. 16). In short, Crozier maintains, the proletarianization process did not seriously affect either men or women: women entering clerical jobs experienced a form of advancement, while men tended to retain the remaining positions of authority. The displacement of male by female labor, however, reduces the value of labor power and is accompanied by a loss of status (Freedman, 1975, p. 52n).

As aspects of economic action, the division of labor, and formal and substantive rationality, the expansion of bureaucracy contributes to condition proletarianization (cf. Weber, 1968, pp. 63ff). This expansion lay in bureaucracy's technical superiority in handling administrative tasks (pp. 956ff). The increasing rationalization of bureaucratic society abetted the proletarianization of labor overall. An abnormal form of the division of labor, and the ultimate state and effect of proletarianization in the "forced" division of labor, occurs when social differentiation develops on the basis of classes or castes, not according to talent (Durkheim, 1933, p. 353ff). The anomic division of labor produces differentiation without consolidation. Exemplified in business failures during industrial crises, and from the antagonism of labor and capital, it creates neither organic solidarity of the normal division of labor nor the mechanical solidarity based on commonality. An excess of anomic division of labor would constitute extreme condition proletarianization.

"Objectively," as Mills noted in *White Collar*, "the structural position of the white-collar mass is becoming more and more similar to that of the wage-workers" (1951, p. 297).

> Both are, of course, propertyless, and their incomes draw closer and closer together. All the factors of their status position, which have enabled white-collar workers to set themselves apart from wage-workers, are now subject to definite decline. Increased rationalization is lowering the skill levels and making their work more and more factory-like. As . . . the skills required for many white-collar tasks become simpler, . . . the white-collar job market will include more wage-worker children. (p. 297)

Mills predicted that "[i]n the course of the next generation," a "social class" would probably be formed between the bulk of lower white-collar workers in salesrooms or offices and wage-workers (p. 297).

In positing the degradation--deskilling and fragmentation--of the labor process occurring as capitalism developed, Braverman (1974) saw two general processes at work. First, the application of technology and machinery reduces the skill levels of craftwork. Second, the application of scientific management (or managerial technology) to the control of the labor process fragments skills and removes control for the worker. The application of the "Babbage Principle" of fragmenting work into unequally paid parts to reduce labor costs assists in both deskilling jobs and in reducing the wage bill to capitalists.

In extensive comments on studies of the white collar labor process, Braverman identified the "mechanization of the office" and movement toward the "office as manual labor" in factory-like conditions as forms of proletarianization (1974, pp. 319, 326). In placing jobs in clerical, sales, and service work among the "growing working-class occupations," Braverman distinguished between "unskilled and semi-skilled" salaried workers (Braverman, 1974, pp. 291, 351; cf. Speier, 1934, pp. 116-18). This underscores both divisions within and similarities between white collar and blue collar labor. Describing keypunching a "'semi-blue-collar' job," Braverman highlights the routinization of office work into a factory-like process (1974, pp. 332, 347). Though Braverman did not consider managerial and professional jobs to be working class, he found aspects of working class conditions at each level.

Labor market pressures reduce the price of labor by erasing the distinctions in skills (Freedman, 1975, p. 52; see also Edwards, 1979). Capital's imperatives are to cheapen the value of labor power and to drive down wages through deskilling in order to further accumulation (Freedman, pp. 51-53). The reduction of labor to common conditions occurs at different times in different sectors.

Machinery and the division of labor proletarianized industrial labor. This occurred before scientific management and technology had affected the office sector subsequent to its dramatic increase in size (p. 52n). In discussing the "proletarianization of the professional," Oppenheimer recognized that lower white collar labor was essentially fully proletarianized (1973, p. 213). "The clerical and sales strata of white collar life have long since been 'proletarianized'" (p. 213). Any further proletarianization would come in the relatively better situated professional labor. For the postwar period through the century's end, segmentation should continue to be the dominant tendency as the current type decays. However, polarization, proletarianization or deproletarianization may all represent manifestations of segmentation. Moreover, the pressures on each segment will not return to homogenization, but to further segmentation in a "reshuffling" of the labor market boundaries and internal changes (Gordon, Edwards, and Reich, 1982, p. 226).

On the other hand, postindustrial theorists hold that there is a constant upgrading of the skill and training levels in jobs (reskilling) as technology develops (Bell, 1973; Kerr, et al., 1964). This contrasts with marxian theorists who hold that there has been a decline in the level of skills and responsibility along with more routinization as capitalism develops (Wright and Singlemann, 1982). Reviewing studies on skill levels and technology, Squires concludes that there is no clear evidence for either overall upgrading or downgrading (1979, pp. 64-74). Spenner's (1983) examination of both the case studies and aggregate analyses also supports the hypothesis of little net change. These conclusions generally challenge the upgrading thesis, and question the impact of automation on job content. Squires (1979, p. 73) and Braverman (1974, Ch. 20), moreover, concluded that the increase in size of various occupational categories (e.g., white collar) which seems to indicate higher skill levels is a misleading indicator of upgrading. This is because the increases in size mask changes in the composition of various occupational categories and the decline in quality of the various jobs within the growing categories.

If proletarianization is occurring, the percentages of empowered employees should be falling, while the percentages of proletarian workers should be rising over time. Wright and Singlemann (1982) found a slight increase in both semi-autonomous employees and in workers in the labor force overall for the decade of the 1960s. Wright and Martin (1987) find an increase in "experts" and a decrease in workers from 1960 to 1980. The latter findings, in particular, indicate deproletarianization.

Contradictory Tendencies

Conflicting analyses in Marx about the change in class structure suggest contradictory possibilities for white collar labor (Speier, 1939, pp. 9-10; Low-Beer, 1978, p. 15). Best known is the classic statement in the *Manifesto* describing the sinking of the lower middle class into the proletariat (Marx, 1977, p. 222). On the other hand, a less familiar prediction in the *Theories of Surplus Value* that the existence and expansion of the middle classes aided the "upper ten thousand" points in the opposite direction (Speier, 1939, p. 10). Moreover, while Marx's more familiar prediction is that "as capital accumulates, the lot of the labourer . . . must grow worse" (1967a, p. 604), he also held that modern industry "compels society . . . to replace the detail-worker of to-day . . . by the fully developed individual . . . ready to face any change of production" (Marx, 1967a, p. 458). Similarly, Dahrendorf (1959, pp. 45-50) questions the rate of labor-process proletarianization, while postindustrial theorists foresee a process of upgrading (Bell, 1973; Kerr, et al., 1964; Fuchs, 1968; Richta, et al., 1969; Gartner and Riesman, 1974).

Although advancing the proletarianization thesis, even Freedman sees the process proceeding at different rates (1975, pp. 52-53). Certain forces counteract or retard the main proletarianization effect. Accumulation has two related tendencies: proletarianization of a few skilled, salaried (and managerial) employees at the top, and the reduced situations of most at lower levels (Braverman, 1974, p. 53). A similar tendency involves the concentration of planning in a few persons, and the actual execution in the larger group. At one point this separation distinguished between mental (white collar) and manual (blue collar) labor, but now the distinction exists within nonmaterial, white collar work as well. Bowles and Gintis (1977), too, question the homogenization thesis and hold to a concept of "heterogeneous labor." In essence, stratification and segmentation are occurring within the working class. Such differentiation is a part of the division within the working class: the various occupations are not homogenized but polarized. A few skilled jobs contrast with the larger, lesser skilled group.

Part of the problem in correctly predicting to what extent white collar proletarianization should occur lies in the question of whether fragmenting processes that occur in manufacture pertain to white collar, administrative labor. The labor of industrial workers produces commodities and profits, while white collar administrative labor decreases realization costs--the expenses of selling and accounting. In production, it may be to the advantage of the capitalist to add employees and increase the rate of surplus value through control and fragmentation of labor. In clerical and sales work, it may, however, be more advantageous in reducing costs to combine more technology with fewer, more skilled technicians than to employ a greater number of less skilled employees. The addition of more industrial labor under proletarianized conditions may provide a capitalist with increased profit. But the addition of more white collar labor, even if proletarianized, may increase realization costs. This does not argue that there is a class difference between productive and unproductive labor, but only that there are different dynamics in fragmenting blue collar industrial and white collar administrative labor.

Moreover, it is "likely that automation does not univocally [sic] either upgrade or downgrade jobs" (Low-Beer, 1978, p. 11). "[A]utomation of blue collar jobs has different consequences from automation of white collar functions" (p. 11). Blue collar automation decreases the division of labor and leaves the worker with an enlarged job and more responsibility. "The findings for white collar work are more contradictory and on the whole less sanguine" (p. 11). Automation is most difficult to develop for the unstructured decisions involved in higher-level managerial jobs. It is also difficult to develop for routine jobs that require the sensing abilities computers lack. Thus the middle level of white collar bureaucracies are the most affected by computerization because decision making there involves a limited number of alternatives that can potentially be handled by computers (p. 11).

It is possible that both theories of deproletarianization and proletarianization are correct: "they may simply describe different situations or different aspects of the same situation" (Low-Beer, 1978, p. 214). Besides unidirectional changes such as proletarianization or deproletarianization, there may be no net change, changes at some levels and not at others or simultaneous proletarianization and deproletarianization that constitute polarization. Moreover, there may be different trends at different points in capitalist development as different social structures of accumulation affect the labor process differently. Initial proletarianization (1820-70), homogenization (1870-1940), and segmentation (1940 to present) have occurred sequentially as dominant trends over the past two centuries. Each trend has an internal lifecycle moving from exploration to consolidation to decay (Gordon, Edwards, and Reich, 1982, Ch. 6). For the current period, there should be general segmentation of white collar labor, but also continuing, though diminished, class proletarianization. In addition, homogenization continues in those areas where machines concentrate occupations at a semiskilled level. The decay of the current mode of segmentation should lead to resegmentation as a new period consolidates (p. 226). The postwar period represents increasingly decaying segmentation that might reveal itself as alternating periods of proletarianization, deproletarianization, polarization or no net change.

The new working class theories, particularly in their European variants, join the strands of the debates on both the course and consequences of proletarianization (Low-Beer, 1978, p. 2). One of these strands maintains that blue collar workers have experienced embourgeoisement to white collar or middle class conditions (cf. Crozier, 1971). The other involves the controversy about the political significance of the growth in white collar employees. Contrary to embourgeoisement theories of the upgrading of industrial workers, new working class theories emphasize the downgrading both of technicians working with rather complex machines and of white collar employees (Mallet, 1963; Belleville, 1963; Gorz, 1964; see also Goldthorpe, Lockwood, et al., 1969 for similar conclusions). Thus convergence occurs between white and blue collar groups. "[T]he manual-nonmanual distinction, so important for centuries, is losing all meaning in our technological age" (Low-Beer, 1978, pp. 217-18). In designating skilled workers and technicians sometimes as white collar and sometimes as blue, new working class theories blur the white collar/blue collar distinction. The fact that both Mallet (1963) and Blauner (1964) describe technicians of the new working class, including skilled workers, as essentially blue collar, while more recent American versions see the new working class as mainly white collar (cf. Oppenheimer, 1972, 1973) also suggests the the blurring of both distinction and the types of labor. Distinctions in conditions and functions are disappearing among the two types of labor. (See Sobel, 1982b, and Chapters 6 here for further discussion.)

These two strands of the debate have historically been separated, but as the blue collar-white collar line has blurred, their referent has come to be the same. One of the groups merging on this fuzzy borderline is the *new working class,* variously defined as educated labor in general or as technicians in particular. In the new working class thesis, the two strands of the debate are reunited. (Low-Beer, 1978, p. 2; emphasis in original)

The theories of embourgeoisement, postindustrialization (upgrading), and proletarianization (downgrading) may be reconciled in the merging of white and blue collar labor (cf. Low-Beer, 1978, p. 2).

The various meanings of the term *new* working class elucidate the implications of new working class and proletarianization theories. The formerly self-employed are new members of the working class. Their autonomy, technical skills, and sometime supervisory functions are newly eroded. With the decline in conditions, even technically skilled white collar employees experience decline in conditions as their work comes to resemble blue collar jobs. In other words, technical labor in the new working class simultaneously experiences simple, intermediary, and condition proletarianization. The basic thrust of the new working class theories is that all three kinds of proletarianization are occurring among white collar labor.

Equally important questions address the various consequences of the new conditions. Some new working class theories stress the loss of status among educated workers as a type of proletarianization; others stress that even seemingly improved conditions produce discontent. Ironically, both embourgeoisement and new working class theorists tend to agree on the merging of conditions of white collar and blue collar labor but differ on the expected consequences. In embourgeoisement theories, better conditions produce workers who are integrated into the middle class mainstream. In the new working class theories, improved conditions for skilled blue collar technicians produce not integration, but discontent, through "conflictual participation" (Mallet, 1975, pp. 52). Rising educational levels produce rising expectations for jobs that are personally involving but come in conflict with overly-structured work situations (see Chapter 7 here).

PROLETARIANIZATION HYPOTHESES

In addressing the proletarianization questions, a simple hypothesis would be that each type of proletarianization--class, intermediary, and condition--should occur at each white collar occupational level. Yet, while the theory clearly predicts class proletarianization, the theoretical predictions for intermediary proletarianization and condition proletarianization are contradictory. Applying the contradictory expectations specifically to the white collar labor produces a set of conflicting hypotheses for the different types of proletarianization. Since class proletarianization is a secular trend, the hypothesis should also predict such proletarianization for white collar labor. Since both postindustrial and marxian theorists predict increases in supervisory labor, the hypothesis here is for intermediary deproletarianization. Since it is unclear whether similar proletarianizing tendencies to those among industrial labor should affect white collar labor, and postindustrial and marxian predictions differ at this most complex level, the hypothesis about condition proletarianization should be for contradictory tendencies,[4] or perhaps segmentation or polarization.

The empirical work that follows in Chapters 5 and 6 tests these theories of white collar proletarianization. Chapter 5 begins with a brief examination of class proletarianization by comparing class proportions among white collar labor over time. The rest of Chapter 5 investigates intermediary proletarianization by comparing the proportions in the class-categories of supervisors (including managers and nominal supervisors) versus nonsupervisory employees over time. Chapter 6 examines both condition proletarianization and the blurring of white collar and blue collar labor. These empirical investigations clarify the theoretical predictions and reveal the extent to which white collar labor has or has not become more proletarian.

NOTES

1. Mills noted that by the 1950s the crisis of property, which had occurred for white collar entrepreneurs prior to World War I, was such an accepted fact that it was no longer experienced as a crisis (1951, p. xiv). A second crisis of unemployment (p. xv) would now threaten white collar employees as well as the prospects of declining working conditions and status.

2. In describing "an emerging white collar proletariat," tied to changes in the educational system, Bowles and Gintis observed that both the system of higher education and those being schooled were being integrated into the system of wage labor (1976, p. 201). This incorporation into dependent conditions is similar to proletarianization in its class sense and stimulates a political response.

3. See Speier (1939, p. 12) on rationalization of organizations and the growth of hierarchy; Schumpeter (1950, p. 131) on the demise of entrepreneurial function in the rationalized corporation that constitutes a type of intermediary proletarianization; and Mills (1951) on "the enormous file," "great salesroom," "managerial demiurge," government and business bureaucracy and hierarchy.

4. One of the theoretical questions that this study was unable to answer involves identifying the neoclassical economic predictions regarding the upgrading or downgrading of jobs. Under the assumption of profit maximization, would neoclassical theory predict general upward skilling or deskilling of jobs? Under what circumstances would capital substitute for labor, deskilled or fragmented jobs substitute for skilled work, or enhanced jobs substitute for deskilled jobs? When would more supervisors tend fewer subordinates and when would skilled technicians tend machines? In the aggregate, what changes would be predicted, and would those constitute proletarianization, deproletarianization, or polarization for both white collar and blue collar labor? Besides considering the substitution of capital for labor, the analysis would explore the effects of transaction costs such as supervision on the organization of work.

Scoville summarizes a neoclassical approach. "Put very simply, the particular 'art'--the industry-specific technology involved--determines the extent to which division of labor *can* be pursued; given the technology, the size of product markets determine how far it *will* be pursued" (1969, p. 36, emphasis in original). Sabel examines the relationship between market structure and industrial structure (1982, pp. 34-36) based on Piore's (1980) analysis of Adam Smith's famous pin-making example. Productivity depends on the division of labor and on the extent of the market. Decomposition of tasks is generally more productive and opens the way to substituting machines to increase productivity. The subdivision of tasks also typically increases total output, but if there is not adequate demand for greater output, the tasks will not be subdivided. Stable, or the lowest level of consistent demand, (as opposed to fluctuating unstable demand) determines the division of labor. However, if the new machinery ultimately destroys workers' dedication to their job, management will not invest in new machines (Sabel, 1982, p. 74). Edwards posits that "considerable choice surrounds any productive techniques," and a range of techniques are available in any industry (1979, p. 179). The decision to use high- or low-skill labor depends on whether it is profitable for a firm to undertake the research and development to convert high- to low-skill production (1979, p. 179).

The pure neoclassical analysis would contrast with the political-economic analysis of the importance of control versus efficiency in production. The need for control might produce greater supervision while the need for efficiency in light of high supervision costs might lessen the amount of supervision. Moreover, the neoclassical approach would provide hypotheses to compare with the Marxist/marxian predictions of proletarianization and the postindustrial predictions of upgrading. Over the long term, what would neoclassical theory predict about the effects of technological development on intermediary or condition proletarianization, on whether supervisors or skilled technicians would oversee automated processes, and whether technology might ultimately displace most workers entirely? While the political implications are outside neoclassical theory, these technological revolutions constitute the bases for fundamental transformation in Marx (1977, pp. 4-5) (see Chapter 7 here), and require an extended exploration of the relationship of technological revolution, knowledge production, and class. (See Bowles and Gintis, 1989 for a microeconomic approach that defines the inherently political in the economics of work relations in the capitalist firm; Bowles and Gintis, 1986, pp. 194-95; and Bowles, Gordon, and Weisskopf, 1983, on increasing enforcement costs.) The attempt to find a collaborator to pursue these theoretical questions was unsuccessful. Initial consultations with both radical and neoclassical economists indicated that this is not a subject for which an established body of microeconomic or labor economic analysis exists.

5 Is White Collar Being Proletarianized?

INTRODUCTION

While white collar labor has clearly changed in the past half century, has it, in fact, become more working class in all its dimensions? Based on the previously developed structural definitions of class and class-categories, Chapter 5 explores changes in the structure and subclass situations of white collar labor over time. In essence, this chapter begins to answer the proletarianization questions: to what extent has white collar labor become more working class and proletarian in the U.S. since 1945? Extending the review of the theories of proletarianization in the last chapter, the chapter begins the empirical investigation of the extent to which white collar labor has or has not come into various working class situations over time. The extent to which white collar labor has become more working class contrasts with the image of white collar as "middle class" (meaning self-employed but connoting general advantage).

The three types of proletarianization parallel the divisions between and within classes discussed in the previous chapters. Class proletarianization consists in the change from ownership to nonownership of productive resources, and involves moving from self-employment into wage or salary employment. Intermediary proletarianization involves the loss of managerial or supervisory responsibility. Condition proletarianization consists in the relative deterioration in the labor process, including decline in authority and conditions of work. It involves a more complex process that encompasses the decline in working conditions toward those of proletarian workers in industry.

In the cross-sectional investigation in Chapter 3, an occupation was essentially proletarian if a significant proportion of its members were in working class conditions or workers. In this chapter change in working class situation is central. On the one hand, an occupation only a quarter working class but with a growing working class proportion is being proletarianized. On the other hand, an occupation more than half working class, with a declining working class proportion, is being deproletarianized. General decreases in supervisory responsibility and decline in work conditions indicate, respectively, intermediary and condition proletarianization. Simultaneous upgrading or downgrading of contrasting categories within white collar occupations indicates polarization. (Referring generally to "proletarianization" questions implies consideration of both proletarianization and deproletarianization.)

Intermediary proletarianization lies "between" class and condition proletarianization. It is measured by a decrease in the proportion of employees with supervisory responsibility and an increase in the proportion of employees without supervisory responsibility. *Intermediary* proletarianization implies both that the process is intermediate between class and condition proletarianization, and that it affects supervisors as intermediaries between capital and labor. Because supervisory responsibility is a proxy for work with significant authority and decision making, and nonsupervisory employment for being proletarian, intermediary proletarianization is a proxy for condition proletarianization. Changes over time in the proportions of supervisors and employees provide an approximation of the change in structural conditions within the working class. Since supervisory responsibility indicates more empowered situations, a decline in the proportion of supervisory employees and an increase in the proportion of nonsupervisory employees indicates intermediary proletarianization. Decline in the proportion of supervisory employees and increase in the proportion of nonsupervisory employees are direct indications of intermediary proletarianization and indirect indications of condition proletarianization. Changes in proportions of managers and nominal supervisors indicate a more complex form of intermediary proletarianization.

In operational terms, the hypothesis of class proletarianization suggests relative decline in the proportion of white collar labor that is self-employed and increase in the proportion that is employed for wages and salaries. The hypothesis of intermediary proletarianization suggests relative increases in the proportions of white collar nonsupervisory employees and relative decreases in supervisory employees. The hypothesis of intermediary deproletarianization suggests relative increases in supervisors and decreases in employees.

The empirical presentations in Chapters 5 and 6 consist of three major analyses. First, there is an examination of class proletarianization of white collar labor based on government data. The question here is the extent to which white collar labor has moved from ownership and self-employment to nonownership and wage or salary employment. Second, there is an examination of intermediary proletarianization through the investigation of changes in proportions of supervisory and nonsupervisory employees in various national sample surveys. In addition, there is a brief examination of the changes in the proportions of managers and nominal supervisors as an indication of more complex intermediary deproletarianization. The findings from seven national surveys from 1945 to 1980 illustrate the trends in supervisory and nonsupervisory employees in the appropriate white collar occupations from World War II through the last complete decade. The findings from the General Social Surveys for 1972 to 1988 provide evidence for the most recent decades.

Third, Chapter 6 examines condition proletarianization through survey evidence on changes in the proportions in the subclasses of authors and workers. Though not referring directly to white collar work, Wright and Singleman (1982) and Wright and Martin (1987) find evidence of condition deproletarianization, while Spenner (1983) finds little net change. Chapter 6 also investigates the blurring of white collar and blue collar labor.

CLASS PROLETARIANIZATION

Class proletarianization, or movement from ownership to nonownership, as measured by changes from self-employment to wage employment, has been occurring continually (cf. Singlemann, Joachim and Wright, 1978, p. 17). Census and CPS figures on self-employment versus wage and salary employment reveal a continuing decline in the ratio of owners to nonowners. From 1950 to 1980 self-employment among white collar labor dropped from 20.8 percent to 8.2 percent. For professionals it dropped from 9.2 percent to 7.7 percent, and for managerial employees from 45.3 percent to 17.7 percent. (The net decline in self-employment among managerial occupations also reflects the inclusion of "employees" of their own corporations among employees after 1970; see Chapter 3.) The related increase in wage employment (employees) (Table 11) indicates class proletarianization. From 1940 to 1980 the proportion of white collar employees grew from 79.2 to 91.2 percent. In the upper white collar level, the increase was from 62.1 to 88.2 percent. The increase among upper white collar employees of 26.1 percentage points is about 40 percent proportionally.

At the lower white collar level there has been virtually no net change during the period 1940 to 1980. After a small apparent decline in working class membership between 1940 and 1950, there was no change between 1960 and 1980. A small decline in the percentages of clerical employees occurred, but wage employment had essentially reached a limit of 95 percent by 1940. The proportion in the working class among sales has been approximately constant near 85 percent employees since 1960. Thus, in the class sense, lower white collar

Table 11. **Working Class as Percentages of White Collar Occupations, 1940-80**

	1940	1950	1960	1970	1980	80−40	80−70
White Collar	79.2	81.5	85.5	89.5	91.2	12.0	1.7
Upper White Collar	62.1	67.4	77.1	84.6	88.2	26.1	3.6
Professional	81.6	86.5	87.9	90.7	92.2	10.6	2.2
Managerial	44.4	48.7	62.6	73.4	82.5	38.1	9.1
Lower White Collar	94.8	94.4	93.2	94.1	94.4	−0.4	0.3
Clerical	98.4	98.2	97.5	97.2	97.3	−1.1	0.1
Sales	89.1	87.2	84.5	86.0	86.0	−3.1	0.0
Total	76.9	81.0	86.7	90.1	90.6	13.7	0.5

Note: Figures are percentages of each white collar occupational group in the working class. Percentages for 1970 include employees of their own corporations as self-employed; for 1980 as employees.
Source: Census, 1940 to 1970; unpublished CPS, 1975 and 1980.

was previously almost fully proletarianized (Oppenheimer, 1973, p. 213). Quite clearly there has been class proletarianization of white collar labor.

By 1980, 52.2 percent of the labor force is white collar labor and 91.2 percent of white collar labor is employed for wages and salaries. This means that the white collar working class encompasses 47.6 percent of all labor. By 1982, 53.7 percent of the labor force is white collar labor though the proportion of employees remains the same. Thus, by 1982, the white collar working class has grown to 49 percent of the labor force. Because of a change in Census (and hence Current Population Survey) occupational coding scheme for 1980 (see Stevens and Cho, 1985), the proportion of white collar occupations cannot be identified after 1982. However, based on an estimate using the General Social Survey, by 1988 the labor force is 58.9 percent white collar labor and 87.4 percent of white collar labor are employees. In other words, by the end of the 1980s, most of the labor force (51.4 percent) is part of the white collar working class. In short, the white collar working class now constitutes the majority of the working population.

INTERMEDIARY PROLETARIANIZATION

Since supervisors are between capital and labor in a higher fraction of the working class than nonsupervisory employees, declines in the relative proportions of supervisors and increases in the proportion of nonsupervisory employees indicate intermediary proletarianization. However, both marxian (Wright and Singleman, 1982, pp. S186-88) and postindustrial theorists (Bell, 1973) predict that supervisors should increase proportionally; such growth in supervisory proportions would indicate intermediary deproletarianization. While supervisory increases constitute the basic form of intermediary deproletarianization, changes in managers and nominal supervisors indicate more complex forms of intermediary proletarianization.

National Sample Surveys

For 1945 to 1980, estimates of the changes in the relative sizes of the class-categories within the white collar occupational groups are drawn from seven nationally representative sample surveys conducted since World War II.[1] For 1972 to 1988, estimates are based on the General Social Survey and, where appropriate, the Panel Study of Income Dynamics, 1975-77. Figure 4 identifies the sources, dates, and sample sizes for the surveys in the time series.[2] Each of the surveys contains the appropriate variables to identify class position through self-employment versus wage employment, and to distinguish supervisors from nonsupervisory employees. Figure 5 identifies the supervisory questions. The data provide estimates over time of the proportions of independents, employers, supervisors, and employees in white collar occupations. Combining the appropriate surveys produces the two time series, respectively, from 1945 to 1980 and from 1972 to 1988 for the class-categories within white collar labor and the total labor force.

Figure 4. National Surveys in the Time Series

Surveys in the Time Series, 1945-80

1) Richard Centers, *The Psychology of Social Classes,* 1949. (OPOR #52, July 1945 data.) N = 1144.

2) Gerald Gurin, et al., *Americans View Their Mental Health* 1960. (Spring 1957 data; updated 1976) (SRC 422, SSA 3503.) N = 290.

3) Melvin L. Kohn, *Class and Conformity, A Study In Values,* 1969. (Spring 1964 data, updated 1974) (NORC 481.). N = 3082.

4) Robert P. Quinn, et al., *The Survey of Working Conditions, 1969-70;* 1973. (1969-70 data.) (SRC 3507) N = 1531.

5) Robert P. Quinn, et al., *The Quality of Employment Survey, 1972-73;* 1975. (1972-73 data; update 1977) (SSA 3510) N = 1496 (1455). Weighted N = 2168 (2068).

6) Joseph Veroff, et al., *Americans View Their Mental Health,* 1980. (1976 data; update of 1957) (SRC 576) N = 2264 (1202).

7) Warren E. Miller and Center for Political Studies, *The American National Election Study,* 1980. (SRC, 1981). N = 1614 (907).

Surveys in the Time Series, 1972-88

1) James A. Davis and Tom W. Smith. *The General Social Survey,* 1972-88. (NORC 9006, April 1972-88 data). N = 1500 (500-1029).

2) James N. Morgan. *The Panel Study of Income Dynamics, 1975-77.* (Waves VIII-X, SRC 7439, 1975-77 data). Unweighted Ns = 5725, 5862, 6007.

Note: Citations are to published studies or codebooks for the surveys. National multistage area probability samples (except 1945, quota control). 1945, white men; 1964, men; 1957 restricted to men. 1945-64, ages 21 and older. 1970-80, ages 16 or older (PSID, 18+, household heads). Effective Ns (in parentheses) restricted to labor force participants.

Figure 5. Wordings on Supervisory Questions, 1945-88

Surveys in the Time Series, 1945-80

Centers, Psychology of Social Classes, 1945. (Q9a, "What do you do for a living?") c. Ask Supervisors, Managers, etc. "About how many people do you have working under your direction?"

Gurin, AVMH, 1957. Q63, "Do you have any people working under you?" (V212).

Kohn, Class and Conformity, 1964. Q18, "Are there employees of the (firm, organization, department) who are under you, either because they are directly under you or because they are under people you supervise?"

Quinn, SWC, 1970. Q33, "Do you supervise anybody as part of your job?" (V127).

Quinn, QES, 1973. Q44, "Do you supervise anyone as part of your job?" (V165).

Gurin, AVMH., 1976. Q. H33, "Do you have any people working under (for) you?" (V361).

Miller, ANES, 1980. Q. Y6a, "Do you supervise any workers or employees as part of your job?" (V460)

Surveys in the Time Series, 1972-88

Davis, GSS, 1972-88. "In your job, do you supervise anyone who is directly responsible to you?" (WKSUP). "Do any of those persons supervise anyone else?" (WKSUPS).

Morgan, PSID, 1975(-77). D14, "Do you supervise the work of others, or tell other employees what to do?" (V179). D16, "Do you have any say about their pay or promotion?" (V181).

Source: Codebooks for the surveys. See Figure 4 for sources for surveys in the time series; see Davis (1982) and Morgan (1975) in the references for sources of those surveys.

Time Series Based on National Sample Surveys, 1945-80

The time series shows the progressions in proportions of white collar independents, employers,[3] supervisors, and employees from 1945 to 1980 (Tables 12 and 13). Supervisors, with authority over others, are a proxy for advantaged employees, while (nonsupervisory) employees, as members of the central working class without authority, are a proxy for proletarians. Relative growth in supervisors and decline in employees indicate intermediary deproletarianization. Relative decline in supervisors and growth in employees indicate intermediary proletarianization.[4] Relative growth (or decline) in both supervisors and employees indicates intermediary polarization.

Differences among the studies had to be reconciled in order to make appropriate comparisons across the surveys. First, the population bases had to be standardized in the largest common group consisting of employed males in civilian occupations.[5] The employed male subgroup, however, is not representative of the entire population since men tend to be household heads and hold higher prestige jobs. Thus employed men tend to have higher class and subclass situations than the excluded groups, for instance, women and the unemployed. The sample sizes also differ, though weighting in the regression analysis compensates for the differences. Respondents generally included employees working at least 20 hours per week. In order to reduce variability based on sampling error, wherever possible (that is, 1945-80 and 1972-82, but not 1984-88), the percentages in each major occupation have been standardized by weighting to the correct occupational percentages by gender based on the appropriate Current Population Survey. The results of aggregating correctly weighted occupations into larger groups produce slightly different distributions among class-categories from the unweighted percentages.

The studies also differ in their procedures and question wordings. The most telling difference comes in questions on supervisory responsibility (Figure 4). For instance, the Survey of Working Conditions asks if respondents "supervise anybody as part of your job?" Americans View Their Mental Health (1957) asks if respondents "have any people working under you?" Different question wordings alone might produce different proportions. Despite the differences, these are the best data available for the longer period (1945 to 1980), and they suggest answers to the questions about the change in class-category proportions over time. Tables 12 and 13 present the respective percentages in the four class-categories for men among white collar occupations from 1945 to 1980.[6]

National Survey Results on Intermediary Proletarianization

As is apparent from Census data, the percentages of self-employed generally decreased. For most occupational groups, both independents and employers declined. On the other hand, total white collar and lower white collar independents increased. Since the samples of self-employed are relatively small, these estimates are approximate, especially for the individual occupations. Because the Census provides better data on self-employment trends and the emphasis here is on the working class, no further analysis of self-employment will be undertaken.

Table 12. Class-categories as Percentages of White Collar Occupational Groups (and Totals), Employed Men, 1945-80

Year	Independents	Employers	Supervisors	Employees	N
		White Collar			
1945	7.1	19.2	20.7	53.1	341
1957	6.2	14.8	34.9	44.2	103
1964	5.1	13.6	43.2	38.2	790
1970	6.7	16.4	50.0	26.9	406
1973	3.6	15.6	49.2	31.5	505
1976	4.2	14.6	48.8	32.4	290
1980	8.9	8.8	45.6	36.6	193
		Upper White Collar			
1945	11.6	34.0	27.9	27.4	197
1957	9.6	22.8	42.0	25.6	76
1964	5.1	16.5	51.6	26.9	790
1970	7.8	22.8	55.3	14.1	279
1973	4.7	19.3	60.8	15.2	346
1976	4.9	19.8	51.8	23.4	203
1980	9.5	12.1	50.6	27.8	140
		Lower White Collar			
1945	1.3	0.0	11.1	87.6	146
1957	0.0	0.0	21.4	78.6	36
1964	5.1	7.8	26.3	60.9	396
1970	4.2	2.5	38.3	55.1	127
1973	1.4	7.6	24.2	66.8	160
1976	2.6	2.6	41.6	53.3	87
1980	7.5	0.0	32.3	60.2	82
		Total			
1945	16.8	11.2	9.2	62.7	1144
1957	9.4	8.9	26.2	55.5	290
1964	8.3	9.3	29.3	53.1	3082
1970	7.1	8.9	40.0	44.0	996
1973	3.9	9.5	38.2	48.3	1270
1976	5.7	8.7	35.9	49.7	691
1980	8.1	6.0	33.9	52.0	459

Note: For the tables in this chapter, occupational groups are weighted to the correct proportions from the Current Population Survey (CPS). Percentages add horizontally to 100 with rounding. Totals for comparison.
Source: See Figure 4.

Table 13. **Class-categories as Percentages of White Collar Occupational Groups, Employed Men, 1945-80**

Year	Independents	Employers	Supervisors	Employees	N
		Professional			
1945	10.6	7.1	19.9	62.4	141
1957	0.0	11.8	44.1	44.2	28
1964	5.2	8.2	41.5	45.2	365
1970	3.5	3.5	68.8	24.1	138
1973	2.1	7.4	68.4	22.2	181
1976	1.6	7.4	47.5	43.4	104
1980	6.8	5.7	40.9	46.6	78
		Managerial			
1945	11.8	51.9	33.2	3.2	187
1957	16.7	31.0	40.4	12.0	39
1964	5.0	23.6	60.4	11.1	424
1970	12.0	41.6	42.2	4.2	141
1973	7.2	31.2	53.2	8.4	173
1976	8.4	32.8	56.3	2.5	99
1980	12.8	20.2	62.8	4.3	62
		Clerical			
1945	---	0.0	---	---	---
1957	0.0	0.0	25.0	75.1	20
1964	0.5	0.0	33.5	66.0	215
1970	0.0	0.0	44.6	55.4	71
1973	0.0	0.0	31.3	68.7	91
1976	2.6	0.0	43.6	53.8	45
1980	0.0	0.0	52.6	47.4	21
		Sales			
1945	---	0.0	---	---	---
1957	0.0	0.0	17.6	82.3	16
1964	10.5	17.1	17.7	54.7	181
1970	9.4	5.7	30.2	54.7	56
1973	2.9	16.2	16.2	64.7	75
1976	2.6	5.3	39.4	52.8	42
1980	12.5	0.0	18.8	68.7	31

Note: See note to Table 11. --- means no data available.

Because the percentages in the time series fluctuate from year to year, it is necessary to use specific statistical procedures to identify trends. For the initial analyses, weighted least squares regression identified possible trends among supervisors and employees in each occupational group for men during the period 1945 to 1980.[7]   This weighting adjusts for differences in sample sizes (as distinguished from weighting as a means of standardizing to correct CPS occupational proportions).   The simple model of respective class-category proportions as a function of time involves regressing the appropriate percentages against time (year). The sign on the slope coefficient indicates the trend, that is, whether the relative size of the class-category is increasing ($+$) or decreasing ($-$).[8] The intermediary proletarianization hypothesis of decreasing proportions of supervisors and increasing proportions of employees implies that the slopes on the regressions for supervisors should be negative and the slopes for employees should be positive. Conversely, the intermediary deproletarianization hypothesis implies positive supervisory and negative employee slopes.[9] Table 14 summarizes the results for intermediary proletarianization from 1945 to 1980. Most tables present analyses of the direction of the regression slopes, rather than the slope coefficients themselves, because the emphasis here is on the direction and not the magnitude of the significant changes.   Those tables in which it is necessary to indicate the magnitude of changes (e.g., Tables 39 and 40 in the Appendix) include regression coefficients.[10]

The tables indicate whether the respective proportions are increasing or decreasing.   Positive supervisory slopes or negative employee slopes indicate deproletarianization, while positive employee or negative supervisory slopes indicate proletarianization.   Slope coefficients significant at p less than .05 are indicated by $++/--$.   Slopes significant at between .05 and .10 are indicated by $+/-$; slopes at between .10 and .25 by $(+)/(-)$; and slopes greater than .25 by $o(-/+)$. o means constant (no slope).   Exact probability values for nearly significant slopes (between .05 and .10) appear in parentheses.

From 1945 to 1980, the slopes for male supervisors among white collar, upper and lower white collar labor (as well as total labor force) were positive ($++$) and significant at p less than .05 (Table 14).   Slopes for white collar and lower white collar (and total) male employees were significantly negative ($--$) at p less than .05. The net increases in supervisors and decrease in employees indicate intermediary deproletarianization among men from 1945 to 1980.   The increases in supervisors predicted by both the marxian and postindustrial theories of deproletarianization appear to be supported by the data analyses. The results are contrary to the thesis of intermediary proletarianization.[11]

By summarizing an overall direction, however, linear regression misses possible increases and decreases during the total period.   For instance, comparing only the two years 1945 and 1980, white collar supervisory percentages increased, but examining the percentages during the period indicates that they rose and fell between the two dates.   The pattern in the figures in Table 12 and 13 suggests that intermediary deproletarianization occurred at first, in the period 1945 to 1970, and that intermediary proletarianization occurred afterwards, in the period 1970 to 1980.   The data suggest that a change in the directions of the trends occurred around 1970. From 1945 to 1970, the proportions of supervisors

Table 14. **Directions of Changes for White Collar Supervisor and Employee Percentages, Regressions, Men, 1945-80**

	Supervisors	Employees
White Collar	+ +	– –
Upper White Collar	+ +	o(–)
Professional	(+)	(–)
Managerial	(+) (.10)	o (–)
Lower White Collar	+ +	– –
Clerical	(+) (.10)	– (.09)
Sales	o (+)	o (–)
Total	+ +	– –

Note: Slope coefficients significant at $p < .05$ are indicated by $+ +/– –$; at $.05 < p < .10$ by $+/–$; at $.10 < p < .25$ by $(+)/(–)$; at $p > .25$ by $o(– / +)$ ($n = 7$, $df = 5$, two-tailed test). Exact probability values between $.05 < p < .10$ are given in parentheses. Regressions are weighted by square root of N, except 1945 by square root of N/2 because of a quota control sample. Series for clerical and sales include only 1957-80 since there are no data for 1945.
Source: See Figure 4.

among total white collar men increased; however, after 1970 the proportions decreased. Similarly, from 1945 to 1970, the proportions of white collar (nonsupervisory) employees decreased, while from 1970 to 1980 they increased.

To determine whether the trends did, in fact, reverse from intermediary deproletarianization from 1945 to 1970 to intermediary proletarianization afterwards, linear regressions have been run on the corresponding class-category percentages separately, first, for the years from 1945 to 1970 and then for the years from 1970 to 1980.[12] From 1945 to 1970, the slopes for supervisors among overall white collar, upper white collar, and lower white collar labor (as well as for the total labor force) among men were positive and statistically significant (Table 15). For the same period, the slopes for employees among overall white collar and lower white collar men were significantly negative. For upper white collar and total men, the slopes for employees were negative though not significant. The relative increases in supervisors and the constancy or relative decreases in employees among white collar men from 1945 to 1970 again indicate intermediary deproletarianization. In other words, the deproletarianization among white collar occurring from 1945 to 1970 appears to be part of the same trend of deproletarianization that occurred for the entire 1945 to 1980 period (Table 14). But the intermediary deproletarianization trend did not necessarily continue into the 1970s.

Table 15.   Directions of Changes for White Collar Supervisor and Employee Percentages, Regressions, Men, 1945-70

	Supervisors	Employees
White Collar	+ +	– –
Upper White Collar	+ +	o(–)
Professional	(+) (.11)	(–) (.10)
Managerial	o(+)	o(+)
Lower White Collar	+ +	– –
Clerical	(+) (.10)	– (.07)
Sales	o(+)	o(–)
Total	+ +	– (.06)

Note: Slope coefficients significant at p < .05 are indicated by + +/– –; at .05 < p < .10 by +/–; at .10 < p < .25 by (+)/(–); at p > .25 by o(–/+) (n = 7, df = 5, two-tailed test). Exact probability values between .05 < p < .10 are given in parentheses.
Source: See Figure 4.

Intermediary Proletarianization in the 1970s

From 1970 to 1980, supervisory proportions for white collar men tend to decrease while employee proportions tend to increase (see Table 16). For white collar, upper white collar, and the total labor force employees the relative increases among men are statistically significant at p less than .05. The other changes are not significant, except for the increase in supervisors in managerial occupations. In general, the signs for the supervisory slopes are negative while those for the employee slopes are positive (Table 16). The combination of decreasing proportions of supervisors and increasing proportions of employees among men from 1970 to 1980 suggests that intermediary proletarianization was occurring among white collar labor during the 1970s.

While the data for men are helpful in analyzing changes in class-category proportions for the entire period of 1945 to 1980, the results based on only one gender are not representative of the entire population. If the trends for women were different from those for men, the conclusions about intermediary proletarianization based on men alone would not apply overall. Unfortunately the surveys for 1945, 1957 and 1964 only provide data for men for the appropriate variables needed in operationalizing class-categories.[13]

Table 16. Directions of Changes for White Collar Supervisor and Employee Percentages, Regressions, Men, 1970-80

	Supervisors	Employees
White Collar	− (.07)	+ +
Upper White Collar	o (−)	+ +
Professional	− (.07)	(+) (.12)
Managerial	+ +	o (−)
Lower White Collar	o (−)	o (+)
Clerical	o (+)	o (−)
Sales	o (−)	o (+)
Total	− −	+ +

Note: Table indicates whether regression slopes are positive (+), and hence category percentages are increasing, or negative (−), and percentages are decreasing. Slope coefficients significant at $p < .05$ are indicated by + +/− −; at $.05 < p < .10$ by +/−; at $.10 < p < .25$ by (+)/(−); at $p > .25$ by o(−/+) (n = 7, df = 5, two-tailed test). Exact probability values between $.05 < p < .10$ are given in parentheses.
Sources: Survey of Working Conditions, 1969-70; Quality of Employment Survey, 1972-73; Americans View Their Mental Health, 1976; American National Election Study, 1980.

Data for Combined Men and Women

Because appropriate data for the examination of the class-categories exist only for men for 1945 to 1964 (1945, 1957, 1964), the investigation over the complete period (1945-80) covers only the one gender. Data do exist for both men and women for 1970 to 1980 (1970, 1973, 1976, 1980) and permit the examination of trends among employees and supervisors in white collar jobs for combined men and women during the later period from 1970 to 1980. Tables 17 and 18 present the data.

The same trend of intermediary proletarianization seen among men for 1970 to 1980 (Table 16 above) appears in the results for combined men and women from 1970 to 1980 (Table 19). In general, there is a relative decline in white collar supervisors and a relative increase in employees. In particular, overall white collar and professional supervisors decrease proportionally. Upper white collar (and total) employees increase proportionally. All of the signs on the regressions for white collar employees (except managers and clericals) are positive.

Table 17. Class-categories as Percentages of White Collar Occupational Groups (and Total), Combined Men and Women, 1970-80

Year	Independents	Employers	Supervisors	Employees	N
		White Collar			
1970	5.2	10.1	43.4	41.3	732
1973	3.2	9.0	41.4	46.4	988
1976	3.5	8.5	39.9	48.0	617
1980	6.4	8.2	39.0	46.4	500
		Upper White Collar			
1970	8.0	18.5	53.9	19.5	381
1973	4.9	15.4	57.6	22.1	500
1976	5.7	14.6	49.4	30.3	315
1980	9.1	12.6	46.5	31.8	318
		Lower White Collar			
1970	2.1	0.9	32.1	65.0	351
1973	1.5	2.5	24.8	71.2	488
1976	1.3	2.1	30.1	66.5	302
1980	1.6	0.5	25.8	72.0	182
		Total			
1970	5.4	6.3	36.1	52.2	1531
1973	3.9	7.1	34.1	54.9	2168
1976	5.1	6.2	31.4	57.3	1202
1980	6.4	5.7	31.2	56.7	907

Note: Occupations weighted to CPS proportions.
Source: See Table 16.

The pattern of increases in employee percentages suggests intermediary proletarianization. In addition, all of the signs on the regression for supervisors (except for managers) are negative. This pattern also suggests intermediary proletarianization. In short, the patterns in the data for both men alone (Table 16) and combined men and women (Table 19) agree in their indications of intermediary proletarianization of white collar labor in the 1970s (Table 20 summarizes the agreements). In sum, these data support the hypothesis of intermediary proletarianization among white collar in the 1970s.

Table 18. Class-categories as Percentages of White Collar Occupations, Combined Men and Women, 1970-80

Year	Independents	Employers	Supervisors	Employees	N
		Professional			
1970	4.0	2.7	62.9	30.3	215
1973	1.9	4.4	62.2	31.5	288
1976	2.3	4.1	45.8	47.8	187
1980	6.7	4.2	38.2	50.9	165
		Managerial			
1970	13.2	39.1	42.2	5.4	165
1973	9.0	30.2	51.3	9.4	212
1976	10.5	30.0	54.6	4.8	128
1980	11.8	21.6	55.6	11.1	153
		Clerical			
1970	0.8	0.0	33.4	65.8	257
1973	0.6	0.0	26.9	72.5	357
1976	0.5	1.9	31.3	66.3	226
1980	0.0	0.7	26.8	72.5	153
		Sales			
1970	5.6	3.4	28.5	62.5	215
1973	3.9	9.4	19.1	67.7	130
1976	3.8	2.9	26.5	66.8	77
1980	10.3	0.0	20.7	69.0	29

Note: Occupations weighted to CPS proportions.
Source: See Table 16.

Both the series for men and for combined men and women suggest that intermediary proletarianization occurred among white collar labor from 1970 to 1980 (Table 20). But this evidence of intermediary proletarianization may be an artifact of different wordings on the supervision questions among the surveys in the time series, or may result from other differences in administering the surveys. The findings of intermediary proletarianization among white collar labor also contradict the predictions among both marxian and postindustrial theorists that supervisors should increase over time (intermediary deproletarianization). The analysis that follows clarifies the situation.

Table 19. Directions of Changes for White Collar Supervisor and Employee Percentages, Regressions, Combined Men and Women, 1970-80

	Supervisors	Employees
White Collar	– –	o(+)
Upper White Collar	(–)	+ +
Professional	– –	+(.09)
Managerial	(+)(.11)	o(+)
Lower White Collar	o(–)	o(+)
Clerical	o(–)	o(+)
Sales	–(.06)	o(+)(.17)
Total	– –	+ +

Note: + +/– – means significant increase/decrease at p < .05. +/– means significant at .05 < p < .10, (–)/(+) means .10 <p < .25; o (–/+) means p > .25.
Source: See Table 16.

Table 20. Agreements on Changes in White Collar Supervisor and Employee Percentages, Men versus Combined, Regressions, 1970-80

	Supervisors	Employees
White Collar	–(.07)	o(+)
Upper White Collar	o(–)	+ +
Professional	–(.07)	+(.12)
Managerial	+(.11)	o(x)
Lower White Collar	o(–)	o(+)
Clerical	o(x)	o(x)
Sales	o(–)	o(+)
Total	– –	+ +

Note: + +/– – means agreement within p < .05; +/– means agreement within .05 < p < .10; (–)/(+) means .10 < p < .15; o(–/+) means p > .15. o(x) means signs differ.
Source: See Table 16.

The General Social Surveys, 1972-88

A time series based on a single common study, the General Social Survey, also exists for combined men and women for most of the years from 1972 to 1988. On several criteria, these are better data than those from the four different studies. Each GSS uses the same question wording, follows essentially the same procedures, has approximately the same question order, and utilizes a similar sample size.[14] In particular, each GSS uses the same wording on the supervision question: *"In your job, do you supervise anyone who is directly responsible to you?"* (cf. Figure 5). These data permit a more consistent examination of intermediary proletarianization over the last two decades, and provide a comparison series to the four studies for the 1970s. The proportions in the unweighted occupations from 1972 to 1988 appear in Tables 21 and 22.

Because of the change in the Census and CPS occupational coding scheme for 1980 weights from the CPS for white collar occupations exist only until 1982. This means that it is impossible to reduce post-1982 variability due to sampling error by standardizing through weighting to the correct occupational proportions. Thus, the time series for the entire 1972-88 period cannot be standardized to the correct proportions. The results using the unweighted occupation data are less reliable than those using weighted data. Since occupational weights do exist through 1982, however, the weighted figures are analyzed for 1972 to 1982 (Table 23 and 24) to provide a comparison both to the figures for 1970 to 1980 from the four different (weighted) surveys and to the unweighted GSS figures for the later period.

The analysis of the data for 1972 to 1988 includes several parts. First, regression analyzes the weighted GSS 1972-82 occupations data to provide comparisons to the findings from the four surveys for 1970-80. To settle disagreements in the findings based on the two different sets of studies for the 1970s, an alternate technique for trend analysis, the chi square goodness-of-fit test, evaluates, in particular, the better (weighted) GSS data for 1972 to 1982.

Second, there is a brief comparison of the results for data based on the slightly different percentages in the weighted versus unweighted GSS occupations data for 1972 to 1982. Relative similarities in results based on the weighted versus unweighted data for 1972 to 1982 establish a basis for drawing conclusions for 1972 to 1988 using only the unweighted GSS. To the extent that weighted and unweighted data produce similar findings, it is possible to use the analyses of the unweighted data to identify trends over the entire 1972 to 1988 period. (Hereafter, *weighted* or *unweighted* data means GSS data for class-categories based on weighted or unweighted occupations data.)

Third, there is the analysis (Table 28) of the entire series of unweighted GSS data from 1972 to 1988 (Tables 21 and 22) to identify the trend for the longest available recent time series. The data are also disaggregated into the two most recent decades. Analysis of 1972 to 1980 data identifies the trend for the 1970s, while analysis of 1982 to 1988 data identifies the trend for the 1980s. These results indicate whether the evidence using the better weighted occupation data for the shorter period (1972-82) is consistent with the disaggregated findings for the 1970s (1972-80) and 1980s (1982-88).

Table 21. Class-categories as Percentages of White Collar and Upper White Collar Occupations, Unweighted GSS, 1972-88

Year	Independent	Employer	Supervisor	Employee	N
		White Collar			
1972	3.7	6.8	38.3	51.2	410
1973	4.6	8.9	40.7	45.8	371
1974	6.3	10.1	36.4	47.2	398
1976	5.0	5.6	39.4	50.0	360
1977	2.3	8.7	40.1	48.9	436
1980	6.8	10.0	41.2	41.9	468
1982	4.4	11.1	39.1	45.4	567
1984	5.9	8.1	41.5	44.6	509
1985	5.0	12.8	38.3	43.9	538
1987	5.5	8.0	39.9	46.5	672
1988	4.1	8.5	38.1	49.3	294
		Upper White Collar			
1972	4.8	9.5	49.4	36.4	231
1973	6.4	11.9	48.5	33.2	202
1974	6.6	15.9	42.7	34.8	227
1976	4.3	9.0	52.1	34.6	188
1977	2.1	13.2	48.9	35.7	235
1980	8.5	10.7	48.5	32.4	272
1982	6.0	17.0	47.0	30.0	296
1984	6.9	12.1	47.8	33.2	289
1985	4.8	17.8	47.9	29.5	332
1987	5.1	10.0	50.4	34.5	451
1988	4.7	12.4	46.2	36.7	169

Note: Occupations not weighted to CPS.
Source: General Social Survey, 1972-88.

To parallel the procedures used in analyzing the 1970-80 data, weighted linear regression provides the initial analysis of trends using the weighted occupations data for 1972-82 (Table 25). Because the findings based on the 1970-80 versus 1972-82 differ, a more complex procedure (chi square goodness-of-fit) is also used on the better weighted data to identify trends.

Weighted GSS, 1972 to 1982

As in analyzing supervisory and employee percentages for men from 1945 to 1980, regression against time provides the initial analysis of trends using GSS for 1972 to 1982 (see Tables 23 and 24). The regression slopes for 1972 to 1982

Table 22. **Class-categories as Percentages of Lower White Collar Occupations (and Totals), Unweighted GSS, 1972-1988**

Year	Independent	Employer	Supervisor	Employee	N
		Lower White Collar			
1972	2.2	3.4	24.0	70.4	179
1973	2.4	5.3	31.4	60.9	169
1974	5.8	2.3	28.1	63.7	171
1976	5.8	1.7	25.6	66.9	172
1977	2.5	3.5	29.9	64.2	201
1980	4.6	9.2	31.1	55.1	196
1982	2.7	4.7	30.3	62.2	271
1984	4.5	2.7	33.2	59.5	220
1985	5.3	4.9	22.8	67.0	206
1987	6.6	3.9	18.7	70.9	222
1988	3.2	3.2	27.2	66.4	125
		Total			
1972	5.6	5.1	29.2	60.0	836
1973	5.4	6.1	32.8	55.7	754
1974	5.3	6.3	31.5	56.9	742
1976	7.2	4.8	33.9	54.1	684
1977	4.2	5.9	32.8	57.1	862
1980	6.8	7.7	36.1	49.3	833
1982	6.4	8.3	34.5	50.9	1029
1984	6.7	7.6	34.1	51.7	869
1985	6.3	9.6	33.3	50.8	930
1987	7.3	7.4	34.9	50.4	1024
1988	5.4	6.2	33.0	55.4	500

Note: Occupations not weighted to CPS.
Source: General Social Survey, 1972-88.

(Table 25) for overall white collar and lower white collar supervisors are positive at p less than .12. The slopes for white collar (p = .10) and lower white collar (p = .11) employees are negative. The slopes for upper white collar supervisors and upper white collar employees are zero, or constant. The high significance levels and constant slopes imply that there have been no net changes in supervisory and employee proportions among white collar labor from 1972 to 1982. On the other hand, the pattern of generally positive slopes for supervisors and generally negative slopes for employees suggest that there is intermediary

Table 23. Class-categories as Percentages of White Collar Occupational Groups (and Totals), Weighted GSS, 1972-82

Year	Independents	Employers	Supervisors	Employees	N
White Collar					
1972	4.3	6.2	34.4	55.1	429
1973	5.7	8.4	37.6	48.3	379
1974	7.3	9.3	33.9	49.5	376
1976	5.6	4.9	35.0	54.5	385
1977	3.6	8.6	37.7	50.0	453
1980	6.7	9.2	39.3	44.8	443
1982	4.7	11.5	37.5	46.4	472
Upper White Collar					
1972	5.3	9.1	46.9	38.7	214
1973	8.9	12.2	45.6	33.3	191
1974	6.9	15.9	41.4	35.8	192
1976	5.7	8.1	45.6	40.6	199
1977	3.9	13.6	46.4	36.1	235
1980	8.8	10.2	46.8	34.2	232
1982	6.1	17.3	44.2	32.5	251
Lower White Collar					
1972	3.3	3.3	22.2	71.3	215
1973	2.4	4.5	29.4	63.7	187
1974	7.6	2.4	26.1	63.8	184
1976	5.6	1.5	23.6	69.3	186
1977	3.3	3.3	28.4	64.9	218
1980	4.3	8.1	31.1	56.5	212
1982	3.1	5.0	29.8	62.1	221
Total					
1972	6.3	4.6	25.2	63.9	897
1973	7.5	5.9	29.4	57.2	792
1974	6.6	6.0	27.5	59.9	775
1976	7.1	4.0	29.0	60.0	801
1977	5.4	5.9	29.9	58.8	907
1980	7.0	6.8	34.1	52.0	849
1982	6.8	8.5	32.2	52.5	879

Note: Occupations weighted to CPS proportions.
Source: General Social Surveys, 1972-82.

Table 24. **Class-categories as Percentages of White Collar Occupations, Weighted GSS, 1972-82**

Year	Independents	Employers	Supervisors	Employees	N
		Professional			
1972	4.8	4.1	39.3	51.7	125
1973	4.4	3.7	45.2	46.7	111
1974	4.8	7.5	34.0	53.7	111
1976	3.7	3.7	38.8	53.7	117
1977	4.3	4.9	42.6	48.1	137
1980	4.8	3.6	47.9	43.6	137
1982	7.3	5.5	42.1	45.1	150
		Managerial			
1972	6.1	16.2	57.6	20.2	88
1973	15.0	23.8	46.2	15.0	81
1974	9.9	27.5	51.6	11.0	81
1976	8.4	14.5	55.4	21.7	81
1977	3.4	25.8	51.7	19.1	97
1980	14.5	19.7	45.3	20.5	95
1982	4.2	34.7	47.4	13.7	101
		Clerical			
1972	2.1	2.1	26.4	69.4	156
1973	0.0	1.6	31.2	67.2	136
1974	1.4	1.4	31.9	65.2	136
1976	3.0	0.8	25.6	70.7	138
1977	1.3	1.9	34.0	62.8	161
1980	2.9	1.4	32.9	62.9	158
1982	1.1	2.2	30.6	66.1	163
		Sales			
1972	6.4	6.4	10.6	76.6	60
1973	8.8	12.3	24.6	54.4	51
1974	25.0	5.0	10.0	60.0	48
1976	12.7	3.6	18.2	65.5	49
1977	9.1	7.3	12.7	70.9	57
1980	8.6	27.6	25.9	37.9	54
1982	8.5	12.8	27.7	51.1	59

Note: Occupations weighted to CPS proportions.
Source: General Social Surveys, 1972-82.

Table 25.   **Directions of Changes for White Collar Supervisors and Employees, Regressions, Combined Men and Women, GSS, 1972-82**

	Supervisors	Employees
White Collar	(+)(.12)	(−)(.10)
Upper White Collar	o (+)	o (−)
Professional	o (+)	(−)(.10)
Managerial	o (−)	o (−)
Lower White Collar	(+)(.11)	(−)(.11)
Clerical	o (+)	o (−)
Sales	(+)(.12)	o (−)
Total	+ +	− −

Note: + + / − − means regression slope significant at two-tailed p < .05. + / − means significant at .05 < p < .10; (−)/(+) means .10 < p < .25; o (−/+) means p > .25. Sample sizes divided by 1.5 to adjust for clustering. Exact probability values near .10 in parentheses.
Source: General Social Surveys, 1972-82.

deproletarianization of white collar labor. (Applying the procedure to the four survey series produces similar results to the regressions. Similar results using the chi square test occur for 1972 to 1980.)

These results do not support the hypothesis of intermediary proletarianization among white collar labor. They indicate at least no change, and provide some evidence for intermediary deproletarianization of white collar labor. These findings contradict those based on the four separate studies for 1970 to 1980 (Table 19 above) that suggested intermediary proletarianization.

Chi Square Goodness-of-fit Analysis

Because the findings on intermediary proletarianization for 1970 to 1980 differ from those for 1972 to 1982 based on regressions (see Tables 32 and 33 in the Appendix), the alternative analytic technique is also applied to weighted occupations GSS data for 1972 to 1982. By testing specific statistical models, this technique overcomes a problem with linear regression analysis. Regression does not explicitly test a model of a constant proportion over time; instead it accepts the null hypothesis of no change when the slope is not significantly different from zero. Initial and final values in chronological series also have particularly strong effects on the linear regression fits.

The alternative analytic technique specifically tests a constant model, and then tests a linear trend model. It is based on chi square goodness-of-fit test, and evaluates the difference between the data (observed values) and the model (expected values). As opposed to regression, which minimizes the sum of squared deviations to create the line of best fit, $[\sum((Y - Ypred)^2)]$, the chi square goodness-of-fit test calculates the sum of the squared deviations between the observed (o) and expected (e) (that is, predicted) values, divided by the expected observed (o) and expected (e) (that is, predicted) values, divided by the expected values: $[\sum((o-e)^2/e)]$, to determine if the total difference between the data and the fit is significant for certain degrees of freedom. The constant model is based on an average (pooled) proportion of all the percentages in the series. The linear model is based on a weighted regression of percentages against time. (Each sum of squares is weighted inversely to the variance before summations. The second stage of the chi square fitting uses a similar approach to the first stage of simple regression analysis of trends.) An insignificant (relatively small) chi square (p *greater* than .05) indicates a good fit because there is little difference between the model and the data. The fits are developed by an analytic computer program, Margie (Smith, 1980b), applied to the General Social Survey, 1972-82 data. It first tests the constant (no change) model (constant proportion); then it tests the linear trend model (see Taylor, 1980).[15] Because similar probability values have different implications in the chi square and regression fits, their interpretations are somewhat complicated. For goodness-of-fit analysis, a small chi square and hence a higher probability value (p greater than .05) is desirable because it indicates a good fit to the constant model; however, significant chi squares (nongood fits, p less than .05) indicate that the model is not constant. For regressions, however, low probability values (p less than .05) are desirable because they indicate linear fits and hence a trend. The complex goodness-of-fit modelling is applied to the better weighted data only.

Because of the additional problems introduced by the inability to weight occupations percentages to the CPS proportions for the post-1982 data, however, using the complex goodness-of-fit analysis would provide false precision with unweighted data. Instead, the analysis uses a simpler chi square test followed by regression. The approach uses the simple chi square test to determine if the percentages are changing. If the chi square is not statistically significant (p greater than .05), the constant model is a good fit. If there is not a good fit to the constant model (p less than .05), regression weighted by the square root of the sample size identifies any trend based on the sign of the slope. (In cases of near significant chi squares, the significance levels for the regression slopes are also reported.) In addition, because of the imprecision due to the impossibility of weighting occupational proportions, the analysis only covers the major white collar occupational groups (white collar, upper white collar, and lower white collar), but not the separate white collar occupations.

Goodness-of-fit analysis on the GSS data indicates that the proportions of combined men and women supervisors for overall white collar from 1972 to 1982 did not change significantly (Table 26, column 2).[16] The constant model fits for white collar, upper white collar, and lower white collar supervisors. The constant model also fits for white collar, upper white collar, and lower white collar employees. The goodness-of-fit analysis tends to agree with the regression findings above (Table 25). Taken together, they suggest that no net change occurred in the proportions of supervisors and employees from 1972 to 1982.

Similar results appeared for the individual white collar occupations. For both regression and goodness-of-fit analyses (Table 26), the constant models fit all supervisory and employee categories among professionals, managers, and clericals. For sales employees, the goodness-of-fit trend is just insignificantly negative (p = .06). Technically this is a constant fit, but the negative sign suggests deproletarianization.

Table 26. **Directions of Change for Supervisor and Employee Percentages, Regression and Goodness-of-fit, Men and Women, GSS, 1972-82**

| | Regressions | | Goodness-of-fit | |
	Supervisors	Employees	Supervisors	Employees
White Collar	(+)(.12)	(−)(.10)	o(+)	o(−)(.12)*
Upper White Collar	o(+)	o(−)	o(−)	o(−)
Professional	o(+)	(−)(.10)	o(+)	o(−)
Managerial	o(−)	o(−)	o(−)	o(−)
Lower White Collar	(+)(.11)	(−)(.11)	o(+)	(−)*
Clerical	o(+)	o(−)	o(+)	o(−)
Sales	(+)(.12)	o(−)	o(+)	(−)(.06)*
Total	+ +	− −	+ +	− −

Note: Notation for regression fits same as Table 25. In a goodness-of-fit model, o(+)/(−) at $p > .10$ indicates constant (o) fit; (+)/(−) marginal constant fit, $.05 < p < .10$; + +/− − significant linear trend fit. Sample sizes divided by 1.5 to adjust for clustering. Fits for regression and goodness-of-fit are same (constant) for all other levels for unadjusted and adjusted variance. Near significant chi square probability values in parentheses. * indicates significant linear fit with unadjusted variance (cf. Note 16).
Source: Tables 23 and 24 and goodness-of-fit analysis on unweighted data.

Even though the directional fits are not significant (Table 26), the pattern of all negative signs on the employee fits suggests a decline in employees, or intermediary deproletarianization. The pattern of generally positive signs for supervisors also suggests an increase in supervisors, or intermediary deproletarianization. In short, there is evidence for no change, but also for intermediary deproletarianization.

Both the regression and goodness-of-fit models for the GSS data indicate that the percentages of white collar supervisors, upper white collars employees, clerical employees, and clerical supervisors did not change from 1972 to 1982. In all but two cases, regression and goodness-of-fit analyses agree in signs. In 10 of 14 cases there is agreement in sign and probability values between the regression and goodness-of-fit analyses. (Table 35 in the Appendix shows agreement on directions and significance of changes between the regression and goodness-of-fit analyses on the weighted GSS data for 1972 to 1982.) In sum, both regression and goodness-of-fit analyses of the GSS data support models of no change. The generally positive signs for supervisors and negative signs for employees, however, suggest intermediary deproletarianization.[17] Contrary to the findings from 1970-80 data, the GSS analyses do not support the intermediary proletarianization hypothesis for white collar in the 1980s. In fact, there is more support for the intermediary deproletarianization hypothesis.[18]

The overall conclusion about intermediary proletarianization or deproletarianization would be clearer if the results for the four studies (1970-80) and the GSS (1972-82) were similar. But the four studies suggest intermediary proletarianization, while the GSS suggests constancy or weak deproletarianization. The signs differ in every case (Table 19 versus Table 25). Even when corresponding fits with probability values greater than .05 are considered constant and thus consistent (ignoring differences in signs), there is little similarity. (Table 33 in the Appendix shows little agreement on regression fits.) Because the General Social Survey weighted occupations data are more consistent and the goodness-of-fit approach is a more appropriate analytic procedure, the results based on the GSS series are more reliable than those using regression and the separate studies.

Weighted versus Unweighted GSS, 1972 to 1982

The corresponding GSS percentages for unweighted versus weighted occupations for 1972-82 (Table 21 versus 23) shows cases in which the respective percentages differ by as much as 4 to 6 points, e.g., for 1976 GSS the weighted percentage of supervisors is 35.0 (Table 23), while the unweighted figure is 39.4 (Table 21). Comparisons of goodness-of-fit models on the GSS weighted versus unweighted occupations data for 1972 to 1982, however, show generally similar results. Analyses of both sets of data indicate generally constant fits with similar signs (Table 27). The analysis of trends after 1982 is less reliable because no CPS data on proportions in various occupations exist for weighting and hence the differences in percentages could be because of sampling errors in the estimate of class-category proportions across occupational groups. However, the results based on unweighted occupations for 1972-82 are consistent with those for weighted occupations, and can be used as a proxy for the better data. This suggests, too, that results based on unweighted 1972-80 and 1982-88 data can serve as proxies for the unavailable weighted figures.

Table 27. Agreement on Fits for White Collar Supervisors and Employees, Men and Women, Weighted versus Unweighted GSS, 1972-82

	Weighted		Unweighted	
	Supervisors	Employees	Supervisors	Employees
White Collar	o(+)	o(−)(.12)*	o(+)	o(−)(.10)
Upper White Collar	o(−)	o(−)	o(−)	o(−)
Lower White Collar	o(+)	(−)*	o(+)	(−)(.09)
Total	+ +	− −	+(.08)	− −

Note: Simple goodness-of-fit with regression. Notation for regression part same as Table 25. See Note to Table 26 for notation goodness-of-fit.
Source: Tables 23 and 24 and goodness-of-fit analysis.

Unweighted GSS, 1972 to 1982

The analysis of the unweighted occupations GSS data for the longest time series from 1972 to 1988 consists of two parts. First, the simple chi square test indicates whether the overall trend is constant (insignificant chi square) or not. Since an insignificant chi square indicates constant fit for most cases, no further analysis is necessary. However, in the cases of significant or nearly significant chi squares, the regressions identify trends based on the signs of the slopes. Following the earlier chi square approach and rules of parsimony, the fit is considered constant if the chi square is insignificant, even if the slope of the regression (weighted by square root of sample size) is positive.

Table 28 shows the findings for 1972 to 1988. The meanings of the symbols here are similar to those for the complex chi square analysis above. The left symbol identifies the chi square fit (either o for constant fit or * for nonconstant). The right symbol identifies the regression slope (+/− indicates positive or negative direction for significant slopes; (−)/(+) indicates directions for insignificant slope (probability values for slopes of p less than .25 are listed below in parentheses). For instance, o − means a constant fit but a significant negative regression slope. Only a significant chi square and significant regression slope (* + or * −) clearly indicate a trend (positive or negative).

The analysis begins with the trends for the entire period, 1972 to 1988. In addition, it disaggregates the findings for 1972 to 1980 to identify trends for the 1970s, and 1982 to 1988 to identify trends for 1980s. Despite the differences in respective percentages for comparable class-categories between weighted versus unweighted occupations data (Tables 21 versus 23), the chi square fits for most of the unweighted 1972 to 1988 GSS data are also insignificant and indicate no net change. Most of the fits for 1972 to 1988, 1972 to 1980, and 1982 to 1988

Table 28. Directions of Change for White Collar Supervisors and Employees, Goodness-of-fit, Unweighted GSS, 1972-88

	1972-88 Supervisors	Employees	1972-80 Supervisors	Employees	1982-88 Supervisors	Employees
White Collar	o (+)	o (−)	o (+)	o (−)	o (−)	o (+)
Upper White Collar	o o	o (−)	o (+)	o (−)	o o	o + (.08)
Lower White Collar	* (−)	* (+)	o (+)	o (+) (.16)	* (−)	o (+) (.06)
Total	o +	* −	o +	* −	o (+)	o (+)

Note: Left symbols, * means chi square significant at p < .05; (*) .05 < p < .10 (marginal constant fit); o p > .10 (constant fit). Right symbols, +/− means regression slope direction p < .05; (+)/(−) p > .05; regression .05 < p < .25 in parentheses. Other p > .25.
Source: Tables 21 and 22, and goodness-of-fit analysis.

are constant and agree with the findings of no change based on the weighted data for 1972 to 1982.

More specifically for the unweighted 1972 to 1988 data, goodness-of-fit tests show insignificant chi squares (p greater than .05), respectively, for overall white collar, upper white collar, and total supervisors. (The chi square fit for total employees is constant, but the regression slope is significantly positive.) For lower white collar employees and supervisors for 1972 to 1988, the chi squares are significant, though the slopes are not; the nonconstant, nonlinear fit suggests fluctuation over the period. The pattern of negative signs for the overall white collar, upper white collar and total employees suggests intermediary deproletarianization. The results for 1972 to 1988 agree generally with those suggesting intermediary deproletarianization based on weighted 1972 to 1982 GSS data alone. However, the significant chi square and positive regression slopes for lower white collar employees and negative slopes for lower white collar supervisors provide weak counter evidence of intermediary proletarianization.

Distinguishing data for 1972-80 versus 1982-88 identifies trends for the 1970s and 1980s, respectively. Again the pattern of insignificant chi squares for both white collar supervisors and employees for 1972-80 suggests no net change for the 1970s. For 1972-80, only total employees have both a significant chi square and significant negative regression slope. The positive signs on all white collar supervisory slopes along with the negative signs for overall white collar, upper white collar, and total employee slopes suggest intermediary deproletarianization as is the case in the weighted 1972-82 data. In short, there appears to have been no net change or perhaps intermediary deproletarianization in the 1970s.

For 1982-88, the mostly insignificant chi squares also suggest no change in the 1980s. However, for lower white collar supervisors, there is a significant chi square and insignificant negative coefficient, suggesting intermediary proletarianization. Similarly, for all white collar employees the positive regression coefficients, including a nearly significant one for upper white collar employees, suggest proletarianization. In short, there appears to have been no net change or perhaps intermediary proletarianization in the 1980s.

In sum, the supervisory versus employee data suggest constancy for the entire 1972-88 period .[19] However, as in the weighted 1972-82 GSS data, the unweighted 1972-82 data do suggest that intermediary deproletarianization might have been the dominant tendency for the entire period and particularly for the 1970s; intermediary proletarianization might have begun in the 1980s. The evidence supports Wright and Martin's (1987) finding of intermediary deproletarianization across the entire period. The evidence of employee growth for the 1980s alone, however, provides support for Wright and Singlemann's (1982) earlier prediction of proletarianization. As a proxy for condition proletarianization, the data on intermediary proletarianization basically challenge the proletarianization hypothesis, and do not entirely support the deproletarianization hypothesis.

Managers versus Nominal Supervisors

Using evidence of intermediary deproletarianization based on supervisory growth as a proxy for deproletarianization is not a fully adequate approach because an increase in supervisors overall might mask a decrease in the proportion of supervisors with real authority, that is, managers. (The class-category of managers differs from the occupational category of managerial labor; see discussion in Chapter 3.) Supervisors here are divided into managers and nominal supervisors. Changes in both are different indicators of more complex intermediary proletarianization. Because managers are not members of the central working class, changes in their proportions are not as meaningful in analyzing the transformation of the working class as are changes in nominal supervisors in the expanded central working class and employees in the central working class. Net decline in the proportion of either managers or nominal supervisors would indicate more complex intermediary proletarianization. Net growth in managers or nominal supervisors would indicate more complex intermediary deproletarianization. Simultaneous growth or decline in the proportions of both managers or nominal supervisors and employees over the same period would indicate polarization.

As Chapter 3 notes, the PSID (1975-77) data distinguish managers from nominal supervisors based on whether a supervisor has a say in pay or promotion of subordinates. PSID data on managers exist only for three years (1975-77) (Table 29) and are not fully comparable to, e.g., the GSS results because the PSID respondents are household heads. From 1975 to 1977, the proportion of white collar managers increased from 19.6 to 24.8 percent. The proportion of

Table 29. Class-categories as Percentages of White Collar Occupations (and Totals), Managers and Nominal Supervisors, PSID, 1975-77

Year	Independents	Employers	Managers	Nominals	Employees	N
		White Collar				
1975	5.0	15.0	19.6	24.3	36.1	43264
1976	5.2	14.6	25.2	18.7	36.4	42469
1977	4.0	15.5	24.8	22.5	33.1	41221
		Upper White Collar				
1975	6.0	19.5	24.8	26.5	23.2	31349
1976	5.9	19.3	30.9	19.5	24.3	30187
1977	4.7	19.4	31.7	23.4	20.8	29786
		Lower White Collar				
1975	2.2	3.2	6.1	18.6	69.9	11915
1976	3.4	2.8	11.3	16.5	65.9	12282
1977	2.2	5.1	6.9	20.4	65.4	11435
		Total				
1975	5.4	9.9	14.3	23.0	47.3	79621
1976	4.8	10.0	17.5	19.9	47.9	81019
1977	4.3	10.9	17.9	23.6	43.3	79750

Note: Occupations not weighted to CPS. Weighted N. Nominals are nominal supervisors.

white collar nominal supervisors declined from 24.3 to 22.5 percent; the proportion of nonsupervisory employees declined from 36.1 to 33.1 percent. The same pattern exists for upper white collar labor between 1975 and 1977. But for lower white collar both managers and nominal supervisors grew. The net increases in managers support the conclusion of intermediary deproletarianization in the 1970s based on the simpler supervisory data, though the decreases in nominal supervisors suggest intermediary proletarianization.

It is also possible to use the GSS data to examine trends in managerial versus nominal supervisor proportions. As Chapter 3 explains, this involves a weaker definition of manager based on the GSS question about whether a supervisor's subordinates supervise other employees. Those supervisors that supervise other supervisors are considered higher level supervisors, or managers. Those supervisors that do not supervise other supervisors are considered nominal supervisors. Because this definition does not specifically identify power over pay or promotion, it is not as powerful as the one based on the PSID. Using the GSS data for 1974-76 provides a comparison for the PSID data for the middle 1970s. Since GSS data on managers and nominal supervisors exist for 1972 to 1988, they can be used to analyze trends for the entire period.

For the period 1974-77, GSS data (Table 30) comparable to the PSID data for 1975-77 (Table 29) also show a net increase in managers and a net decrease in nominal supervisors. Overall white collar (18.7 to 21.7 percent), lower white collar (5.4 to 10.1 percent), and total managers (9.5 to 10.7 percent) grew, while overall white collar, lower white collar collar (12.7 to 16.4 percent), upper white

Table 30. Class-categories as Percentages of White Collar Occupations (and Totals), Managers and Nominal Supervisors, GSS, 1974-77

Year	Independents	Employers	Managers	Nominals	Employees	N
		White Collar				
1974	6.3	10.1	12.7	23.3	47.6	395
1976	5.0	5.6	15.6	23.7	50.1	359
1977	3.3	8.8	16.4	23.5	49.1	434
		Upper White Collar				
1974	6.6	15.9	18.1	24.7	34.8	227
1976	4.3	9.1	22.5	29.5	34.8	187
1977	2.1	13.2	21.7	27.2	35.7	235
		Lower White Collar				
1974	6.0	2.4	5.4	21.4	64.9	168
1976	5.8	1.7	8.1	17.4	66.9	172
1977	2.5	3.5	10.1	19.1	64.8	199
		Total				
1974	5.3	6.4	9.5	21.6	57.3	737
1976	7.2	4.8	12.5	21.1	54.3	681
1977	4.2	5.9	10.7	21.9	57.3	859

and total nominal supervisors stayed the same or declined. Only lower white collar nominal supervisors grew. The general increase in managers suggests more complex intermediary deproletarianization in the 1970s. This is the same conclusion as that based on the PSID data.

Since GSS data for managers and nominal supervisors exist for 1972 to 1988, they can also be the basis for investigating change over the entire period. Examining the change in proportions of managers in the GSS for 1972 to 1988 identifies patterns of more complex deproletarianization (or proletarianization) based on managerial responsibility (see Tables 36 and 37 in the Appendix). Over the longer period 1972-88, there is little net change among white collar managers or nominal supervisors (Table 31). The evidence of a decrease in managers suggests complex intermediary proletarianization over the longer period, but the evidence for nominal supervisors suggests intermediary deproletarianization. For 1972-88, the slight net decrease in lower white collar managers suggests complex intermediary proletarianization, but the other manager slopes are also significantly negative. The slopes for nominal supervisors are mixed, but the nearly significant positive increase for lower white collar nominal supervisors suggests intermediary deproletarianization. For 1972-80 for all white collar occupations, the chi squares suggest no change. However, the positive slopes for overall white collar and lower white collar nominal supervisors suggest intermediary deproletarianization in the 1970s. On the other hand, for 1982-88, the almost significant net decline in lower white collar nominal supervisors and other negative supervisory slopes suggest deproletarianization in the 1980s.

Table 31. **Directions of Change for White Collar Manager and Nominal Supervisor Percentages, Goodness-of-fit, GSS, 1972-88**

	1972-88		1972-80		1982-88	
	Managers	Nominals	Managers	Nominals	Managers	Nominals
White Collar	o (−)	o (−)	o (−)	o +	o (+)	o (−)
Upper White Collar	o (−)	o (−)	o (−)	o (+)	o (−)	o (−)
Lower White Collar	(*) −	(*) (+)	o o	o + (.15)	o (+)	* (−) (.06)
Total	o (+)	* (+)	o (−)	* +	o (+)	o (−) (.16)

Note: Nominals mean nominal supervisors. For the left symbols, * means chi square significant at p < .05; (*) means .05 < p < .10 and hence a marginal constant fit; o means chi square p > .10 and hence a constant fit. For the right symbols, +/− means regression slope direction p < .05; (+)/(−) means p > .05; regression probability values .05 < p < .25 in parentheses. Other nonsignificant p > .25. o o means constant fit, no slope.
Source: Tables 39 and 40 and analysis.

Again the clearest conclusion is no net change. The findings based on managers contradict the conclusion based on overall supervisor and employee changes. The data for all supervisors (combined managers and nominals) suggest intermediary deproletarianization for 1972-88 for the entire period and for the 1970s, but intermediary proletarianization in the 1980s. On the other hand, the data for managers suggest intermediary proletarianization over the entire 1972-88 period and in the 1970s, with intermediary deproletarianization in the 1980s. The data for nominal supervisors suggest intermediary deproletarianization for the 1970s and perhaps over the longer period, and proletarianization for the 1980s.

Possibilities of Intermediary Proletarianization in the 1980s

Since the data on managers and nominal supervisors clarify a distinction blurred in the analysis of the overall supervisory data alone, the conclusion about modest intermediary proletarianization overall is somewhat stronger. On one level, an increase in managers suggests an overall upgrading of those with supervisory responsibility. However, an increase in managers may not be a meaningful measure of change within the working class. In fact, increase in overall supervisors or simply nominal supervisors may more appropriately suggest upgrading of the working class *per se*. This may be so because, to the extent that nominal supervisors are members of the central working class, their decline over time may more clearly reflect changes within the working class--or proletarianization in its fundamental working class sense--than changes in managers, whose responsibility (and, in some cases, ownership) puts them closer to employers. Since managers are not in the central working class and are closer to employers than to general employees, their relative increase suggests a general upgrading of the labor force but not necessarily of the working class. In this sense, the increase in nominal supervisors, in fact, is a better representation of general upgrading of the working class. The increase in nominal supervisors would then suggest intermediary deproletarianization, or upgrading of the central working class, in the 1970s, and would be consistent with findings based on the overall supervisory data. This approach indicates that relative increases in both supervisors as a whole and nominal supervisors would suggest overall intermediary deproletarianization for 1972 to 1988 and for the 1970s alone, but the decreases indicate intermediary proletarianization for the 1980s.

The earlier data on supervisors, moreover, provide some evidence for recent intermediary proletarianization of white collar labor. In light of previous evidence of deproletarianization (1945-70 in Table 15), the pattern of no significant change in the 1972-82 (Table 24) and 1972-88 (Table 26) data may indicate the beginning of a new trend toward proletarianization. The data for men alone (1945-80 in Tables 12 and 13) indicate that intermediary deproletarianization for 1945-70 preceded proletarianization beginning around 1970 (Table 16). The data for combined men and women for 1970 to 1980 also indicate intermediary proletarianization in 1970-80 (see Table 19). The GSS data for men and women for 1972 to 1982 (Tables 23 and 24) indicate at most weak deproletarianization if not constancy. Together the data suggest that a transformation began around 1970 from strong deproletarianization (as evidenced for 1945-70 for men) to a different model: constancy, deproletarianization, or perhaps proletarianization. The rate of deproletarianization among men appears to have slowed around 1970. (See regression coefficients in Tables 39 and 40.)[20]   The change away from strong deproletarianization to weaker deproletarianization or constancy may indicate movement toward proletarianization. In other words, underlying the decrease in deproletarianization may be proletarianization.

Changes within industries in the direction of proletarianization may account for the slowing of the rate of deproletarianization and thus movement toward proletarianization over all (cf. Wright and Singlemann, 1982). On the other hand, the evidence in Wright and Martin (1987) suggests that deproletarianization, in fact, became stronger in the 1970s. The indications of expansion in the overall supervisory (and perhaps nominal supervisory) proportions for GSS 1972-88, and of managers in the 1980s generally support the deproletarianization conclusions. The proletarianizing tendencies may as yet be too subtle to demonstrate a clear aggregate trend.

CONCLUSION: CLASS PROLETARIANIZATION AND INTERMEDIARY DEPROLETARIANIZATION

Contrary to its image, white collar labor has not become consistently more "middle class." In the simple sense of class position, white collar has become increasingly working class. But it is difficult to provide definitive answers to the intermediary proletarianization questions since the findings are imprecise, the analyses involve complex identifications of managerial, supervisory, and employee proportions over time, and the results are contradictory. The seven survey time series for men from 1945 to 1980 suggests intermediary deproletarianization over the long term. Both the four survey time series for men and combined men and women for 1970 to 1980 suggest intermediary proletarianization in the 1970s.

However, both the weighted occupations GSS series for 1972-82 and unweighted[21] series for 1972-88 suggest no net change or perhaps intermediary deproletarianization over the two decades. From the start of the 1970s to the end of the 1980s, the GSS data show neither the net decrease in supervisors nor the net increase in employees among white collar labor that the intermediary proletarianization hypothesis implies. The GSS data for the 1980s do suggest slight intermediary proletarianization, as do the findings for nominal supervisors. The findings for managers challenge this conclusion. Because the General Social Surveys provide better data than the separate survey and the goodness-of-fit analysis provides clearer results, the more likely conclusion is that there has been intermediary deproletarianization after 1970.

The overall evidence of intermediary deproletarianization beyond 1970 is consistent with both the postindustrial and marxian predictions of a net increase in supervisors. Neither the findings of supervisory growth nor those of no net change support the thesis of intermediary proletarianization. But evidence for the 1980s indicates the possibilities of intermediary proletarianization over the most recent decade.   Over the long term, however, white collar has not undergone general intermediary proletarianization. But what is happening within the white collar working class?

APPENDIX

Table 32. Agreement in Regression Fits Between White Collar Men and Combined Men and Women, 1970-80 versus 1972-82

	Supervisors	Employees
	1970-80	
White Collar	o(−)(.07)	o(+)
Upper White Collar	o(−)	+ +
Professional	−(.07)	o(+) (.12)
Managerial	(+)(.11)	o(x)
Lower White Collar	o(−)	o(+)
Clerical	o(+)	o(x)
Sales	o(−)	o(+)
Total	−(.06)	o(+)(.13)
	1972-82	
White Collar	+(.12)	−(.10)
Upper White Collar	o(x)	o(−)
Professional	o(+)	o(−)(.13)
Managerial	o(−)(.19)	o(x)
Lower White Collar	+(.11)	(−)(.11)
Clerical	o(x)	o(−)
Sales	o(+)(.12)	o(−)(.14)
Total	+ +	− −

Note: + +/− − means agreement within $p < .05$. +/−, $.05 < p < .10$; (+)/(−), $.10 < p < .15$; o(+/−), $p > .15$. o(x), signs differ.
Source: Table 19 and 25.

Table 33. Agreement on Fits on White Collar Supervisors and Employees, Combined Men and Women, Regressions, 1970-80 and 1972-82

	Supervisors	Employees
White Collar		
Upper White Collar		
Professional		
Managerial		o
Lower White Collar		
Clerical	o	o
Sales		o
Total		

Note: o means regression for 1970-80 versus 1972-82 agree on constant fit at $p > .05$, with sign ignored.
Source: Tables 19 and 25.

Table 34. Comparisons of Trends, White Collar Men and Combined Men and Women, Regressions, 1970-80 and 1972-82

	Men Supervisors	Men Employees	Men and Women Supervisors	Men and Women Employees
		1970-80		
White Collar	o(−)(.07)	++	−−	o(+)
Upper White Collar	o(−)	++	o(−)	++
Professional	−(.07)	(+)(.12)	−−(.05)	+(.09)
Managerial	++	o(−)	(+)(.11)	o(+)
Lower White Collar	o(−)	o(+)	o(−)	o(+)
Clerical	o(+)	o(−)	o(−)	o(+)
Sales	o(−)	o(+)	o(−)	o(+)(.17)
Total	−−	++	−(.06)	++
		1972-82		
White Collar	++	−−	(+)(.12)	(−)(.10)
Upper White Collar	o(−)	o(−)(.19)	o(+)	o(−)(.26)
Professional	o(+)(.20)	o(−)(.13)	o(+)	(−)(.10)
Managerial	o(−)(.12)	o(+)	o(−)(.19)	o(−)
Lower White Collar	++	−−	+(.11)	(−)(.11)
Clerical	o(+)(.13)	−(.06)	o(+)	o(−)(.28)
Sales	+(.08)	−(.06)	(+)(.10)	o(−)(.13)
Total	++	−−	++	−−

Note: $++/--$ significant at one-tailed $p < .05$; $+/-$ at $.05 < p < .10$; $(-)/(+)$ at $.10 < p < .15$; o $(-/+)$ at $p > .15$; o constant.
Source: Tables 16 versus 19; analysis of men versus Table 25.

Table 35. Agreement on Supervisor and Employee Fits, White Collar Occupational Groups, Combined Men and Women, GSS, 1972-82

	Supervisors	Employees
White Collar	o(+)(.10)	o(−)(.12)
Upper White Collar	o(x)	o(−)
Professional	o(+)	o(−)(.10)
Managerial	o(−)	o(x)
Lower White Collar	o(+)	o(−)
Clerical	o(+)	o(−)
Sales	o(+)	o(−)
Total	++	−−

Note: Agreements on changes in supervisors and employees, using regression and goodness-of-fit for men and women, 1972-82. o where regression and goodness-of-fit agree. o(x) signs differ.
Source: Table 26 and analysis.

Table 36. **Class-categories as Percentages of White and Upper White Collar Occupations, Managers and Nominals, Unweighted GSS, 1972-88**

Year	Independents	Employers	Managers	Nominals	Employees	N
			White Collar			
1972	3.7	6.9	15.0	23.0	51.5	408
1973	4.7	9.0	16.2	23.6	46.6	365
1974	6.3	10.1	12.7	23.3	47.6	395
1976	5.0	5.6	15.6	23.7	50.1	359
1977	2.3	8.8	16.4	23.5	49.1	434
1980	6.9	10.1	12.9	28.1	42.1	466
1982	4.4	11.1	12.3	26.5	45.6	564
1984	5.9	8.1	16.0	25.1	44.9	506
1985	5.1	12.9	14.4	23.4	44.2	534
1987	5.6	8.1	15.1	24.6	46.7	670
1988	4.1	8.6	14.1	23.4	49.8	291
			Upper White Collar			
1972	4.8	9.6	19.6	29.6	36.5	230
1973	6.5	12.0	19.5	28.5	33.5	200
1974	6.6	15.9	18.1	24.7	34.8	227
1976	4.3	9.1	22.5	29.4	34.8	187
1977	2.1	13.2	21.7	27.2	35.7	235
1980	8.5	10.7	15.5	32.8	32.5	271
1982	6.0	17.1	19.1	27.5	30.3	293
1984	6.9	12.2	21.5	26.0	33.3	288
1985	4.8	17.9	19.7	27.9	29.7	330
1987	5.1	10.1	20.6	29.5	34.7	448
1988	4.7	12.6	18.6	26.9	36.1	167

Note: Nominals mean nominal supervisors. Weighted N for 1982 and 1987 due to subsample.
Source: General Social Surveys, 1972-88.

Table 37. **Class-categories as Percentages of Lower White Collar Occupations (and Totals), Managers and Nominals, Unweighted GSS, 1972-88**

Year	Independents	Employers	Managers	Nominals	Employees	N
			Lower White Collar			
1972	2.2	3.4	9.0	14.6	70.8	178
1973	2.4	5.5	12.1	17.6	63.4	165
1974	6.0	2.4	5.4	21.4	64.9	168
1976	5.8	1.7	8.1	17.4	66.9	172
1977	2.5	3.5	10.1	19.1	64.8	199
1980	4.6	9.2	9.2	21.5	55.4	195
1982	2.7	4.7	11.4	17.4	62.2	271
1984	4.6	2.8	11.0	21.0	60.1	218
1985	5.4	4.9	9.5	21.6	67.6	204
1987	6.6	3.9	10.7	21.9	70.9	222
1988	3.2	3.2	9.9	26.1	66.9	124
			Total			
1972	5.6	5.2	11.4	17.4	60.3	832
1973	5.5	6.2	11.0	21.0	56.3	746
1974	5.3	6.4	9.5	21.6	57.3	737
1976	7.2	4.8	12.5	21.1	54.3	681
1977	4.2	5.9	10.7	21.9	57.3	859
1980	6.9	7.7	9.9	26.1	49.5	831
1982	6.4	8.3	10.4	23.9	51.0	1026
1984	6.7	7.6	12.4	21.5	51.8	866
1985	6.4	9.6	10.9	22.1	51.0	926
1987	7.3	7.4	12.2	22.6	50.5	1121
1988	5.4	6.2	12.1	20.5	55.7	497

Note: Nominals mean nominal supervisors. Weighted N for 1982 and 1987 due to subsample.
Source: General Social Surveys, 1972-88.

Table 38. Regression Trends for White Collar Men versus Combined Men and Women, 1945-80, 1945-70, 1970-80, 1972-82

| | Men | | Men and Women | |
	Supervisors	Employees	Supervisors	Employees
1945 – 70	+ +	– –	---	---
1945 – 80	+ +	– –	---	---
1970 – 80	– (.07)	+ +	– –	o(+)(.25)
1972 – 82	+ +	– –	o(+)(.12)	– (.10)

Note: See Note to Table 32. --- means no data available.

Table 39. Unstandardized Regression Coefficients, White Collar Trends, Men versus Combined, 1945-80, 1945-70, 1970-80, 1972-82

| | Men | | Men and Women | |
	Supervisors	Employees	Supervisors	Employees
1945 – 80	0.799	– 0.614	---	---
1945 – 70	1.206	– 1.031	---	---
1970 – 80	– 0.407 (.07)	0.909	– 0.443	0.498 (.25)
1972 – 82	0.690 (.05)	– 1.508 (.04)	0.353 (.12)	– 0.703 (.10)

Note: See Table 38 for significance levels. --- means no data available.

Table 40. Standardized Regression Coefficients, White Collar Trends, Men versus Combined, 1945-80, 1945-70, 1970-80, 1972-82

| | Men | | Men and Women | |
	Supervisors	Employees	Supervisors	Employees
1945 – 80	0.900	– 0.815	---	---
1945 – 70	1.000	– 0.961	---	---
1970 – 80	– 0.933 (.07)	0.969	– 0.972	0.704
1972 – 82	0.763	– 0.774	0.646	– 0.676

Note: See Table 38 for significance levels. --- means no data available.

NOTES

1. Federal wage and hour surveys of industry permit an initial distinction between supervisory (that is, exempt) and nonsupervisory employees (U.S. Department of Labor, 1972, 1977). By incorporating Census data for self-employment with wage and hour data on supervisors, it is possible to divide relevant industries into three class categories: self-employment, supervisory employment, and nonsupervisory employment. Because certain industries in the services sector (e.g. finance) have high proportions of white collar jobs, it is possible to approximate the class category changes in white collar occupations by using those industries as proxies (cf. Sobel, 1982a, p. 141, Table 4 and Appendix 3.1, pp. 338-51). For 1968-77, there was an increase in supervisory labor in each service industry. This indicated a general intermediary deproletarianization of white collar labor (1982a, pp. 211-15, and Appendix 4.3, pp. 381-84). In services overall and trade, however, there were also increases in the proportions of nonsupervisory employment, indicating proletarianization. Other examinations of these tendencies use the trends in nonproduction employment or the ratios of nonproduction to overall employment (cf. Gordon, Edwards, and Reich 1982, p. 196-97).

2. Other studies also ask self-employment and supervisory questions. The Panel Study of Income Dynamics, 1975-77, though based on a large sample (unweighted N greater than 5000), is not used in the longer time series because the respondents are household heads. Kohn's 1974 follow-up study (see Kohn and Schooler, 1983) also asks self-employment and supervisory questions, but reinterviews only the respondents who were still working ten years later (it also interviews their wives). It is unrepresentative of the 1974 population, in part, because of mortality in the second wave of the panel. The American National Election Study, 1976, American National Election Study, 1984 and American National Election Study, 1985 Pilot also include self-employment and supervisory questions (cf. Kamieniecki and O'Brien, 1984; Sobel, 1986), but the supervisory question was dropped from the ANES after 1985.

3. In some surveys (e.g., Survey of Working Conditions), employers are identified by the employment of others; in others (e.g., Quality of Employment Survey, 1972-73), they are identified as self-employed who supervise. The latter operationalization overstates the size of the employer category because some self-employed who say they supervise are not actually employers (see Smith, 1980b) but independents who also supervise employees for other employers or in a second job.

4. Using supervisory growth as a proxy for deproletarianization might mask a decrease in the proportion of supervisors with real authority, that is, managers. Similarly, an increase in the proportion of (nonsupervisory) employees alone might mask an increase in the percentage of authorized employees, that would indicate condition deproletarianization. Simultaneous growth or decline in the proportions of both supervisors and employees over the same period would indicate polarization.

5. Because the six (1957-80) other surveys include both white and black men, and the percentage of black males was relatively small (9.6 percent) in 1945, the Centers data for white men alone are included in the series on all males.

6. The Kohn data were not publicly available, so the statistical analysis (e.g., crosstabulations) were run at National Institute of Mental Health under specifications supplied by the author. I would like to thank Melvin Kohn for permission to use the data and Carrie Schoenback for the computer analysis.

7. Two major difficulties arise in trying to analyze survey data to identify trends. First, rather than an exact figure, each percentage is associated with a sampling error; the difficulty then lies in determining the fit under uncertainty over not just one, but a series of points. Second, percentages based on different sample sizes may exhibit heteroskedasticity unless corrected by using weighted least squares regression. The GSS sample sizes for weighting are divided by 1.5 to reflect the lack of efficiency in cluster sampling for demographic factors (suggested by Smith, 1980a). (See Note 16 here.) To determine the trends (slopes), the percentages of supervisors and employees were regressed against time.

8. Comparing initial and final years only from 1945 to 1980, the percentages of male supervisors in most white collar groups increased and the percentages of employees decreased from 1945 to 1980, indicating deproletarianization. Between the initial and final years, however, there are cyclical patterns. Specifically, among overall white collar men supervisory percentages increased and employees percentages decreased from 1945 to 1970, and from 1970 to 1980 superviory percentages decreased and employee percentages increased. The longer term results (1945-80) suggest intermediary deproletarianization among men. This is clearest between 1945 and 1970. Between 1970 and 1980, however, intermediary proletarianization appears.

9. Because the hypotheses for intermediary proletarianization are directional (deproletarianization) and imply positive supervisory and negative employee slopes, one-tailed test should be applied to the regression coefficients. However, to be conservative and because the simple hypothesis of proletarianization at all levels challenges the research hypothesis of deproletarianization, two-tailed significance values are used (doubling the significance levels over one-tailed tests, and reducing the probability value, or alpha, for rejecting the null hypothesis to .025). For two-tailed probability values with seven years of data in the 1945 to 1980 time series, the loss of one degree of freedom for each coefficient estimate (constant and slope) produces 5 degrees of freedom for the t and F (denominator) statistics. For 7 data points (5 df), a t statistic of more than about 2.5 ($t > 2.571$, $p < .05$), two-tailed, (F $1/5 > 6.6$) for the slope coefficients indicates a significant slope. The regressions of the percentages of supervisors and employees among the white collar occupational categories against time (year) are weighted by the square root of the sample size (N) (N/2 for 1945 quota control sample) to compensate for differences in sampling errors, though even if autocorrelation were present, the slope estimates would be unbiased.

10. Time series data present the possibility of autocorrelation in the error terms. For example, in Table 14, the positive slopes for upper white collar and lower white collar supervisors show possible autocorrelation that could leave the regression coefficients nonsignificant. But autocorrelation would produce underestimated standard errors of the slopes; this would suggest that the slopes were significant when, in fact, they were not significantly different from zero. The possibility of autocorrelation supports the null hypothesis of no net change.

The series here are generally too short for analysis of autocorrelation. Weighting by the square root of the sample size compensates for the potential differences in variances. Autocorrelated equations could also be reestimated with Generalized Least Squares (GLS) regression.

11. Noting potential problems from the differences in wordings of the supervisory questions and differences in the samples, Wright and Singlemann (1982, p. S202) cited data on the decline in supervisory percentages provided by the author in personal communication (cf. Sobel, 1982a, p. 144) as evidence of intermediary proletarianization. See also Spenner (1983, pp. 834-35) and Oppenheimer (1985, p. 107) for similar comments.

12. This is similar to the use of splines, or piecewise linear regressions. In this case, however, 1970, the terminal year of the earlier series (1945-70), is also used as the initial year of the later series (1970-80).

13. The data for men must serve as a proxy for the unavailable data for both men and women prior to 1970s. Although Americans View Their Mental Health for 1957 included women, it did not ask them the supervisory question. See Nie, Verba, and Petrocik (1979, Ch. 11) for an example of estimating trends for periods before comparable data exist.

14. The General Social Survey began in 1972 and has been conducted every year except 1979 and 1981. The supervisory question (WKSUP) was not asked, however, in 1975, 1978, 1983 and 1986, so the proportions of supervisors and employers could not be determined for those years. Because of the separate analysis of the GSS for 1972 to 1988, GSS figures for men alone were not used in the 1945 to 1980 series. The 1972 to 1974 GSS and half of the 1975 and 1976 GSS used quota sampling at the block level instead of the full probability sampling used afterwards. The GSS occupations data were weighted to the CPS proportions only from 1972 to 1982 since CPS proportions do not exist for the 1970 Census occupational categories after 1982.

15. If both a constant and linear model fit the data, the laws of parsimony dictate accepting the simpler model (constant). But in some cases, the linear fit has a much lower significance level and a higher R^2. The bias toward the constant model particularly creates questions when there is a monotonic linear increase or decrease in the proportions, though all the proportions are within the confidence interval for the mean. Goodness-of-fit modelling would define such a pattern as a constant fit, though the likelihood of such a pattern is $1/N!$, e.g., for seven data points, $1/7! = 1/5040 = 0.00002$. The bias of the goodness-of-fit model toward the constant fits contrasts with the bias of regression toward linear fits. More work is needed on when to ignore a constant fit in favor of the linear model when both models fit well.

16. Dividing the GSS sample sizes by 1.5 to compensate for inefficiency from clustering in multistage sampling is a conservative approach that increases the sampling error. When not adjusting the variance for clustering (that is, goodness-of-fit 1.0 versus 1.5), the fits for overall white collar and lower white collar employees for 1972-82 are significantly negative, while sales employees show only a component of a negative trend. If the sample sizes were larger, the trends might be significant (see Table 26).

17. Though most of the slopes for 1972 to 1982 are not significant, analysis of the patterns of signs on the slopes using nonparametric sign tests (Blalock, 1979, pp. 166-68) provides further evidence on the directions of possible trends.

There are seven white collar occupational levels for the regressions. In all cases, at least six signs agree. The nonagreeing signs typically occur for managers (upper white collar) or clericals (lower white collar). If these regression results were independent (which they are not since, for instance, upper white collar includes professional and managerial), a non-parametric sign test for seven out of seven signs in agreement would be significant at $p < .05$ ($p = .0078$). For six out of seven, it would be significant at $p = .0525$. (The four individual white collar occupations are independent, and the probability of four out of four signs in agreement is .0625.) For male employees 1972-82, seven out of eight signs are negative (managers are positive). For combined men and women for 1970 to 1980, all the employee signs are positive (proletarianization); for 1972 to 1982, all are negative (deproletarianization). While the 1970 to 1980 data show opposite results, the 1972 to 1982 GSS data are more consistent and thus a better basis for drawing conclusions. Though the significance levels are too high to be conclusive, the pattern of signs suggests deproletarianization.

18. A number of marxian theorists suggests that the increase in the proportion of supervisors represents a massive increase in the cost of maintaining corporate power over employees in a burgeoning bureaucratic apparatus (Bowles, Gordon, and Weisskopf, 1983, pp. 254-55; Gordon, Edwards, and Reich, 1982, Ch. 5). These are not simply the transaction costs of production, but enforcement costs of capital over labor (Bowles and Gintis, 1986, pp. 107, 194-96). In evaluating the "the microeconomics of the Great Repression," Bowles, Gordon, and Weisskopf (1983, p. 164) estimate that surplus supervisory hours constitute a waste burden of $174 billion in 1980 or 6.6 percent of GNP (p. 177). The problem is particularly severe in the U.S. which has a much higher proportion of supervisory to nonsupervisory employees (cf. Wright, 1982; Harbison, et al., 1955). The costs of corporate power in increased supervisory expenses are an aspect of the conflict of the force and relations of production that Marx (1977, pp. 4-5) identified as leading to fundamental economic and social transformation (see Chapter 7 here).

19. Because the supervisory (WKSUP) question was only asked on two of three GSS ballots (A and C) in 1988, and there was a notable increase in no answers on WKSUP due to incorrect skip instructions on ballot A, the results for 1988 are not fully comparable to earlier years (Davis and Smith, 1988, pp. 670, 773) Because of these problems with the 1988 supervisory estimates, analyses were also done using 1987 as the end point of the time series. Goodness-of-fit tests show nonsignificant chi squares (p greater than .05) for total, white collar, and upper white collar 1982 to 1987. As in the results for 1972 to 1982, these suggest no change. In particular, the results for supervisors for the 1982 to 1987 data in most cases showed no significant changes. There are, however, for 1982 to 1987 a notable increase in upper white collar supervisors (3.4 percentage points), suggesting intermediary deproletarianization, and a large decrease (probably due to sampling error from relatively small subsample sizes) for lower white collar supervisors (11.6 percentage points) and modest almost significant increase in the proportion of employees, suggesting intermediary proletarianization.

20. Tables 38, 39 and 40 in the Appendix to this chapter support the idea that the rate of deproletarianization slowed around 1970, and that proletarianization may have begun about then. The slope on male supervisors

decreased from 1.206 from 1945 to 1970, to .0690 for 1972 to 1982 (or -0.407 for 1970 to 1980). The same pattern occurs for standardized regression coefficients for men. On the other hand, the slope for male employees increased in absolute value from -1.031 to -1.508. The standardized regression coefficient for male employees actually decreased in absolute value from -0.961 to -0.774. While there are no comparable data for combined men and women for 1945 to 1970, the slopes for combined men and women supervisors (0.353 versus 0.690 for men) and employees (-0.703 versus -1.508 for men) for 1970 to 1980 are both smaller and less significant than for men alone. These suggest weakening of the deproletarianization process. In other words, the rate of intermediary deproletarianization, at least among supervisors, appears to have declined, and may indicate the start of intermediary proletarianization of white collar labor around 1970.

21. It is theoretically possible to use the post-1982 CPS to develop estimates of the approximate proportions in white collar occupations (professionals, managerials, clericals, and sales) after 1982 (see Andes and McGinnis, 1984). This would involve disaggregating all the new 1980 categories and reaggregating them into 1970 categories. These estimates of white collar proportions could then be used to standardize (weight) the post-1982 figures from surveys like the GSS that use 1970 occupations codings. Unfortunately, since some 1980 categories correspond to more than one 1970 code, and there are new occupations for 1980, the relationships are not exact, and the estimates would be only approximate.

6 Is White Collar Being Deproletarianized?

CONDITION PROLETARIANIZATION: COMPARISONS OVER TIME

While white collar has become more working class, it has not necessarily become more proletarian. The examination of intermediary proletarianization in Chapter 5 served as a proxy for specifically investigating condition proletarianization within the working class. This chapter directly explores the question of whether the white collar labor process has become increasingly proletarian, that is, whether white collar labor has become increasingly concentrated in working class conditions. Investigating changes in the labor process, including authority relations and working conditions, provides a more precise way to identify condition proletarianization among white collar labor. The chapter also explores whether changes in both white and blue collar working conditions constitute a blurring of the white collar/blue collar line.

Estimates of Condition Proletarianization

This analysis explores condition proletarianization among white collar labor by examining changes over time in the relative proportions of empowered employees versus proletarian workers in white collar labor. A growing proportion of empowered employees and declining proportion of proletarians would support the postindustrial prediction of deproletarianization (Bell, 1973). A declining proportion of empowered employees and a growing proportion of proletarian workers would support the marxian prediction of proletarianization (Braverman, 1974). Changes in the sizes of the respective groups over time suggest changes in the white collar labor process.

By examining the changes in the relative sizes of the semi-autonomous employee and worker categories across industries, Wright and Singlemann (1982) explored condition proletarianization overall between 1960 and 1970. Applying the class-category distributions from the Survey of Working Conditions to industry figures, Wright and Singlemann compared proportions of semi-autonomous employees and workers in 1960 and 1970.[1] Between the two dates there were small increases in both semi-autonomous employees (10.95 to 11.05 percent) and workers (43.65 to 45.60 percent) (Wright and Singlemann, 1982, p. S193). Managers (supervisors) also grew (32.7 to 35.6 percent), while small employers (6.6 to 4.0 percent) and independents (6.1 to 3.7 percent) declined. The increase in semi-autonomous employees (0.1 percentage points or 1.3 percent proportionally) indicates slight deproletarianization. The larger increase in workers (1.95 percentage points or 5.5 percent proportionally) indicates proletarianization.[2] Together they suggest polarization.

Wright and Singlemann hypothesized that as the rate of growth of service industries and the state would decline over time the rate of proletarianization would increase both within and between industries (1982, pp. S201-2). This would produce net proletarianization for the rest of the century (pp. S179, S202). Using a modified class conception and slightly different empirical approach, Wright and Martin (1987), however, find both a net increase in "experts" (akin to semi-autonomous employees) and a net decrease in workers both from 1960 to 1970 and 1970 to 1980. They ascribe the deproletarianization to the internationalization and technological upgrading of the class structure. For 1950 to 1970, Gordon, Edwards, and Reich found that independent primary (27.8 to 32.8 percent) and secondary (35.0 to 36.2 percent) labor markets increased proportionally, but that the subordinate primary decreased (37.2 to 31.0 percent) (1982, p. 221). On the one hand, the contrasting increases suggest polarization in skilling and deskilling; on the other hand, the subordinate primary decrease suggests movement away from homogenization at semiskilled levels.

Spenner's (1983) examination of both the case studies and aggregate analyses on deskilling also supports the hypothesis of no net change. Changes (upgrading, downgrading, mixed effects or no change) are measured along two dimensions of skills: skill as substantive complexity of work (see Kohn, 1977) and skill as autonomy-control (Spenner, 1983, pp. 828-29); the latter is related to but distinct from formal authority or supervisory responsibility in a hierarchy. For compositional shifts in substantive complexity there was no net change. For shifts in skill as content and substantive complexity, there was no net change or slight upgrading (Mueller, et al., 1969; Karasek, et al., 1982). For content and autonomy-control, there was both upgrading and downgrading (Mueller, et al., 1969; Sobel, 1982a). For composition shifts in skill as autonomy-control, there was slight downgrading (Wright and Singlemann, 1982). In the aggregate, though skill as autonomy-control has declined slightly, skill as substantive complexity has stayed the same or increased. Although Spenner (1983, pp. 834-35) draws no firm conclusions, the studies overall provide evidence of no net change or slight deproletarianization.

Examination of Condition Proletarianization

The empirical analysis here investigates condition proletarianization, or the increase in working class condition, by examining changes over time in relative proportions of the author and worker subclasses. Chapter 3 identified authors and workers using questions on work conditions from the Survey of Working Conditions and Quality of Employment Survey. Similar specifications are developed here for two other studies in the time series. Comparing proportions of authors is particularly appropriate because authority is a central component of the labor process and subclass definition. Comparing proportions of workers is appropriate in investigating relative absence of authority and deterioration in the labor process. Comparing proportions of authors and workers in two similar studies identifies changes in net sizes of the subclasses over time. Two pairs of comparable studies, Americans View Their Mental Health (in 1957 versus 1976) and the Survey of Working Conditions, 1969-70 versus the Quality of Employment Survey, 1972-73 provide evidence on condition proletarianization. Like the examination of intermediary proletarianization from 1970 to 1980, the focus is on possible condition proletarianization in the 1970s.

Americans View Their Mental Health (Gurin, 1957 versus Veroff, 1976)

One pair of studies consists of two replications of Americans View Their Mental Health (1957 and 1976). Both contain the supervisory variable for small subsamples of men (N = 290 and N = 703), as well as variables about self-employment and working conditions. Though the variety of condition related questions is less rich than in the Survey of Working Conditions, this pair offers an initial opportunity to examine proportional changes in male authors and workers over time.[3] (See Tables 41 and 42).

Table 41. Changes in Relative Class-category Sizes, White Collar Occupational Groups, Men, Gurin (1957) versus Veroff (1976)

	Independents	Employers	Supervisors	Authors	Normals	Workers	N
			White Collar				
1957	6.2	14.8	34.9	19.8	15.4	9.0	103
1976	4.2	14.6	48.8	15.6	10.7	6.0	290
Diff.	− 2.0	− 0.2	13.9	− 4.2	− 4.7	− 3.0	
Sign.	(−)	(−)	+ +	(−)	(−)	(−)	
			Upper White Collar				
1957	9.6	22.8	42.0	14.0	3.9	7.7	76
1976	4.9	19.8	51.8	10.0	9.2	4.2	203
Diff.	− 4.7	− 3.0	9.8	− 4.0	5.3	− 3.5	
Sign.	(−)	(−)	(+)	(−)	(+)	(−)	
			Lower White Collar				
1957	0.0	0.0	21.4	30.7	36.5	11.4	36
1976	2.6	2.6	41.6	28.6	14.3	10.4	87
Diff.	2.6	2.6	19.9	− 1.8	− 22.2	− 1.0	
Sign.	(+)	(+)	+ +	(−)	− −	(−)	
			Total				
1957	9.4	8.9	26.2	24.5	16.6	14.4	290
1976	6.4	9.0	35.4	20.2	16.7	12.2	703
Diff.	− 3.0	0.1	9.2	− 4.3	0.1	− 2.2	
Sign.	(−)	(+)	+ +	(−)	(+)	(−)	

Note: + + or − − means differences significant at $p < .05$. (+) or (−) means nonsignificant. Occupations weighted to CPS proportions.

The comparisons indicate that between 1957 and 1976, the relative proportions of male authors among all white collar groups declined, and the relative proportions of workers except among clericals also declined (see Tables 32 and 33). But none of the differences among men in either the author or worker proportions is significant at the .05 level largely because of the small subsample sizes. A plausible interpretation is that there have been no significant changes in relative subclass sizes from 1957 to 1976. But the pattern of decreases among authors suggests slight condition proletarianization, while the pattern of decreases among workers suggests condition deproletarianization. A nonparametric sign test indicates, moreover, that the probability that all the signs on the author changes and virtually all on the worker changes would be so consistent by chance is extremely low (p less than .01). The indications that from 1957 to 1976 both authors and workers decreased relatively provides evidence for both condition proletarianization and deproletarianization. This suggests slight condition polarization for overall white collar.

Table 42. **Changes in Relative Class-category Sizes, White Collar Occupations, Men, Gurin (1957) versus Veroff (1976)**

	Independents	Employers	Supervisors	Authors	Normals	Workers	N
			Professional				
1957	0.0	11.8	44.1	26.5	5.9	11.8	28
1976	1.6	7.4	47.5	18.9	17.2	7.4	104
Diff.	1.6	− 4.4	3.4	− 7.6	11.3	− 4.4	
Sign.	(+)	(−)	(+)	(−)	(+)	(−)	
			Managerial				
1957	16.7	31.0	40.5	4.8	2.4	4.8	39
1976	8.4	32.8	56.3	0.8	0.8	0.8	99
Diff.	− 8.3	1.8	15.8	− 4.0	− 1.6	− 4.0	
Sign.	(−)	(+)	(+)	(−)	(−)	(−)	
			Clerical				
1957	0.0	0.0	25.0	31.3	37.5	6.3	20
1976	2.6	0.0	43.6	28.2	15.4	10.3	45
Diff.	2.6	0.0	18.6	− 3.1	− 22.1	4.0	
Sign.	(+)	(o)	(+)	(−)	(−)	(+)	
			Sales				
1957	0.0	0.0	17.6	29.4	35.3	17.6	16
1976	2.6	5.3	39.5	28.9	13.2	10.5	42
Diff.	2.6	5.3	21.9	− 0.5	− 22.1	− 7.0	
Sign.	(+)	(+)	(+)	(−)	(−)	(−)	

Note: See Note to Table 5.1.

Survey of Working Conditions, 1969-70 versus Quality of Employment Survey, 1972-73

Another pair of studies, the Survey of Working Conditions, 1969-70 (SWC), and the companion, Quality of Employment Survey, 1972-73 (QES), provides the basis for a second comparison (see Tables 43 and 44). The operationalizations for condition proletarianization follow the procedures for the SWC and QES in Chapter 3 and use only variables shared by both studies for the discriminant analyses.[4] Because the sample sizes are larger than in the previous (AVMH) comparison, there is a greater possibility of statistically significant differences. Because these surveys include both men and women, the results are more representative.

Table 43.   Changes in Relative Class-category Sizes, 1970 versus 1973, White Collar Occupational Groups, Men and Women, SWC versus QES

	Independents	Employers	Supervisors	Authors	Normals	Workers	N
			White Collar				
1970	5.2	10.1	43.4	16.3	15.1	9.8	732
1973	3.2	9.0	41.4	20.0	15.9	10.5	988
Diff.	− 2.0	− 1.1	− 2.0	+ 3.7	+ 0.8	+ 0.7	
Sign.	(−)	(−)	(−)	+	(+)	(+)	
			Upper White Collar				
1970	8.0	18.5	53.9	9.4	6.7	3.5	381
1973	4.9	15.4	57.6	11.5	6.2	4.5	500
Diff.	− 3.1	− 3.1	+ 3.7	+ 2.1	− 0.5	+ 1.0	
Sign.	(−)	(−)	(+)	(+)	(−)	(+)	
			Lower White Collar				
1970	2.1	0.9	32.1	23.9	24.3	16.8	351
1973	1.5	2.5	24.8	28.7	25.8	16.7	488
Diff.	− 0.6	1.6	− 7.3	+ 4.8	+ 1.8	− 0.1	
Sign.	(−)	(+)	ns	(+)	(+)	(−)	
			Total				
1970	5.4	6.3	36.1	18.6	18.3	15.3	1531
1973	4.0	7.1	34.1	22.2	19.7	12.9	2068
Diff.	− 1.4	0.8	− 2.0	+ 3.6	+ 1.4	− 2.4	
Sign.	− −	(+)	(−)	+ +	(+)	− −	

Note: + + or − − means significant at p < .05; + or − means significant at p < .10; (−) or (+) means not significant.

The data analysis finds proportional increases among white collar authors during the early 1970s. While only the increase for the total labor force is significant at p less than .05, there have been modest increases for each white collar occupational group. A nonparametric sign test on the pattern of (all) positive signs indicates a small likelihood of such a pattern occurring by chance (p less than .05). In short, the increases in authors are evidence for white collar condition deproletarianization.

There are no statistically significant changes among workers in white collar occupations. Upper white collar workers did increase by 1.0 percentage point and sales workers by 7.2 percentage points. Overall white collar workers increased an insignificant 0.7 point. The distribution of signs for changes in the

Table 44. Changes in Relative Class-category Sizes, 1970 and 1973, White Collar Occupations, Men and Women, SWC versus QES

	Independents	Employers	Supervisors	Authors	Normals	Workers	N
			Professional				
1970	4.0	2.7	62.9	13.8	11.1	5.4	215
1973	1.9	4.4	62.2	15.6	8.6	7.3	288
Diff.	− 2.1	1.8	− 0.7	+ 1.8	− 2.5	+ 1.9	
Sign.	(−)	(+)	(−)	(+)	(−)	(+)	
			Managerial				
1970	13.2	39.1	42.2	3.5	0.9	1.0	165
1973	9.0	30.2	51.3	5.9	2.9	0.6	212
Diff.	− 4.2	− 8.9	9.1	+ 2.4	+ 2.0	− 0.4	
Sign.	(−)	−	+	(+)	(+)	(−)	
			Clerical				
1970	0.8	0.0	33.4	21.0	25.5	19.3	257
1973	0.6	0.0	26.9	26.6	29.2	16.6	357
Diff.	− 0.2	0.0	− 6.5	+ 5.6	+ 3.7	− 2.7	
Sign.	(−)	(=)	−	(+)	(+)	(−)	
			Sales				
1970	5.6	3.4	28.5	31.9	21.0	9.7	94
1973	3.9	9.4	19.1	34.5	16.3	16.9	130
Diff.	− 1.7	6.0	− 9.4	+ 2.6	+ 4.7	+ 7.2	
Sign.	(−)	(+)	(−)	(+)	(+)	(+)	

Note: + +/− − means significant at p < .05; +/− means significant at p < .10; (−)/(+) means not significant at p < .10. = means no change. N weighted by square−root of sample size.

worker percentages shows an equal number of increases and decreases, and thus no statistically significant pattern. The probable conclusion is that during the early 1970s authors increased but workers stayed the same. The clear increase in authors suggests deproletarianization of white collar labor in the early 1970s.

The patterns in the data overall both challenge and support Oppenheimer's (1973) hypothesis that, because lower white collar jobs were already proletarianized, any future proletarianization must occur in the upper sectors. The largest, though not statistically significant, growth in workers (proletarianization) occurred among the lower white collar sector (7.2 points for sales), but upper white collar workers also grew insignificantly. The pattern of increases for both authors and workers suggests polarization for upper white collar labor and for professionals in particular. There may have been deproletarianization among managers and clericals, however, since authors increased and workers decreased. The pattern in the results indicates both condition proletarianization and deproletarianization in the early 1970s, but it is too weak to support a clear conclusion of polarization. Without more conclusive evidence, the overall trends are not possible to determine.[5]

The Gurin-Veroff (1957-76) comparisons for men indicate that the proportions of both authors (proletarianization) and workers (deproletarianization) decreased. The SWC-QES (1970-73) comparisons indicate that authors increased significantly (deproletarianization) and some worker categories increased insignificantly (proletarianization). Taken together these two pairs of studies suggest a pattern over time of, first, polarization, and, then, slight deproletarianization (or polarization). The evidence for polarization would be stronger, but the small decreases in both authors and workers from 1957 to 1976 are offset by the small increase in both categories from 1970 to 1973. The combination suggests no net change.

Perhaps, as Wright and Singlemann hypothesized (1982, p. 202), proletarianization began to develop in the late 1970s.[6] However, the pattern in which both authors and workers decrease may represent polarization, as Bowles and Gintis (1977) indicate, or resegmentation, as Gordon, Edwards, and Reich (1982) predict. There appear to have been the changes in both directions that Spenner (1983) and Squires (1979) identify. Some evidence exists for deproletarianization, no change, or polarization, but little for proletarianization. Similarly, the analyses of data on supervisory responsibility showed intermediary deproletarianization through 1970 (Table 15), and little change or slight proletarianization (Table 28) afterwards. In any case, the data analyses provide little support for the hypothesis of overall proletarianization.[7]

COMPARING WHITE COLLAR AND BLUE COLLAR LABOR

Blurring the White Collar/Blue Collar Line

Although this study concentrates on white collar labor, comparing white collar with blue collar labor reveals growing similarities between the sectors. The two types of labor are increasingly alike in class situations and work conditions. While the theoretical analysis in Chapter 2 indicates that both white collar and blue collar labor are largely working class, white and blue collar are often considered to have different class positions and different work situations. White collar is often considered to be middle class; blue collar is typically considered to be working class. Similarly, white collar working conditions are typically considered better than blue collar conditions. White collar has an aura of middle class professionalism and mental work; blue collar seems manual and proletarian. In the U. S. in the 1970s, however, much white collar labor, particularly clerical work, is in similar structural class and work situations to blue collar personnel (Sobel, 1982b). In short, the class and work situations of white and blue collar labor have blurred.

There are several types of similarity between white collar and blue collar labor. For instance, upper white collar technicians and upper blue collar craftworkers are both involved in technical activities. Lower white collar clericals and lower blue collar operatives are both semiskilled in that they work on machine processes like text editing and printing. New working class technicians in French industries have become similar to blue collar technical workers (Mallet, 1963, p. 57). Many specialized technical jobs in "an uncertain border area" of industry "involve a measure of manual work" (Low-Beer, 1978, p. 13). This is not simply homogenization to a common semiskilled level but segmentation in which both white and blue collar are upgraded at different rates to similar outcomes (cf. Gordon, Edwards, and Reich, 1982). The embourgeoisement, postindustrial (upgrading), and proletarianization (downgrading) theories may also be reconciled in the merging of white and blue collar labor (cf. Low-Beer, 1978, p. 2).

The central concern here is whether there has been a blurring of the class and work situations of clericals and blue collar labor. This would occur if clericals were like operatives (and others in the blue collar sector) in class position and conditions of work. This does not, however, mean that white collar jobs have been proletarianized to blue collar conditions. The similarities may derive from greater rates of upgrading in the blue collar sector. Conditions in both clerical and operative jobs may have converged to a common level.

The comparison between white and blue collar labor focuses on clericals versus operatives in particular and clericals versus blue collar in general. Clericals are the largest occupational group in the U.S. labor force, and thus among white collar. In 1980, for instance, 18.1 million of a 97.3 million labor force (18.6 percent) are clericals. Most clericals (80.1 percent) are women (who comprise 42.4 percent of the labor force). In fact, 35.1 percent of all working women are in clerical jobs (versus only 6.4 percent of men). Thus changes in the structural conditions of white collar work have a major impact on women in the labor force. The similar situations for clericals and operatives underscore the similar class and work situations between white and blue collar labor.

This section demonstrates four points about the blurring of white collar and blue collar labor (see Table 46). First, white collar clericals and blue collar operatives generally share the same working class position. Second, they share similarly structured work situations. Third, the class situations of white collar clericals and blue collar operatives are merging. Fourth, the work situations of white and blue collar labor are also merging. Overall, these changes indicate a blurring of the white collar/blue collar line.

As in the above comparisons of white collar class-categories and subclasses across time, and because the definitions here of subclasses such as authors or workers are structural, it is possible to compare class and work situations between white collar and blue collar occupations. Such comparisons can be made by examining relative proportions in the various class-categories and subclasses both at one point and over time. Tables 50 and 51 in the Appendix divide white collar and blue collar occupations into all the class-categories (independents, employers, supervisors, authors, normals, and workers) for 1970 and 1973, respectively. Tables 45 and 46 focus on the subclasses among white collar labor (e.g., authors) that identify work conditions in 1970 and 1973.

Comparisons of Clericals with Operatives and Blue Collar Labor

Table 45 indicates that roughly the same high proportions of clericals, operatives, and blue collar labor (between 94.9 and 99.2 percent) are in the same working class situation. Their work situations are also similar. The proportions of authors and normals are virtually the same among clericals and operatives. For instance, the proportions of workers in the clericals and operative occupations differ by only about 6 nonsignificant percentage points.[8] Thus clericals overall are in similar situations to operatives.

For clericals versus blue collar as a whole, the differences in worker proportions are less than 2 percentage points. There is virtually the same distribution of authors among clericals and blue collars (0.7 points difference). In short, in class and work situations, clericals and blue collars are similar. Their situations essentially blur.

Table 46 also shows blurring of the white collar and blue collar line over time by comparing class and work situations for 1970 and 1973. The data both for 1970 alone and for 1970 versus 1973 indicate similar class situations and work structures. (Because the 1977 QES does not include the same supervisory variable, it is impossible to operationalize authors and workers in the same way to make valid comparisons with the SWC and earlier QES figures.)

Table 45. **Comparisons of Working Class and Subclasses as Percentages of Clericals versus Operatives and Blue Collar Labor, 1970**

	Working Class	Authors	Normals	Workers
Clerical	99.2	21.0	25.5	19.3
Operatives	96.8	21.3	26.5	25.2
Clerical – Operatives		– 0.3	– 1.0	– 5.9
		o	o	o
Clerical	99.2	21.0	25.5	19.3
Blue Collar	94.9	21.7	20.8	21.2
Clerical – Blue Collar		– 0.7	4.7	– 1.9
		o	o	o

Note: o means differences are not significant (p > .10). Percentage in working class equals the sum of author, normal, worker, and supervisory percentages (see Table 49).
Source: Survey of Working Conditions, 1969-70.

Table 46.   Comparisons of Working Class and Subclasses as Percentages of Clericals versus Operatives and Blue Collar Labor, 1970 and 1973

	Working Class	Authors	Normals	Workers
1970				
Clerical	99.2	21.0	25.5	19.3
Operatives	96.8	21.3	26.5	25.2
Clerical − Operatives		− 0.3	− 1.0	− 5.9
		o	o	o
Clerical	99.2	21.0	25.5	19.3
Blue Collar	94.9	21.7	20.8	21.2
Clerical − Blue Collar		− 0.7	4.7	− 1.9
		o	o	o
1973				
Clerical	99.4	26.6	29.2	16.6
Operatives	98.7	28.6	29.4	21.1
Clerical − Operatives		− 2.0	− 0.2	− 4.5
		o	o	o
Clerical	99.4	26.6	29.2	16.6
Blue Collar	97.4	25.0	23.6	18.4
Clerical − Blue Collar		1.6	5.6	− 1.8
		o	*	o

Note: o means differences not significant ($p > .10$); ** means $p < .05$; * means $.05 < p < .10$. See note to Table 45.
Sources: Survey of Working Conditions, 1969-70, and Quality of Employment Survey, 1972-73.

Table 47 compares the changes in percentages in the working class and in various subclasses between 1970 and 1973. For clericals and operatives, the differences in the working class membership have gotten smaller from 1970 to 1973. In 1970, the percentages in the working class differed by 2.4 percentage points, but by 1973 this difference had declined to 0.7 points. Similarly, working class membership among clericals and all blue collars differed by 4.3 percentage points in 1970 and declined to only 2.0 points in 1973. There is a mixed pattern for changes in work situations across time. For clericals and operatives, in two of three cases, work situations became more alike. For clericals and blue collar labor, two of three work situations became more divergent.

Table 47.   Summary Table: Comparisons of Percentage Differences, Clericals versus Operatives and Blue Collars, 1970 versus 1973

	Working Class	Authors	Normals	Workers	|Sum|
Clerical – Operative, 1970	(2.4)	– 0.3	– 1.0	– 5.9	7.2
Clerical – Operative, 1973	(0.7)	– 2.0	– 0.2	– 4.5	6.7
Direction	–	+	–	–	–
Clerical – Blue Collar, 1970	(4.3)	– 0.7	4.7	– 1.9	7.3
Clerical – Blue Collar, 1973	(2.0)	1.6	5.6	– 1.8	9.0
Direction	–	+	+	–	+

Note: Entries are percentage in the first occupation minus that in the second. + means increase in percentage differences; – means decrease in percentage differences. \|Sum\| means the sum of the absolute values of the author, normal and worker percentages across each occupation comparison.
Source: Survey of Working Conditions, 1969-70, and Quality of Employment Survey, 1972-73

For clericals and operatives, 1970 versus 1973, the differences in percentages decreased for both normal employees and workers. Normals declined from a 1.0 point difference in 1970 to a 0.2 point difference in 1973. Workers declined from 5.9 percent in 1970 to 4.5 percent in 1973. The difference in percentage of clerical and blue collar workers decreased from 1.9 to 1.8 percent. On the other hand, the differences for authors in both comparisons, and normals for the clerical and blue collar comparisons increased in 1973. These latter data indicate slightly diverging work situations between white collar and blue collar labor.

The sums of the absolute values of the differences across the occupational comparisons for all the three central working class subclasses (authors, normals, and workers) measure the overall change in work situation. Table 47 indicates that the overall sum of differences for clericals versus operatives for 1970 and 1973 declined from 7.2 to 6.7 percent. On the other hand, the overall sum of differences for clericals versus blue collar increased from 7.3 to 9.0 percent. In the first case, the decline indicates that work situations have become closer over time. In the second case, the growth indicates greater differentiation over time.

The blurring of the white collar/blue collar line has not developed because of proletarianization of clerical work. Instead, there has been a merging of work situations in the two sectors through simultaneous upgrading. The blurring occurs through both a slight upgrading of clerical labor and a greater upgrading of operatives and overall blue collar labor.[9] Table 48 shows, for instance, that from 1970 to 1973 for clericals, there was a net, though insignificant, upgrading (deproletarianization) of work situations. Not only have authors increased among clericals 5.6 percent, but workers have declined by 2.7 percent. Both figures suggest an upgrading of clerical work.

Table 48.   Comparisons of Class-categories among Clerical, Operatives and Blue Collar Occupations, 1970 versus 1973

	Independents	Employers	Supervisors	Authors	Normals	Workers	N
			Clerical				
1970	0.8	0.0	33.4	21.0	25.5	19.3	257
1973	0.6	0.0	26.9	26.6	29.2	16.6	357
Diff.	− 0.2	0.0	− 6.5	+ 5.6	+ 3.7	− 2.7	
Sign.	o	o	*	o	o	o	
			Operatives				
1970	2.8	0.4	23.8	21.3	26.5	25.2	273
1973	1.3	0.0	19.5	28.6	29.4	21.1	347
Diff.	− 1.5	− 0.4	− 4.3	+ 7.3	+ 2.9	− 4.1	
Sign.	o	o	o	**	o	o	
			Blue Collar				
1970	3.5	1.6	31.2	21.7	20.8	21.2	550
1973	1.6	1.0	30.4	25.0	23.6	18.4	732
Diff.	− 1.9	− 0.6	− 0.8	+ 3.3	− 2.8	− 2.8	
Sign.	**	o	o	o	o	o	

Note: ** means significant at $p < .05$;   * means significant at $p < .10$; o means not significant.
Sources: Survey of Working Conditions, 1969-70 and Quality of Employment Survey, 1972-73.

The pattern of condition deproletarianization occurs in operatives and blue collar labor as well.   For operatives, authors increased by a statistically significant 7.3 percent from 1970 to 1973; workers decreased by 4.1 percent in the same period. Both changes indicate upgrading, and both are larger in magnitude than the upgrading among clericals $(7.3 > 5.6; |−4.1| > |−2.7|)$ (Table 49). Similarly, blue collar labor as a whole experienced deproletarianization. Blue collar authors increased by 3.3 percent and workers decreased by 2.8 percent. Though neither change is significant at the .05 level, the directions suggest that both blue collar and clericals were upgraded. Again this indicates that the blurring of white collar and blue collar labor has occurred not because of a proletarianization of white collar labor, but because of greater blue collar deproletarianization to conditions similar to those of white collar labor.

Table 49. Comparisons of Percentage Changes in Authors and Workers, Clericals versus Operatives and Blue Collar, 1970 versus 1973

	Authors $\lvert1970-1973\rvert/1970$	Workers $\lvert1970-73\rvert/1970$
Operatives	7.3/21.3 (0.343)	4.1/25.2 (0.163)
	> >	> >
Clericals	5.6/21.0 (0.267)	2.7/19.3 (0.140)
Blue Collar	3.3/21.7 (0.152)	2.8/21.2 (0.132)
	< <	< <
Clericals	5.6/21.0 (0.267)	2.7/19.3 (0.140)

Note: > (<) means upper figure is larger (smaller) than lower. Figures in parentheses are proportional changes (percentage in 1970 minus 1973 divided by 1970 percentage).
Source: Table 48.

The conditions of clericals and operatives have merged because of the greater rate of upgrading among operatives. Table 49 shows in more detail that, in both absolute and proportional terms, operatives have experienced greater upgrading than clericals. On the other hand, though both experienced upgrading, the absolute and relative rate of upgrading among blue collar as a whole tended to be less than for clericals. The changes among workers are approximately the same, but they differ among authors. Upgrading among operatives (increase in authors) proceeded at a higher rate than among clericals but to similar results. Blue collars and clericals have upgraded at about the same rate, so that there exist similar work conditions between them. This is, in part, because the proportions of clerical and blue collar authors and workers were close in 1970, and they have changed at close enough rates to remain relatively similar in structure (cf. Tables 47 and 48).

The evidence supports the hypothesis that there has been a blurring of the class and work situations of clericals and blue collar labor. Clericals are in similar working class positions to both operatives and blue collar labor as a whole. They are also in similar work conditions as measured by proportions of authors and workers. And the class situations of clericals and blue collars have become more similar over time, while the work conditions of clericals, operatives, and blue collars have also become closer. Clericals have not been proletarianized to similar conditions of white collar labor. Instead, clerical, operative and blue collar labor overall have all been upgraded. These consequently blur the white collar/blue collar line and suggest general deproletarianization across the entire labor force.

CONCLUSION: WHITE COLLAR AND
DEPROLETARIANIZATION

Contrary to the middle class image that white collar retains, white collar labor has an essentially working class nature. White collar employees do not constitute a separate new middle class but are part of the stratified working class. Some clericals and salespeople are in working class conditions like those of classic proletarians in industry. However, the exact changes that have occurred within the white collar working class are difficult to demonstrate because the three forms of proletarianization have been occurring at the same time. The evidence on class, intermediary, and condition proletarianization sustain some of the theory of proletarianization, but leaves many questions unanswered.

White collar labor has experienced class proletarianization from 1940 to 1980 in the growing proportion of white collar employees. This trend is particularly clear among upper white collar professional and managerial personnel. In the lower white collar sector, there has been a net stability in the percentages in the working class over the last third of a century.[10] This supports the thesis of class proletarianization of white collar labor.

Intermediary proletarianization has not occurred among white collar labor over the longer term. In fact, there may have been intermediary deproletarianization in the growth of supervisors. The proportion of male supervisory employees increased from 1940 through 1970, while the proportion of male nonsupervisory employees decreased during the same period. Both changes signal intermediary deproletarianization. Regressions and chi square fits for combined men and women between 1972 and 1988 suggest that there has not been intermediary proletarianization, though data on managers suggest otherwise. The likely conclusion is that there has been no change or slight deproletarianization over time. The changes for males from deproletarianization between 1945 and 1970 to slower deproletarianization or constancy in the last decade suggest that intermediary proletarianization might have begun in the 1970s, and the relative increase in employees suggests it might predominate in the 1980s. The overall evidence, however, contradicts the intermediary proletarianization thesis, but supports both the postindustrial and marxian predictions of upgrading or deproletarianization for white collar labor.

The evidence on condition proletarianization among white collar labor somewhat parallels that for intermediary proletarianization. There has been slight deproletarianization to upgraded conditions, or perhaps polarization. While the decrease in the proportion of authors among men since the late 1950s suggests condition proletarianization, the increase in authors in the 1970s suggests deproletarianization. The apparent decrease in workers suggests deproletarianization since the end of the 1950s. But the constancy or slight increase in workers in the 1970s also suggests intermediary proletarianization. The possible increases in both authors and workers suggest slight condition polarization within the white collar working class.

Moreover, the class situations and work conditions of white collar and blue collar labor have become more similar over time. White collar and blue collar have become closer. This has occurred due to the greater upgrading of blue collar labor to situations similar to those of white collar labor. As deproletarianization occurred among blue collar labor, the white collar/blue collar line has blurred.

These developments generally contradict the condition proletarianization thesis, while moderately supporting the deproletarianization or polarization theses. The similarities of clerical work situations to those of operatives and blue collar labor as a whole, moreover, underscore the generally proletarian conditions of female employment concentrated in the lower white collar sector.

Wright and Singlemann predicted in 1982 that condition proletarianization would accelerate overall as the previously uncrystallized class structures became more proletarianized. Wright and Martin recognized by 1987 that, in fact, condition deproletarianization has occurred. Figures here for the longer period support the hypothesis of class proletarianization, while generally providing evidence for the more complex theses of intermediary and condition deproletarianization or polarization, except perhaps in the 1980s.

The combination of class proletarianization with intermediary deproletarianization, and slight condition deproletarianization or polarization leaves open the question of whether the overall trend is toward upgrading or downgrading of white collar labor. The findings, however, provide little support for the proletarianization theses beyond the class and, perhaps, for the 1980s, the intermediary kind. At this point, the best long term conclusion is no net change, or perhaps slight intermediary deproletarianization and condition polarization.

White collar has not become more middle class, either in class or conditions, and exactly how the white collar working class has changed remains unclear. There are white collar proletarians, like workers on the assembly line, but they do not give current white collar labor its dominant character. Not matter how the class structure of white collar labor is changing, the structure of class itself, as the final chapter indicates, influence its actions in the political arena.

APPENDIX

Table 50.   Class-categories and Subclasses as Percentages of White and Blue Collar Occupations, Survey of Working Conditions, 1969-70

	Independents	Employers	Supervisors	Authors	Normals	Workers
White Collar	5.2	10.1	43.4	16.3	15.1	9.8
Upper White Collar	8.0	18.5	53.9	9.4	6.7	3.5
Professional	4.0	2.7	62.9	13.8	11.1	5.4
Managerial	13.2	39.1	42.2	3.5	0.9	1.0
Lower White Collar	2.1	0.9	32.1	23.9	24.3	16.8
Clerical	0.8	0.0	33.4	21.0	25.5	19.3
Sales	5.6	3.4	28.5	31.9	21.0	9.7
Blue Collar	3.0	1.4	30.8	20.7	22.2	21.9
Upper Blue Collar/Crafts	4.0	3.1	48.3	22.3	10.3	11.9
Lower Blue Collar	3.2	0.7	21.4	21.3	26.8	26.5
Operatives	2.8	0.4	23.8	21.3	26.5	25.2
Laborers	4.3	2.1	12.9	21.5	27.9	31.2
Service	1.5	0.8	29.5	17.7	26.5	24.0
Farm	36.1	18.1	12.5	21.7	8.8	2.8
Total	5.4	6.3	36.1	18.6	18.3	15.3

Note: Occupations are weighted to the Current Population Survey percentages for 1970. N = 1533.
Source: Survey of Working Conditions, 1969-70.

Table 51. Class-categories and Subclasses as Percentages of White and Blue Collar Occupations, Quality of Employment Survey, 1972-73

	Independents	Employers	Supervisors	Authors	Normals	Workers
White Collar	3.2	9.0	41.4	20.0	15.9	10.5
Upper White Collar	4.9	15.4	57.6	11.8	6.2	4.5
Professional	1.9	4.4	62.2	15.6	8.6	7.3
Managerial	9.0	30.2	51.3	5.9	2.9	0.6
Lower White Collar	1.5	2.5	24.8	28.7	25.8	16.7
Clerical	0.6	0.0	26.9	26.6	29.2	16.6
Sales	3.9	9.4	19.1	34.5	16.3	16.9
Blue Collar	1.6	1.0	30.4	25.0	23.6	18.4
Upper Blue Collar/Crafts	2.0	1.6	46.0	21.8	16.1	12.5
Lower Blue Collar	1.3	0.6	20.9	27.0	28.1	22.0
Operatives	1.3	0.0	19.5	28.6	29.4	21.1
Laborers	1.3	2.7	25.3	22.0	24.0	24.7
Service	7.4	2.1	25.1	28.7	26.2	10.4
Farm	23.6	56.9	8.3	2.8	8.3	2.8
Total	4.0	7.1	34.1	22.2	19.7	12.9

Note: Occupations are weighted to the Current Population Survey percentages for 1970. Weight N = 2068.
Source: Quality of Employment Survey, 1972-73.

NOTES

1. To explore underlying trends, Wright and Singlemann (1982, p. S184, Appendix A) decomposed the changes in the class structure into industry-shift effects and class-composition shift effects. Industry-shift effects involve shifts between industries in relative sizes of employees, and class-composition shift effects involve changes in class structure within industries. Within industries overall there were large class composition shift effects (Wright and Singlemann, 1982, Tables 6 and 8). Semi-autonomous employees declined and workers increased, indications of proletarianization. But supervisors increased, suggesting deproletarianization. The greater industry-shift effects, however, masked the class composition changes. For instance, there has been a shift from manufacturing, which was already heavily proletarianized (that is, with a high proportion of workers) to much less proletarianized service industries. While Wright and Singlemann did not have survey data on class category for 1960, they did use Census data for both 1960 and 1970 to calculate the shifts in occupation and industry compositions. Wright and Singlemann computed class structure data for 1960 by applying the class structure found in the Survey of Working Conditions, 1969-70 for each of the 11 occupations within 37 major industries to the corresponding industry-specific Census occupations in 1960. Contrary to the expected results, this procedure assumes that there was no change within industries in the class compositions for various occupations between the two dates. Summing the industry-specific figures for 1960 and 1970 produced estimates for the aggregate changes. Since Wright and Singlemann assumed no change in class composition within industry-specific occupations, the evidence they find for deproletarianization is all the more surprising.

2. There are several problems with the approaches in Wright and Singlemann (1982) and Wright and Martin (1987). First, their operationalizations of class-categories are very general. In the 1982 article, the semi-autonomous category is only generally specified by the choice of the two variables (decision making and freedom), and in the 1987 article, "experts" are identified by certain professional/technical occupations (that is, not a class specification). In both articles, the worker category is a residual of non-semi-autonomous/expert employees. The estimates rely on data by industries, moreover, and they do not examine changes in specific occupational categories. Using data in both Wright analyses, it would be possible to estimate white collar class-category proportions by choosing white collar concentrated industries (cf. Chapter 5, Note 1 here). Chapters 3 and 5 here offer an alternative approach that more directly operationalizes worker and directly analyzes white collar labor. The Wright and Singlemann (1982) findings are consistent with the interpretation used in the analysis of the 1970-80 and 1972-82 data here that the rate of deproletarianization slowed around 1970. Wright and Martin's (1987) analysis, however, also indicates the continuing deproletarianization this chapter describes. Moreover, though the Wright and Singlemann analyses assume no change in class structure within industry-specific occupations because they had no survey data for 1960 on class proportions, as Chapter 5 here indicates, earlier studies (e.g., Kohn, 1964) exist, though since they include only men are not fully comparable.

3. Discriminant analysis identified the set of variables that best distinguish between the authorities and subordinates. For the Gurin (1957) and Veroff (1976) data, the best discriminators are (1) years on the job (tenure), (2) having a supervisor (boss), (3) the degree of supervision, and (4) the good aspects of the job.

4. The best discriminators for both SWC/QES are: (1) having a boss, (2) being allowed to make decisions, (3) having the opportunity to be creative, (4) years on the job (tenure), (5) having enough authority to tell people what to do, (6) having repetitious work, (7) belonging to a union. For the SWC/QES discriminant equations, see Chapter 3, Note 13. Both Survey of Working Conditions, 1969-70 and Quality of Employment Survey, 1972-73 were coded to 1960 Census occupation categories for comparability.

5. For men alone there appears to be a growth in workers in upper white collar jobs. In particular, there is a statistically significant increase of 5.3 percent in workers among professionals. For women alone there is also a growth of workers in clerical work, though women appear to be experiencing deproletarianization in terms of upgrading in upper white collar jobs.

6. Along with a proportional increase in white collar authors, there is a slight decrease in supervisors. To the extent that a decrease in supervisors is tied to an increase in authors, who are by definition nonsupervisory, the pattern may indicate a decline in authority overall, and hence a type of proletarianization. Supervisors may be losing supervisory authority over others, and becoming authors, with authority over only themselves.

7. The Quality of Employment Survey for 1977 (a followup to QES, 1972-73, and Survey of Working Conditions, 1969-70) could not be used to compare percentages of authors and workers over time because the wording of the supervision question, as well as some on work conditions, changed. The earlier studies (SWC, QES) asked respondents "Do you supervise anybody as part of your job?" The 1977 QES asks "Is supervising other people a *major* part of your job" (emphasis in original). (I have requested that any later QES studies include both questions.) The General Social Survey, begun in 1972, has a limited number of questions on employment conditions (for example, whether one is supervised) that are not detailed enough to identify authors or workers.

It might be possible to develop more current estimates of subclass proportions of authors, normals, and workers, however, using both the QES 1977 and the fall 1985 Pilot survey of the American National Election Study. For the Quality of Employment Survey, 1972-73 1977, this would involve identifying supervisors by inference from related questions and using the differently worded work condition questions to approximate those in Survey of Working Conditions, 1969-70 and Quality of Employment Survey, 1972-73. The ANES 1985 Pilot includes most of the discriminating variables about working conditions from the Survey of Working Conditions and Quality of Employment Survey, although the supervisory question in the ANES is slightly different (see Figure 5). However, the Pilot sample size is small (N = 329) and the labor force subsample has only about 200 respondents. The occupational proportions are only representative of those in the second wave of the 1984 post-election sample. Weights could be estimated from the 1980-82 CPS and applied to the occupational proportions. The discriminant analyses would also have to be rerun for the SWC, QES, QES77, and ANES Pilot using only the commonly shared variables. Given the small size for the 1985 subsample, the results would almost certainly not be statistically significant.

8. About 5 to 6 percentage points is the minimum significant difference between percentages in a random sample of 1500; most of the differences here are both smaller and based on smaller subsamples, and therefore are not statistically significant (cf. Blalock, 1979, p. 232).

9. Most of the percentages are not significantly different even at a probability value between .05 and .10 (see Table 46). Statistically most subclass sizes are not significantly different, and could be the same sizes. In substantive terms, there are probably small differences in the conditions between the occupations (cf. Note 8 above).

10. Among professionals, clericals, and especially sales, there may have been small net declines in wage employment and related increases in self-employment. The increase in self-employment may be particularly prominent among women in recent years.

7 Beyond the White Collar Working Class: From Structure to Politics

POLITICAL AGENDA

Conjuring up images of labor militancy and workers on the barricades, the words "working class" are inherently political. Notwithstanding white collar's image as middle class, the notion of a "white collar working class" also raises political issues. Two basic questions motivate the discussion in this final chapter about the relations between structural class and politics. First, what is political about structural class? And second, how does structural class affect white collar political activity? The chapter identifies the political aspects of structural class, brings evidence to the relationship between structure, white collar, and participation, and raises issues for future inquiry.

This study emerged from interest in new theories of white collar labor, the working class, and white collar political action. In particular, the new working class theories identified changes in class structure, the blurring of white collar and blue collar lines, and the generation of political activity as central issues about class and politics.[1] The idea in new working class theories that the contradictory dynamics of being both white collar and working class should produce "conflictual participation" (Mallet, 1975, p. 52) among advantaged groups, including students, facing loss of status, suggested structural links between occupation, new class position, and political behavior. These theories implied that involvement in work leads to increasing involvement in other aspects of life (Low-Beer, 1978, p. 20). The structural and political strands of the analysis of white collar labor were united in the new working class theories (p. 2). In short, both more general theories of white collar class and new working class theories hold that essential political insights derive from structural analysis of white collar class and subclass situations.

The focus of this chapter is on the ways in which structural class implies and influences various forms of political activity. Political involvement here lies essentially in the daily politics of power relationships in the workplace and the implications for politics outside. In short, the discussion focuses on the "politics of production" (Burawoy, 1979) at work and the implications for politics outside of work. The distinctive issue is how objective class and subclass positions contribute to observable political outcomes. This approach recognizes, moreover, that the absence of political activity, or disengagement, is also a form of structured political behavior. However, the emphasis is on the generation of political activity *per se,* not on its ideological or partisan direction. Moreover, the model stresses the political effects of class structure, but recognizes that other traditional factors influence political outcomes. In addition, it recognizes that new factors such as the growing concentration of more highly educated women in white collar work provide potential bases for new political and union activity. The realities versus the expectations of white collar jobs, particularly among women, and the willingness to cooperate with others may undergird new forms of workplace involvement.

This discussion distinguishes traditional issues about working class politics from specific connections between structural class and political outcomes (cf. Wright, 1982, p. 321; 1985, p. 286; see also Katznelson, 1981, pp. 202-9). The discussion does not focus on politics as expressed through unionization or strike activity. Nor does it emphasize politics in terms of the state as essential to setting the legal framework in property rights or in terms of contract, or as reproducing the structure of economic class (Wright, 1982, p. 321). It only speculates briefly about class conflict, class struggle, progressive or reactionary movements (see Oppenheimer, 1985, pp. 181-93; Wright, 1985, pp. 285-91). In the emphasis on the structural bases of politics, the analysis only briefly mentions political aspects of attitudes, class consciousness or community solidarity (see Burris, 1987; Oppenheimer, 1985; Vallas, 1987). And it does not explore whether subjective positions emerge from objective class positions (see Oppenheimer, 1985, p. 181; Vallas, 1987).

STRUCTURAL CLASS AS POLITICAL

An essentially political aspect of white collar class situation derives from the conceptualization of political interactions as being tied to structural, economic class and the structural dimensions within it such as subclass structure. The class and subclass structures of work coincide with the authority structure within the workplace. In fact, the authority structure of work is the political structure of work (Eckstein, 1966; Burawoy, 1985). In other words, the structural aspects of economic class are political in their nature and consequences.

Political aspects of class include power relationships, relationships of domination and subordination, and relationships of control (Wright, 1982, p. 321). "The authority structure is primarily a political relationship in that it systematically limits the capacity of workers to transform the relations within which they work" (1982, pp. 322-24; 1985, p. 290). Class as relations of domination and subordination involve political relationships and power. "In these terms, the relations of domination and subordination are quintessentially political" (Wright, 1982, p. 325). "The work of management and supervision . . . is the direct reproduction, within the process of production itself, of the political relations between the capitalist class and the working class" (Poulantzas, 1975, pp. 227-28). Supervisory activity and the authority relations within the enterprise represent the political domination of capital over the working class

(Wright, 1978, p. 36). "[T]he command of capital over labor represents a socially significant exercise of power" (Bowles and Gintis, 1986, p. 69). In short, class relations are political relations (but see Roemer, 1988).

The concept of class formation as "social relations within each class that determine its capacity to produce its interests" (Wright, 1982, p. 322; 1985, p. 286) links class structure to class politics. "The underlying structure of class relations limits the possible forms of collective class organization, which in turn limit the possible forms of class struggle" (p. 323). The "process of class formation" involves the transition from "class-in-itself" as an economic category to "class-for-itself" as a political outcome (p. 339). The "structuration of class relationships" involves the translation of economic relations into social relations (Giddens, 1973, p. 105), or more boldly, economic and structural class into class formation. Particularly related to "proximate" structuration, the division of labor, while also a basis of fragmentation, may undergird "the consolidation of class relationships" (p. 108). The division of labor "furthers the formation of classes to the degree to which it creates homogeneous groupings which cluster along the same lines" (p. 108). However, though class is an inherently political concept, classes are not necessarily politically mobilized (cf. Roemer, 1988; Burawoy, 1985). "If class is defined in a Marxist sense as a group of persons who share a position in the division of labor, who *for that reason* share political views then . . . [white] collar workers do not form a class" (after Sabel, 1982, p. 187).

THE POLITICS OF THE WHITE COLLAR WORKING CLASS

Is there a type of politics that is generally connected to the working class, and, specifically, to the white collar working class? In other words, is there a form of political involvement that is particularly congruent with the nature of the white collar working class? For instance, the process of unionizing involves a working class activity in assisting dependent employees to sustain collective action. But creating a union is different from joining an established union, so being a union member does not necessarily involve a working class form of politics. Different class formations contribute to different political formations (Wright, 1982, p. 339). Around the political dimensions of work organization, or production relations, develop syndicalist politics. Around the state sphere develops reformist or social democratic politics of governmental processes and practices. And around the coincidence of production politics with state politics develop revolutionary action (p. 339).[2] Edwards suggests that different class fractions have different associated forms of political expression (1979, p. 203; but see Oppenheimer, 1985, p. 181). "The middle layers" (Edwards, 1979, p. 191) or "the new middle class" (p. 192), including lower level administrative workers in white collar jobs, express their concerns most intensely in class fraction politics such as draft opposition, consumer activism and the taxpayer revolt (p. 204). Independent primary workers are likely to focus on political issues regarding the quality of life, individual autonomy, civil liberties and personal freedoms (Gordon, Edwards, and Reich, 1982, p. 213). Giddens suggests that the "institutional . . . *manifestation* of class conflict in the industrial and political spheres," for instance, in worker protest, "*is the normal mode of the structuration of class conflict in capitalist society*" (1973, p. 202, emphasis in the original). The nontraditional conjunction of being both white collar and working class suggests that being white collar working class should contribute to nontraditional forms of politics; thus protest may be the typical form of expression for the white collar working class. Following Edwards's approach, consistency between form and expression should contribute to engagement in protest by the white collar working class. Following Wright's analysis of the nature of working class politics, moreover, both syndicalism and revolution occur, respectively, in the production and state spheres.

At the most basic level of class transformation, the growth of the white collar working class creates the foundation for majoritarian electoral politics. By the middle 1980s, more than half of the labor force was white collar and roughly 90 percent of white collar was working class.[3] This means that white collar working class is now a majority of the entire labor force. More important politically, white collar workers vote at a higher rate than both blue collar workers and those outside of the labor force (Wolfinger and Rosenstone, 1980, pp. 23, 28). Quite simply, the majority white collar working class potentially constitutes an electoral majority.   Because of a contradiction between majoritarian and working class appeals (Przeworski and Sprague, 1986, pp. 34-35), however, this is not sufficient to create the working class majority for socialism that has eluded electoral advocates of the working class parties in Europe for a century. But it does provide an essential basis for white collar working class power within the electoral system. Obviously the heterogeneity of white collar working class, including the segmentation and internal, structural stratification, have contributed to its political quiescence (cf. Gordon, Edwards, and Reich, 1982, p. 213-15; Przeworski and Sprague, 1986, p. 183), and make its widespread political mobilization unlikely. But the opportunity lies open for whatever party--political, union, or social--understands the potential unities within the changing nature of the white collar working class, and seeks thereby to mobilize white collar political power.

FROM STRUCTURE TO POLITICS

Traditionally recognizable kinds of politics also develop from structural class. Structural class organizes work roles with differential opportunities for participation in decisions at work that encourage politics outside of work. In other words, the structure of work permits or inhibits opportunities to participate in the exercise of authority and decision making both within and outside of the workplace. This occurs through political socialization on the job that influences politics off the job. Active involvement in work, which structural class permits or discourages, leads to active politics outside. Though class structure is not the only factor involved, it organizes a propensity for activity or inactivity. Pursuing persistent ideas in democratic theory, Eckstein (1966), Almond and Verba (1963), Pateman (1970), and Mason (1982) hold that participation at work should lead to participation and involvements in the larger political sphere. Congruence in authority relations across spheres should lead to similar behaviors. Internal politics should have external consequences.

The limits and possibilities that class imposes on work also structure specific opportunities to exercise authority and make decisions in the workplace. Thus political activity exercised in the workplace should have effects outside. Occupational involvements, such as exercising authority in the workplace and making decisions about one's own job, should lead, *ceteris paribus*, to political involvement. Those who participate in decision making on the job should participate in decisions off the job. Simply, participation should lead to participation.

More specifically according to the "proximity hypothesis" (Mason, 1982, pp. 70ff.), the transference from work to politics occurs most directly from similarly formal types of work to similarly formal types of politics. Formality or informality resides in the relatively structured or unstructured organization of interactions or relationships that authority patterns or activities encompass (cf. Almond and Verba, 1963, pp. 272, 304; Mason, 1982, pp. 71, 77). Like formal organizations, formality at work lies in set rules, roles, and procedures that constitute a system of interrelationships. Authority patterns are formal to the extent that they occur in organized and usually hierarchical structure within an organization or institution. Like formal democracy, formality in politics lies in set institutional arrangements and procedures which characterize and structure the activities within them. In the sense of formal authority leading to formally organized politics, analogous formality should correspond across spheres. The closer in structure and kind are authority relations and decision making at work to formality and decision making in outside politics, the stronger should be the transference.

Direct effects between spheres occur across congruent lines of authority at corresponding levels of formality. Those who participate in authority and decisions at work should participate in analogously formal or informal decisions in outside politics. For instance, formal occupational involvement such as exercising authority at work should affect formal politics outside like voting in public elections. Less formal occupational involvement such as having a say in workplace decisions (work participation) should affect less formal involvements like community activity. Finally, informal occupational involvement such as having control over one's own job (job participation) should lead to informal politics like protest. For the labor force as a whole and the more formal types of involvements, both U.S. and crossnational research generally finds this pattern (see Sobel, 1986, 1987).

Empirical investigation demonstrates that, for instance, those in class situations that involved greater exercise of authority tend to vote at higher rates than those in more restricted situations. The bivariate correlation between structural class-categories and whether one votes or not, for instance, is positive though modest (tau $c = .09$). The relationship between having authority on the job and voting is about the same (.12). More specifically, in the 1984 national elections, a higher proportion of employers (85.1 percent) reported voting than non-supervisory employees (71.0 percent) (American National Election Study, 1984). Among those who have adequate authority on the job, 81 percent reported voting while only 71.2 percent without authority voted.[4] Scales of occupational involvement, which identify continuous differences similar to those in discrete subclass positions like authors or workers, have moderate positive relationships with outside forms of political participation. In short, though other factors such as socioeconomic, political mobilization, and personal tendency to participate are involved, class-connected levels of authority and participation within the workplace relate modestly to outside political activities.

In order to investigate the impact of structural class on white collar politics, it is important to identify, separately and in interaction, the effects on political activity of participating at work, of being white collar, and of being working class, controlling for others factors.[5] Because white collar jobs typically involve at least limited advantage and nonmaterial resources such as prestige, being white collar should contribute to political involvement.   Because working class situation typically involves subordinate and dependent positions, being working class should discourage political involvement.   Though the individual effects of being white collar and being working class on political involvements then are contradictory, the interaction of being both white collar and working class should increase political involvement since the contradiction should induce action.   In other words, because being both white collar and working class may involve disquieting inconsistencies, this intersection of class and occupation should, in fact, constitute a political impetus.   This has traditionally been seen as directed toward politics of resentment or restoration rather than innovation (cf.   Mills, 1951; Bowles and Gintis, 1976; Oppenheimer, 1985; but see Hamilton, 1982).[6]

The relationships, then, between structural class, subclass, and politics should be different for white collar, the working class, and the white collar working class.   The relationship between occupational involvements and political participation should, in general, be stronger for more advantaged white collar labor, and weaker for the more dependent working class.   The relationship between forms of occupational involvement and political action should be stronger for the contradictory combination of white collar labor within the working class.   The relationship between congruent forms of occupational and political involvements should be stronger still for the white collar labor within the working class.

Specifically, being white collar, being working class, and the interaction of being white collar with being working class should each have separate effects. Being white collar should produce a positive effect on politics.   Being working class should produce a negative effect.   Being white collar working class should also produce a positive effect.   Reflecting differences within the working class, higher levels of occupational involvement (measured on scales of work participation or job participation), *ceteris paribus,* should generate greater political activity.[7]

In the general investigation of how white collar and the working class express themselves politically, bivariate correlations should show positive relationships overall between various forms of occupational involvement and political participation.   For the congruent forms of informal involvements, such as work participation with community involvement or job participation with protest, the relationships should be stronger.   The relationship between informal occupational involvement and protest should be especially strong for the white collar working class.

Bivariate correlations show modest positive relationships overall between community activity and work participation (tau c = .12), and between community activity and job participation (.17) (American National Election Study Pilot, 1985).   The relationships between work and politics are roughly the same, however, for white collar, the working class, or the white collar working class.

The relationships between protest and both work participation and job participation, however, are quite different in relationship to white collar and the working class. While the correlation between work participation and protest overall is .07, for white collar it is .08. For the working class it grows to .19, and for the white collar working class it reaches .24. Similarly, while the overall correlation between job participation and protest is .06, for white collar it is .09. For the working class it grows to .14, and again for the white collar working class it reaches .23. In other words, as predicted, the strength of the relationship between informal occupational participation and protest is three to four times stronger for the white collar working class than for the overall labor force.

Multivariate analysis generally supports these findings, and generally indicates the hypothesized effects of congruence, class, and collar. Holding constant socioeconomic status (measured separately as education, income, and occupation), mobilization by organizations, the personal propensity to participate, and other background factors (see Sobel, 1986), being white collar working class has a positive effect (b = .26) on voting. Authority (.18) and supervision (.35), both of which are relatively formal involvements, also have positive effects on voting; being white collar or working class alone has no impact. For protest, too, work participation has a modest, though insignificant, effect. Being white collar working class has a positive impact on protest. The coefficient for white collar alone is significant, although negative (b = −.23). As predicted for the working class, the coefficient is negative (−.15). The coefficient for white collar working class on protest is strongly positive (.33), and has the largest standardized coefficient of any in the equation (B = .49).[8]

These results provide modest support for the hypothesis that occupational involvement, *ceteris paribus*, affects political participation, and these effects occur across congruent levels of formality. Formal authority at work affects formal politics in voting. Informal work participation affects informal protest. This is especially true in interaction with being white collar working class. For voting, being white collar working class has a significant impact. For protest, being white collar and working class, separately and together, have a moderately strong impact. Protest may, in fact, be the congruent kind of politics[9] for the white collar working class, and may be expressed in increasingly active electoral ways. This suggests that there may be increases in protest both at the workplace and polling place for those who are both white collar and working class.

Moreover, to the extent that those who participate more in decisions at work participate more in outside politics, greater democracy at work promises greater democracy in the polity.[10] Democratic and participatory theory since Mill has generally suggested that by participating one learns to participate (but see Katznelson, 1981, p. 6). However, the participatory relationship between spheres does not necessarily imply that there will be more *democratic* participation. Unless all participate, the minority that participates in some social spheres will tend to participate in others, while the majority that does not participate in any sphere will tend to be inactive in all (see Witte, 1980). This pattern persists for new participators as well as those who were already active. In short, the opportunities to participate must be equally distributed, and those presently inactive must be motivated to begin the involvements that should be self-reinforcing. However, the spread of higher educational levels among white collar personnel provide a greater base for greater democratic involvement and more widespread involvement in politics in the workplace and beyond.

POLITICS BEYOND

Other important implications of class structure for white collar politics exist in theory, but extend beyond the scope of this empirical investigation. For instance, changes in class situation over time should also have political consequences of both the traditional and more radical kind. If proletarianization strips away the middle class aura of professionalism, it may reduce inhibitions to politics among the white collar working class. Such deterioration might make individual white collar employees, particularly those in higher status occupations, more receptive to collective efforts toward regaining lost status. For instance, reduced inhibition might contribute to greater involvement in collective organization such as unionization or political mobilization (see Oppenheimer, 1985, p. 181; Sobel, 1984, p. 748). Since dependent professionals must now seek collective security where once occupants of similar higher status positions would have expected individual success from their positions alone (Oppenheimer, 1985), unionization should expand among white collar labor, particularly professionals experiencing proletarianization. Such political activities may, however, be conservative in attempting to regain lost privileges by retaining material advantages or prestige (see Mills, 1951; Derber, 1982). To the extent that white collar activities include the pursuit of the collective reorganization of the work process and the modification of the class relations of work, however, they may lead to progressive change in work and class structure.

The theories of proletarian revolution suggest that there should be greater class conflict as more labor enters working class conditions. Specifically for better situated white collar, extensive proletarian and degraded white collar labor should lead to revolutionary solidarity and action directed toward socialism. To the extent that the working class has a stake in transforming a proletarian situation, moreover, proletarianization should be a basis for its political action (Wright, 1976b, p. 17; Wright and Singlemann, 1982, p. S179). However, because proletarianization as a loss of position involves a form of downward mobility in accompanying reductions in resources and decline in the conditions of white collar work, it should decrease the likelihood of political involvement. In fact, theories of social and political advantage suggest precisely the opposite of the Marxist predictions: *de*proletarianization should lead to political activity. Because deproletarianization involves both movement to a more advantaged situation and a gain in social and economic resources (Verba, Nie, and Kim, 1978), it should lead to increased political involvement. Improvements in conditions, along with rising expectations, are more likely than degradation to produce radical political change.[11] Because the empirical evidence on condition proletarianization and deproletarianization does not point to a single direction, the investigation of their political consequences both in traditional and radical politics must await clearer demonstration of trends. However, while the general indication of intermediary and condition deproletarianization over time points to an impetus for increased political involvement, the possibly weakening deproletarianization of the 1970s and proletarianization in the 1980s have coincided with periods of declining activism.

Contrary to prediction, Wright and Martin (1987) discovered that there has been condition deproletarianization of labor over time. Marx, in fact, suggested that it is when labor is fully deproletarianized and people stand at the side of production that fundamental change will occur (1971, p. 142). Thus deproletarianization rather than proletarianization may be the indirect instigator of social transformation to the benefit of the white collar working class.

In fact, Marx's predictions in the Preface to *A Contribution to the Critique of Political Economy* and the *Grundrisse* actually point in the same progressive direction. The increasing proportion of supervisors that indicates intermediary deproletarianization has differing short and long term political implications for work domination and social transformation. In the short term, intermediary deproletarianization implies closer oversight and hence greater domination over the working class. In the long term, however, more supervision may be transformed into greater political change to the benefit of the working class.

The growth in supervision as capitalism develops involves, at least in the short term, more supervisors in closer control of fewer employees.[12] The structural conflict between the authority relations that supervisors represent and the productive forces that workers embody may lead to fundamental transformation of social organization. As the Preface notes,

> at a certain stage of their development, the material productive forces of society come in conflict with the existing relations of production, or--what is but a legal expression for the same thing---with the property relations within which they had been at work hitherto. From forms of development of the productive forces these relations turn into their fetters. Then begins an epoch of social revolution. With the change of the economic foundation the entire immense superstructure is more or less rapidly transformed. (Marx, [1859] 1977, pp. 4-5)

The constraint of workers' self-coordinated productivity and initiative by supervisory control embodies Marx's impersonal fetters in personal structural relations. In short, the conflict between forces and relations of production embodied in the conflicts between employees and supervisors may lead not to maintenance of the present order, but instead to change toward a more efficient and equitable social organization.

On the other hand, if the growth of supervisors (or of more empowered employees) involves oversight of automated processes, a less conflictual but nonetheless profound transformation may be in the offing. When the production of goods depends less on the "quantity of labor utilized than on the power of mechanical agents that are set in motion during labor time," as the *Grundrisse* explains, no longer is labor "an essential part of the process of production." The individual stops being the "principal agent" of the production process and "exists along side" it (Marx, 1971, p. 142). At this point human involvement is "restricted to watching and supervising" production.

> As soon as labor, in its direct form, has ceased to be the main source of wealth, then labor time ceases . . . to be its standard of measurement. . . . [T]he immediate process of material production finds itself stripped of its

impoverished, antagonistic form. Individuals are then in a position to develop freely. (Marx, [1859] 1971, p. 142)

"Reducing the necessary labor of society to a minimum" is a precursor to personal liberation. The change from productive labor to greater supervision bodes then, by a different process, similar fundamental transformation.

The deproletarianization that appears problematic from a traditional Marxist perspective may, in fact, lead by a different route to Marx's ultimate goal of social revolution. Rather than socialism's arising from proletarian situations, the desired future may arise from the deproletarianization of labor.[13] Both the decrease in proletarian conditions and the increase in supervisory oversight of either machines or people may lead to progressive and democratic political change.

On a more specific level, political action may lie at the intersection of structural situation and consciousness among white collar labor in the working class. Political action is especially likely when the limitations and opportunities that class structure creates collide with subjective perceptions about one's situation. While class structures the conflict, the coincidence of class position and class identification may well catalyze the generation of class-oriented political action. The interaction of consistent identification and structural position may increase the likelihood of fundamental political conflict along class lines. Those in the working class whose conscious identification with that class is strong may be more likely to act in a solidarily collective way (Przeworski in Wright, 1980, p. 369; Wright, 1985) or, in other words, create "cultures of solidarity" (Fantasia, 1988). Those in the working class who identify with the middle class may be more likely to act individually. These cross-class identifiers may, however, ultimately recognize the importance of collective action if their situations either deteriorate or improve significantly. Only those who in unchanging situations and who do not identify are likely to be inactive.

Moreover, the questions of both political involvement and political mobilization rest not only on the Lasswellian questions of who gets what but the Bowlesian questions of who gets to become what (Bowles and Gintis, 1986). The very process itself of attaining essential political and cultural goals becomes an important determinant of the kinds of change likely to occur in interaction with changing class structure. And higher education, particularly among women, creates the expectations of both skills and personal attainment, which may lead to additional expectations and demands.

Moreover, educationally based expectations and rising aspirations may prove to be a future form of class-related consciousness. Higher education and professional training may raise expectations for challenges and participation at work (cf. Vallas, 1987, p. 253; but Gallie, 1978, pp. 305-7). These expectations may conflict with structural limitations that restrict opportunities for decision making and advancement. For white collar people, by different dynamics than for the blue collar personnel with which they merge, the combination of expectations and structural limitations, as new working class theories suggest, may produce future conflict between white collar employees and their managers (but see Burris, 1983, Mackenzie, 1974). Political action is most likely to occur when the patterns of class-imposed limitations clash with educationally-induced expectations for challenge, responsibility, and mobility. Higher education and skills create among white collar people expectations of decency in a vision of a just society (cf. Sabel, 1982, p. 19). Class-related subjective perceptions and identifications may someday be as important explanatory variables for understanding and generating nontraditional politics and electoral insurgency as party identification is today for traditional electoral behavior.

The combination and contradictions of structural limitations with rising but unmet expectations may have particularly strong effects on women. As a group, women are concentrated in subordinate white collar jobs, yet are increasingly more highly educated, with accompanying higher expectations. Women as a group will feel the contradictions more fully and have a greater stake in transforming them through solidary actions. Again both the analysis that proletarianization has not degraded women's jobs and the predictions of passivity may eventually stand on their heads as the feminization of white collar labor (Crozier, 1971) situates women, who are willing to act in solidary ways, as transforming agents (cf. Fantasia, 1988). Increasingly, those who say white collar politics say women, with major implications for labor force and electoral change.

CONCLUSION

White collar still looms large in the social imagination and the social organization as the twentieth century wanes. As the white collar working class becomes increasingly economically central--and either increasingly simple or increasingly complex--its social and political significance grow larger. Political action among white collar labor, likely led by women in protest or in electoral surges, may well characterize the first part of the twenty-first century.

The essentially working class nature of white collar labor structures its current politics and creates the potential for an increasingly active role in the economic and political spheres. Inherent in the white collar working class and the deproletarianization it may be experiencing is the potential for profound social transformation. The white collar working class is not experiencing embourgeoisement but emboldening. As the white collar working class encompasses ever more people, even as the distinction between white collar and blue blurs, white collar enters increasingly strategic positions to engender transformations for an ever wider constituency.

As white collar is changing, so must the intellectual tools that assist the understanding of its course and consequences. New theories of class, of stratification, of consciousness, and of action must be constructed through social and political inquiry. To the extent that deepening insights develop a political formula both from the analysis and for the organization of white collar labor, they unfetter white collar contradictions and enable white collar labor to become a decisive factor in the contemporary social and political environments. When the theory of white collar is manifest and united with action in white collar mobilization, white collar people will prominently announce their new place in an ever more active social consciousness and even more transformed political arena.

NOTES

1. The French new working class theories (Belleville, 1963; Mallet, 1963; and Gorz, 1964) recognized that structural conflicts may create the potential for political action among technicians in technologically advanced industries. The American formulations of the new working class theories (Calvert, 1967; Davidson, 1967; Gottlieb, Gilbert, and Tenney, 1967; Gintis, 1970) were too restricted in their concentration on professionals or university students (educated labor). In general, the theories focused inappropriately on the "dependent" variable of education (see Sobel, 1982) rather than on the "independent" variable of class (Stinchcombe in Wright, 1979, p. 3). The application of new working class theories to both explaining and organizing student activism in the United States (Calvert, 1967; Calvert and Neiman, 1971; Davidson 1967a; Denitch, 1970; Gintis, 1970; Miles, 1971; and Oppenheimer 1972) suggested the pertinence of the theories for elucidating the bases of more general political behavior of white collar groups in the U.S. See also Gouldner (1979, pp. 70-73) on student rebellion as a political response among "trainee" members of the new class.

2. As Chapter 2 suggests, however, recognizing that the authority relations of work are political is not the same as defining class as authority relations (Dahrendorf, 1959, p. 138). "The participation in or exclusion from the exercise of authority within any imperatively coordinated association" (p. 138) involves politics that flows from class. But authority relations are not the same as class. However, political practice can produce and transform social and authority relations (Wright, 1982, p. 324).

3. Because there are no Current Population Survey occupational data after 1982 it is difficult to identify the proportion of the labor force that the white collar working class constitutes. As Chapter 5 here notes, for the CPS in 1982, 53.7 percent of the labor force is white collar, and 91.2 percent of white collar is working class. Thus 49.0 percent of the labor force is white collar working class. Using the unweighted estimates for 1988 from the GSS, 58.8 percent is white collar and 87.4 percent of white collar is working class, for an estimate of 51.4 percent majority for the white collar working class.

4. This analysis holds constant other factors such as socioeconomic status (measured separately as education, income and occupation), political interest, efficacy, trust, ideology, party and class identification, as well as basic background factors like age, sex, and race (see Sobel, 1986). In particular, it controls for organizational mobilization and the tendency to participate, which could otherwise account for the participatory patterns. It cannot hold constant important variables like social solidarity because the survey does not measure it.

5. In electoral surveys, typically more people report voting (overreport) than actually do vote. The empirical relationships are usually similar for reported and actual voters (see Traugott and Katosh, 1981). Other factors are obviously involved in voting, most prominently socioeconomic resources, attitudes of political efficacy, and political mobilization by organizations such as parties and unions; all are controlled in the empirical investigation (see Note 4). See Nie, Verba, and Kim, 1978, and Sobel, 1986 for fuller descriptions of the models.

6. The literature on status inconsistency is inconsistent in its political predictions (see Mills, 1951; Lipset, 1960; Hamilton, 1972, 1982; Oppenheimer,

1985, Ch. 9). Most, however, focus on an ideological (e.g., reactionary) or conservative partisan direction that status mobility panic generates among those in white collar occupations. The focus here is on the generation of political activity or passivity, not a particular direction.

7. Few research studies include data on structural class, occupational involvement, and political participation. The best is the three decade old *Civic Culture Study* (see Almond and Verba, 1963). The American National Election Study, 1984 (N = 1173), only includes the basic variables to identify class-categories. The two-wave fall 1985 Pilot survey (N1 = 429, N2 = 345) based on the 1984 American National Election Study includes a selection of work and politics variables that permit preliminary investigation of these issues. Because the work participation questions are asked only on the second wave and respondents were restricted to labor force members, the number of respondents with occupation codes is only about 200. Unfortunately, there is no current American or cross-national survey with which to examine these issues using a larger sample. Even Wright's (cf. 1980, 1985) survey for the "Comparative Project on Class Structure and Class Consciousness" though rich in class variables, has no variables on political behavior. The Quality of Employment Survey, 1972-73, 1977 does include a few political variables. Ideally there should be a panel across the lifecycle like Jennings and Niemi's (1981) that explores the effects of earlier participation (e.g., family, school, organization) on later life participation (e.g., work, politics).

8. The results here are for both reported voting and reported protest activity. Regression is used with the linear probability model rather than probit because regression coefficients are more easily understandable as estimates of the population parameters. Because the standard errors may be underestimated due to heteroskedasticity in regression with a dichotomous dependent variable, the significances of these coefficients may be overstated. However, probit analysis on the data finds that being white collar working class is statistically significant, that being working class is near significant, but that being white collar is not.

9. Though Mallet suggests that advantaged situations lead to conflictual participation (1975, p. 22), Low-Beer suggests that congruent types of work and organizational structures (e.g., work that is personally involving and organizations that encourage participation) tend to encourage political satisfaction, and hence inactivity, among employees (1978, pp. 83, 118, 211). Workers in incongruent situations (partially participatory, partially restrictive) are likely to participate, for instance, in strikes. Low-Beer finds little support for the "spillover" hypothesis from work to politics. and only limited support for the new working class hypotheses regarding political involvement (cf. Gallie, 1978).

10. Eckstein (1966), Pateman (1970), and Mason (1982) elaborate the theoretical connections between spheres. Bowles and Gintis note that there is no "isomorphism of sites and practices" (1986, pp. 98, 100).

11. Low-Beer suggests that the appropriate perspective on organizational activities like strike participation is to see "man as active within his environment and at the same time subject to its influences" (1978, p. 117-19; cf. Bowles and Gintis, 1989). This involves a mixture of the socialization perspective that sees attitudes and behaviors as molded at earlier stages, and "rational action" perspective that considers "man as an active, thinking, rational being." For example, a job socializes those individuals holding it who "follow rational

strategies based on . . . the immediate situations and on preexisting values." People pursue rational strategies based on their organizational situations, but since the process of defining a situation is socially created and maintained, all approaches are not equally likely to be adopted.

12. See Chapter 4 here and Wright and Singlemann (1982) on the factors behind an increase in supervisors in the U.S. and the extent to which these imply closer supervision and more proletarian conditions for employees.

13. Under certain circumstances, however, the combination of degraded conditions and rising consciousness may lead to political activity, what Low-Beer (1978, p. 108) calls the "compensatory hypothesis." "A version of the compensatory hypothesis has been used as an explanation for the intense participation of otherwise nonparticipatory groups in revolutionary movements" (p. 108). An important goal for theorists of equality and activists alike is to identify under what conditions of everyday life those in subordinate situations organize politically.

References

Almond, Gabriel, and Sidney Verba. 1963. *The Civic Culture.* Princeton: Princeton University Press.

Andes, Nancy, and Robert McGinnis. 1984. "An Intermediate-level Classification of American Occupations: A Description and Validations." *Proceedings of the Social Science Section.* Philadelphia: American Statistical Association. August.

American National Election Study, 1984: Pre- and Post-Election Survey File. [Machine-readable data file.] 1986. Conducted by the Center for Political Studies of the Institute for Social Research, The University of Michigan and the National Election Studies, under the overall direction of Warren E. Miller. 2d ICPSR ed. Ann Arbor, Michigan: Inter-university Consortium for Political and Social Research.

American National Election Study, Fall 1985 Pilot Survey File. [Machine-readable data file.] 1986. Conducted by the Center for Political Studies of the Institute for Social Research, The University of Michigan and the National Election Studies, under the overall direction of Warren E. Miller. 1st ICPSR ed. Ann Arbor, Michigan: Inter-university Consortium for Political and Social Research.

Americans View Their Mental Health, 1957. Survey File. [Machine-readable data file.] 1960. Principal Investigator, Gerald Gurin. Conducted by the Survey Research Center of the Institute for Social Research, The University of Michigan under the overall direction of Gerald Gurin. 1st ICPSR ed. Ann Arbor, Michigan: Inter-university Consortium for Political and Social Research.

Americans View Their Mental Health, 1976. Survey File. [Machine-readable data file.] 1980. Principal Investigator, Joseph Veroff. Conducted by the Survey

Research Center of the Institute for Social Research, The University of Michigan under the overall direction of Gerald Gurin. 1st ICPSR ed. Ann Arbor, Michigan: Inter-university Consortium for Political and Social Research.

Aronowitz, Stanley. 1971. "Does the United States Have a New Working Class?" In *The Revival of American Socialism.* Edited by George Fischer, pp. 199-216. New York: Oxford University Press.

Barbalet, J. M. 1986. "Limitations of Class Theory and the Disappearance of Status: The Problem of the Middle Class." *Sociology* 20(4): 557-575.

Bazelon, David. 1963. *Power in America: The Politics of the New Class.* New York: New American Library.

Becker, James F. 1973. "Class Structure and Conflict in the Managerial Phase: I." *Science and Society* 37(3): 259-277.

----------. 1974. "Class Structure and Conflict in the Managerial Phase: II." *Science and Society* 37(4): 437-453.

Bell, Daniel. 1960. *The End of Ideology.* Glencoe, Illinois: Free Press.

----------. 1973. *The Coming of Post-Industrial Society.* New York: Basic Books.

Belleville, Pierre. 1963. *Une nouvelle classe ouvrière.* Paris: R. Juilliard.

Bendix, Reinhard, and Seymour Martin Lipset. 1966. *Class, Status, and Power.* New York: Free Press.

Bingham, Alfred M. 1935. *Insurgent America* New York: Harper.

Birnbaum, Norman. 1969. *The Crisis of Industrial Society.* New York: Oxford University Press.

Blalock, Hubert. 1979. *Social Statistics.* rev. 2d ed. New York: McGraw Hill.

Blauner, Robert. 1960. "Work Satisfaction and Industrial Trends in Modern Society." In *Labor and Trade Unionism.* Edited by Walter Galeson and Seymour Martin Lipset, pp. 339-360. New York: Wiley.

----------. 1964. *Alienation and Freedom.* Chicago: University of Chicago Press.

Bowles, Samuel, and Herbert Gintis. 1976. *Schooling in Capitalist America.* New York: Basic Books.

------------. 1977. "The Marxian Theory of Value and Heterogeneous Labor: A Critique and Reformulation." *Cambridge Journal of Economics* 1(2): 173-192.

------------. 1986. *Democracy and Capitalism.* New York: Basic Books.

------------. 1989. "Contested Exchange: New Microeconomic Foundations of Political Economy." *Politics and Society*, Forthcoming, 1990.

Bowles, Samuel, David Gordon, and Thomas Weisskopf. 1983. *Beyond the Waste Land* Garden City, New York: Doubleday.

Braverman, Harry. 1974. *Labor and Monopoly Capital.* New York: Monthly Review Press.

Bridier, Manuel. 1966. "New Working Class or New Bourgeoisie?" *International Socialist Journal* January/February.

Britten, Nicky, and Anthony Heath, 1983. "Women, Men and Social Class." In Eva Gamarnikov, et al. *Gender, Class and Work.* London: Heinemann.

Budish, Jacob. 1962. *The Changing Structure of the Working Class.* New York: International Publishers.

Bruce-Briggs, B. 1978. *The New Class.* New Brunswick: Transaction.

Burawoy, Michael. 1979. *Manufacturing Consent.* Chicago: University of Chicago Press.

----------. 1985. *Politics of Production.* London: Verso.

Burnham, James. 1941. *The Managerial Revolution.* New York: John Day.

Burris, Val. 1983. "The Social and Political Consequences of Overeducation." *American Sociological Review* 48(4): 454-467.

----------. 1987. "Class Structure and Political Ideology." *Insurgent Sociologist* 14(2): 5-46.

Calvert, Gregory. 1967. "In White America: Radical Consciousness and Social Change." *Guardian* March 25.

----------. 1968. "Internationalism New Left Style." *Guardian* June 8-22.

----------, and Carol Neiman. 1971. *A Disrupted History: The New Left and Capitalism.* New York: Random House.

Calvert, Peter. 1982. *The Concept of Class: An Historical Introduction.* New York: St. Martins.

Carchedi, G. 1975a. "On the Economic Identification of the New Middle Class." *Economy and Society* 4(1): 1-86.

----------. 1975b. "Reproduction of Social Classes at the Level of Productive Relations." *Economy and Society* 4(4): 362-417.

Centers, Richard. 1949. *The Psychology of Social Classes.* Princeton: Princeton University Press.

Chinoy, Eli. 1955. *Automobile Workers and the American Dream.* New York: Random House.

Chomsky, Noam. 1969. *American Power and the New Mandarins.* New York: Pantheon.

Clawson, Dan. 1980. *Bureaucracy and the Labor Process.* New York: Monthly Review Press.

Coleman, Richard, and Lee Rainwater. 1978. *Social Standing in America.* New York: Basic Books.

Corey, Lewis. 1935. *The Crisis of the Middle Class.* New York: Covici, Friede.

Cottrell, Aidan. 1984. *Social Classes in Marxist Theory.* London: Routledge and Kegan Paul.

Coyle, Grace L. 1928. *Present Trends in Clerical Occupations.* New York: Women's Press.

Coyner, Sandra J., and Martin Oppenheimer. 1976. "Scholars and White Collars: A Social History of the Great Debate." Presentation to the annual meeting of the American Sociological Association, New York City, September.

Crompton, Rosemary, and Gareth Jones. 1984. *White Collar Proletariat: Deskilling and Gender in Clerical Work.* Philadelphia: Temple University Press.

Crompton, Rosemary, and Michael Mann. 1986. *Gender and Stratification.* Cambridge, England: Polity Press.

Crompton, Rosemary, and Stuart Reid. 1982. "The Deskilling of Clerical Work." In *The Degradation of Work: Skill, Deskilling and the Labour Process.* Edited by Stephen Hill, pp. 163-78. London: Hutchinson.

Croner, Fritz. 1954. *Die Angestellten in der modernen Gesellschaft.* Frankfurt a.M.: Humboldt-Verlag.

Crozier, Michael. 1971. *The World of the Office Worker.* Chicago: University of Chicago Press.

Dahrendorf, Ralf. 1959. *Class and Class Conflict in Industrial Society.* Stanford, California: Stanford University Press.

Davidson, Carl. 1967. *The Multiversity: Crucible of the New Working Class.* Chicago: Students for a Democratic Society.

Davis, James A. 1975. *The General Social Survey.* Chicago: National Opinion Research Center.

----------. 1976. *Studies of Social Change Since 1948.* Chicago: National Opinion Research Center.

----------, and Tom W. Smith. 1982. *The General Social Survey, Cumulative Codebook, 1972-1982.* Chicago: National Opinion Research Center.

----------, and Tom W. Smith. 1988. *The General Social Survey, Cumulative Codebook, 1972-1988.* Chicago: National Opinion Research Center.

Davis, Mike. 1986. *Prisoners of the American Dream.* London: Verso.

Denitch, Bogdan. 1970. "Is There a 'New Working Class'?" *Dissent* January/February.

Derber, Charles. 1982. "Managing Professionals: Ideological Proletarianization and Mental Labor." In *Professionals at Work: Mental Labor in Advanced Capitalism,* pp. 167-190. Boston: G.K. Hall.

Djilas, Milovan. 1957. *The New Class.* New York: Praeger.

Dreyfuss, Carl. 1938. *Occupation and Ideology of the Salaried Employee.* 2 Vols. New York: Works Progress Administration and Columbia University.

Durkheim, Emile. 1933. *The Division of Labor in Society.* New York: Free Press.

Eckstein, Harry. 1966. *Division and Cohesion in Democracy.* Princeton: Princeton University Press.

Edwards, Richard. 1979. *Contested Terrain.* New York: Basic Books.

Ehrenreich, John, and Barbara Ehrenreich. 1977. "The Professional-Managerial Class." *Radical America* Part I, March/April: 2-22, Part II, May/June: 3-31.

Erikson, Robert. 1984. "Social Class of Men, Women and Families." *Sociology* 18: 500-14.

Fantasia, Rick. 1988. *Cultures of Solidarity: Consciousness, Action, and Contemporary American Workers.* Berkeley: University of California Press.

Freedman, Francesca. 1975. "The Internal Structure of the American Proletariat: A Marxist Analysis" *Socialist Revolution* 5(4): 41-83.

Fuchs, Victor. 1968. *The Service Economy.* New York: Columbia University Press.

Gallie, Duncan. 1978. *In Search of the New Working Class: Automation and Social Integration within the Capitalist Enterprise.* Cambridge, England: Cambridge University Press.

Galbraith, John Kenneth. 1967. *The New Industrial State.* New York: New American Library.

Garnsey, Elizabeth. 1978. "Women's Work and Theories of Class and Stratification." *Sociology* 12(2):223-243.

Gartner, A. and F. Riesman. 1974. *The Service Society and the Consumer Vanguard.* New York: Harper & Row.

Geiger, Theodore. 1949. *Die Klassengesellschaft im Schmelztiegel.* Cologne and Hagan: G. Kiepenheuer.

General Social Survey Survey File, 1972-88 Survey File. [Machine-readable data file]. 1988. Principal Investigator James A. Davis. Study Director, Tom W. Smith. Sponsored by the National Science Foundation. NORC ed. Chicago: National Opinion Research Center (producer), Storrs, CT. Roper Public Opinion Research Center, University of Connecticut (distributor).

Giddens, Anthony. 1973. *The Class Structure of the Advanced Societies.* London: Hutchinson.

Gintis, Herbert. 1970. "The New Working Class and Revolutionary Youth." *Socialist Revolution,* May.

Glenn, Evelyn Nakano, and Roslyn L. Feldberg. 1979. "Proletarianizing Clerical Work: Technology and Organization Control in the Office." In *Case Studies on the Labor Process.* Edited by Andrew Zimbalist, pp. 51-72. New York: Monthly Review Press.

Goldthorpe, John H., David Lockwood, Frank Bechhofer, and Jennifer Platt. 1968. *The Affluent Worker: Industrial Attitudes and Behavior.* Cambridge: Cambridge University Press.

----------. 1968. *The Affluent Worker: Political Attitudes and Behavior.* Cambridge: Cambridge University Press.

----------. 1969. *The Affluent Worker in Class Structure.* Cambridge: Cambridge University Press.

Goldthorpe, John H. 1983. "Women and Class Analysis: In Defence of the Conventional View." *Sociology* 17: 465-88.

Gordon, David M., Richard Edwards, and Michael Reich. 1982. *Segmented Work, Divided Workers: The Historical Transformation of Labor in the United States.* New York: Cambridge University Press.

Gorelick, Sherry. 1977. "Undermining Hierarchy: Problems of Schooling in Capitalist America." *Monthly Review* 29(5): 20-36.

Gorz, Andre. 1964. *Strategie ouvrière et neocapitalisme.* Paris: Editions du seuil.

----------. 1965. "Capitalist Relations of Production and the Socially Necessary Labour Force." *International Socialist Review* August: 415-429.

----------. 1967. *Strategy for Labor.* Boston: Beacon Press.

----------. 1972. "Technical Intelligence and the Capitalist Division of Labor." *Telos* 12: 27-41.

Gottlieb, Robert, David Gilbert, and Gerry Tenney. 1967. "Toward a Theory of Social Change in America--The Port Authority Statement," Presentation to the SDS Conference, Princeton University, February.

Gottlieb, Robert, and Marge Piercy. 1967. "Beginning to Begin to Begin." In *The New Left: A Documentary History.* Edited by Massimo Teodori. Indianapolis: Bobbs-Merrill.

Gouldner, Alvin. 1979. *The Future of Intellectuals and the Rise of the New Class.* New York: Seabury.

Gurin, Gerald, Joseph Veroff, and Sheila Feld. 1960. *Americans View Their Mental Health: A Nationwide Interview Survey.* New York: Basic Books.

----------. 1960. *Americans View Their Mental Health.* [Codebook]. Ann Arbor, Michigan: Institute for Social Research.

Guttman, Louis. 1965. "Facets of Job Evaluation." In *Measures of Occupational Attitudes and Characteristics.* Edited by John Robinson. Ann Arbor, Michigan: Institute for Social Research.

Halberstam, David. 1972. *The Best and the Brightest.* New York: Random House.

Hamilton, Richard F. 1972. *Class and Politics in the United States.* New York: Wiley.

----------. 1982. *Who Voted for Hitler?* Princeton: Princeton University Press.

Harbison, Frederick H., E. Kochling, Frank Cassell and H. Ruebmann, 1955. "Steel Management on Two Continents." *Management Science,* Vol. 1-2, pp. 31-39.

Hill, Stephen (ed.). 1982. *The Degradation of Work: Skill, Deskilling and the Labour Process.* London: Hutchinson.

Hobbes, Thomas. 1985. *Leviathan.* Princeton: Princeton University Press.

Hodges, Donald. 1971. "Old and New Working Classes." *Radical America* 5(1): 11-32.

Howard, Dick. 1969. "French New Working Class Theories." *Radical America* 3(2): 1-19.

----------. 1975. "Preface." In *Essays on the New Working Class,* by Serge Mallet. St. Louis: Telos.

Howe, Louise K. 1977. *Pink Collar Workers.* New York: Avon.

Hyman, Richard, and Robert Price. ed. 1983. *The New Working Class? White-Collar Workers and Their Organizations: A Reader.* London: Macmillan Press.

Jenkins, G. Douglas., et al. 1975. "Standardized Observation: An Approach to Measuring the Nature of Jobs." *Journal of Applied Psychology* 60: 171-81.

Jennings, M. Kent, and Richard G. Niemi. 1981. *Generations and Politics.* Princeton: Princeton University Press.

Kamieniecki, Sheldon, and Robert O'Brien. 1984. "Are Social Class Measures Interchangeable?" *Political Behavior* 6:1.

Karasek, Robert, J. Schwartz and C. Pieper. 1982. "A Job Characteristics Scoring System of Occupational Analysis." Unpublished manuscript. Center for Social Sciences, Columbia University.

Katznelson, Ira. 1981. *City Trenches: Urban Politics and the Pattern of Class in the United States.* New York: Pantheon.

Kautsky, Karl. 1971. *The Class Struggle.* New York: Norton. 1910.

Kerr, Clark, John T. Dunlop, Frederick H. Harrison, and Charles A. Myers. 1964. *Industrialism and Industrial Man.* New York: Oxford University Press.

Klecka, William R. 1980. *Discriminant Analysis.* Beverly Hills: Sage.

Klingender, F. D. 1935. *The Condition of Clerical Labour in Britain.* London: Martin Lawrence.

Kocka, Jurgen. 1980. *White Collar Workers in America, 1890-1940.* Beverly Hills: Sage.

Kohn, Melvin L. 1977. *Class and Conformity: A Study in Values,* revised ed. Homewood, Illinois: Dorsey.

----------. 1976. "Occupational Structure and Alienation." *American Journal of Sociology* 82: 111-129.

----------, and Carmi Schooler. 1983. *Work and Personality.* Norwood, New Jersey: Ablex.

Kraft, Philip. 1979. "The Industrialization of Computer Programming: From Programming to Software Production." In *Case Studies in the Labor Process.* Edited by Andrew Zimbalist, pp. 1-17. New York: Monthly Review Press.

Larson, Magali Serfatti. 1977. *The Rise of Professionalism: A Sociological Analysis.* Berkeley: University of California Press.

Lederer, Emil. 1912. "The Problem of the Modern Salaried Employee: Its Theoretical and Statistical Basis." In *Die Privatangestellten in der modernen wirtschaftensentwicklung.* Tübingen: J.C.B. Mohr (P. Siebeck). [New York, 1937].

Lederer, Emil, and Jacob Marschak. 1926. "The New Middle Class" ("Der neue Mittelstand,") In *Grundriss der Sozialeokonomik.* Sect. IX, Part 1. Tübingen: J.C.B. Mohr (P. Siebeck). [New York, 1937].

Lenin, V. I. 1939. *Imperialism: The Highest Stage of Capitalism.* New York: International Publishers.

----------. 1947. "A Great Beginning." In *Essentials of Lenin.* London: Lawrence and Wishart.

Lipset, Seymour Martin. 1981. *Political Man: The Social Bases of Politics.* exp. ed., Baltimore: Johns Hopkins.

Lockwood, David. 1958. *The Blackcoated Worker.* London: Allen and Unwin.

Loren, Charles. 1977. *Classes in the United States.* Davis, California: Cardinal.

Low-Beer, John R. 1978. *Protest and Participation: The New Working Class in Italy.* Cambridge: Cambridge University Press.

Lundberg, Ferdinand. 1968. *The Rich and the Superrich.* New York: Lyle Stuart.

Mackenzie, Gavin. 1974. "The 'Affluent Worker' Study: An Evaluation and Critique." In *The Social Analysis of Class Structure.* Edited by Frank Parkin. London: Tavistock.

Mallet, Serge. 1963. *La nouvelle classe ouvrière.* Paris: Editions du seuil.

----------. 1975. *Essays on the New Working Class.* St. Louis: Telos.

Mandel, Jay. 1970. "Some Notes on the American Working Class." *Review of Radical Political Economy* Spring: 48-60.

Il Manifesto. 1972. "Technicians and the Capitalist Division of Labor." *Socialist Revolution* 2(3): 65-84.

Mann, Michael. 1986. "A Crisis in Stratification Theory? Persons, Households/Families/Lineages, Genders, Classes and Nations." In Crompton and Mann, 1986.

Marcuse, Herbert. 1972. *Counterrevolution and Revolt.* Boston: Beacon Press.

Marglin, Stephen. 1974. "What Do Bosses Do? The Origins and Functions of Hierarchy in Capitalist Production." *Review of Radical Political Economics* 6: 33-60.

Marx, Karl. 1964. *Selected Writings in Sociology and Social Philosophy.* Edited by Tom Bottomore. New York: McGraw-Hill.

----------. [1867]. 1967a. *Capital, Volume One.* New York: International Publishers.

----------. [1894]. 1967b. *Capital, Volume Three.* New York: International Publishers.

----------. [1857]. 1971. *The Grundrisse,* Edited and translated by David McLellan. New York: Harper Torchbooks.

----------. [1867]. 1976. *Capital, Volume One.* New York: Vintage Press.

----------. 1977. *Karl Marx, Selected Writings.* Edited by David McLellan. Oxford: Oxford University Press.

----------. 1978. *The Marx-Engels Reader,* 2d ed. Edited by Robert Tucker. New York: Norton.

Mason, Ronald. 1982. *Participatory and Workplace Democracy.* Carbondale, Illinois: Southern Illinois University Press.

Meiksins, Peter. 1986. "New Classes and Old Theories: The Impasse of Contemporary Class Analysis." In *Recapturing Marxism: An Appraisal of Recent Trends in Sociological Theory,* Edited by Rhonda Levine and Jerry Lembke, pp. 37-63. New York: Praeger.

----------. 1987. "A Comment on Erik Olin Wright's *Classes.*" Presentation to the annual meeting of the American Sociological Association, Chicago.

Warren E. Miller and Center for Political Studies. 1981. *American National Election Study, 1980.* Ann Arbor, Michigan: Institute for Social Research.

----------. 1985. *American National Election Study, Fall 1985 Pilot Survey.* Ann Arbor, Michigan: Institute for Social Research.

Miles, Michael. 1971. *The Radical Probe: The Logic of Student Rebellion.* New York: Atheneum.

Mills, C. Wright. 1951. *White Collar.* New York: Oxford University Press.

----------. 1959. *The Sociological Imagination.* New York: Oxford University Press.

Morgan, James N. 1977. *The Panel Study of Income Dynamics, Waves VIII-X, Procedures and Tape Codes, Interviewing Years, Supplements, 1975-1977.* Ann Arbor, Michigan: Institute for Survey Research.

--------. 1975. *The Panel Study of Income Dynamics, 1968-1975.* Ann Arbor, Michigan: Survey Research Center.

Mueller, Eva, with Judith Hybels, et al. 1969. *Technological Advance in an Expanding Economy: Its Impact on a Crosssection of the Labor Force.* Ann Arbor, Michigan: Survey Research Center.

Nicolaus, Martin. 1967. "Proletariat and Middle Class in Marx: Hegelian Choreography and the Capitalist Dialectic." *Studies on the Left* 7: 22-49.

Nie, Norman, C. H. Hull, Jean G. Jenkins, Karin Steinbrenner, Dale H. Brent, 1975. *Statistical Package for the Social Sciences,* 2d ed. New York: McGraw-Hill.

Nie, Norman, Sidney Verba, and John Petrocik. 1979. *The Changing American Voter.* enl. ed. Cambridge: Harvard University Press.

O'Connor, James. 1973. *The Fiscal Crisis of the State.* New York: St. Martins.

Oppenheimer, Martin. 1972. "What Is the New Working Class?" *New Politics* 15: 29-43.

----------. 1973. "The Proletarianization of the Professional." In *Professionalization and Social Change, Sociological Review Monograph, Vol. 20.* University of Keele.

----------. 1985. *White Collar Politics.* New York: Monthly Review Press.

Ossowski, Stanislaw. 1963. *Class Structure and the Social Consciousness.* London: Routledge and Kegan Paul.

Packard, Vance. 1959. *The Status Seekers.* New York: McKay.

Panel Study of Income Dynamics Survey File, [Machine-readable data file.] Procedures and tape codes. Waves VIII-X, 1975-77 interviewing years. Principal

Investigator, James N. Morgan. Ann Arbor, Michigan, University of Michigan, Survey Research Center.

Parkin, Frank. 1971. *Class Inequality and Political Order: Social Stratification in Capitalist and Communist Societies.* New York: Praeger.

Pateman, Carole. 1970. *Participation and Democratic Theory.* Cambridge: Cambridge University Press.

Poulantzas, Nicos. 1973. *Political Power and Social Classes.* London: New Left Books.

----------. 1975. *Classes in Contemporary Capitalism.* London: New Left Books.

Piore, Michael J. 1980. "The Technological Foundations of Dualism and Discontinuity." In S. Berger and M. Piore, *Dualism and Discontinuity in Industrial Societies.* Cambridge, England: Cambridge University Press.

Przeworski, Adam. 1977. "Proletariat into a Class: The Process of Class Formation from Karl Kautsky's *Class Struggle* to Recent Controversies." *Politics and Society* 7(4): 343-401.

----------. 1985. *Capitalism and Social Democracy.* Cambridge: Cambridge University Press.

----------, and John Sprague. 1986. *Paper Stones: a History of Electoral Socialism.* Chicago: University of Chicago Press.

Quality of Employment Survey, 1972-73. [Machine-readable data file]. 1975. Data originally collected by Robert P. Quinn, Thomas W. Mangione and Stanley E. Seashore for the Survey Research Center, Institute for Social Research, University of Michigan. Ann Arbor, Mich.: ISR Social Science Archive.

Quinn, Robert P., Stanley E. Seashore, and Thomas W. Mangione. 1975. *Quality of Employment Survey, 1972-1973.* [Codebook]. Ann Arbor, Michigan: Institute for Social Research.

----------, Thomas W. Mangione, and Stanley E. Seashore. 1975. *The Survey of Working Conditions, 1969-1970.* [Codebook]. Ann Arbor, Michigan: Institute for Social Research.

Richta, Radovan, et al. 1969. *Civilization at the Crossroads: Social and Human Implications of the Scientific and Technological Revolution.* White Plains, New York: International Arts and Sciences Press.

Robinson, Robert V., and Jonathan Kelley. 1979. "Class as Conceived by Marx and Dahrendorf." *American Sociological Review* 44: 33-58.

Roemer, John. 1982. *A General Theory of Exploitation and Class.* Cambridge, Massachusetts: Harvard University Press.

----------. 1986. *Analytical Marxism.* Cambridge, Massachusetts: Harvard University Press.

---------. 1988. *Free to Lose: An Introduction to Marxist Economic Philosophy.* Cambridge: Harvard University Press

Roper, Elmo. 1947. *The American Factory Worker.* Fortune Survey Number 58. New York: Roper Associates.

Roslender, Robin. 1981. "Misunderstanding Proletarianization: A Comment on Recent Research." *Sociology* 15(3): 428-430.

Rossi, Peter, et al. 1974. "Measuring Household Social Standing." *Social Science Research* 3: 169-190.

Sabel, Charles. 1982. *Work and Politics: The Division of Labor in Industry.* Cambridge, England: Cambridge University Press.

Schumpeter, Joseph. 1950. *Capitalism, Socialism, and Democracy.* New York: Harper.

Scoville, James G. 1969. "A Theory of Jobs and Training." *Industrial Relations* 9 (October): 36-53.

Shaw, K. E. 1987. "Skill, Control, and the Mass Professions." *Sociological Review* 35(4): 775-94.

Singlemann, Joachim, and Erik Olin Wright. 1978. "Proletarianization in Advanced Capitalist Societies: An Empirical Intervention into the Debate Between Marxist and Post-Industrialist Theorists Over the Transformation of the Labor Process." Presentation to the Conference on the Labor Process. SUNY-Binghamton.

Smith, David N. 1974. *Who Rules the University?* New York: Monthly Review Press.

Smith, Tom W. 1980a. *A Compendium of Trends on General Social Survey Questions.* Chicago: National Opinion Research Center.

----------. 1980b. "Self-Employment: An Analysis of General Social Survey Measures of Employment Status." GSS Technical Report #20. Chicago: National Opinion Research Center.

Sobel, Richard. 1982a. "White Collar Structure and Class." Unpublished dissertation. University of Massachusetts, Amherst.

----------. 1982b. "Working Class Clericals: Blurring the White Collar/Blue Collar Line." Presentation to the World Conference of Sociology, Mexico City, August.

----------. 1984. Review of *The New Working Class? White Collar Workers and Their Organizations*, Edited by Richard Hyman and Robert Price. *Contemporary Sociology* 13 (November): 747-48.

----------. 1986. "From Job Participation to Work Participation to Political Participation: Results from the 1985 Fall NES Pilot." Presentation to the annual meeting of the American Political Science Association, Washington, D.C., August.

----------. 1987. "The Effects of Work Participation on Political Participation: Crossnational Evidence." Presentation to the International Society of Political Psychology, San Francisco, July.

Speier, Hans. 1934. "The Salaried Employee in Modern Society." *Social Research* 1: 111-133.

----------. 1939. *The Salaried Employee in German Society*. New York: Works Progress Administration and Columbia University.

Spenner, Kenneth I. 1983. "Deciphering Prometheus: Temporal Change in the Skill Level of Work." *American Sociological Review* 48(6): 824-837.

Squires, Gregory D. 1979. *Education and Jobs: The Imbalancing of the Social Machinery*. New Brunswick, New Jersey: Transaction.

Stabile, Donald. 1984. *Prophets of Order*. Boston: South End Press.

Stevens, Gillian and Joo Hyun Cho, 1985. "Socioeconomic Indexes and the New 1980 Census Occupational Classification Scheme," *Social Science Review*, 14 (June, 1985), pp. 142-68.

Stone, Katherine. 1974. "The Origins of Job Structures in the Steel Industry." *Review of Radical Political Economics* 6: 113-73.

Survey of Working Conditions, 1969-70. [Machine-readable data file]. 1970. Data originally collected by Robert P. Quinn, Stanley E. Seashore and Thomas W. Mangione for the Survey Research Center, Institute for Social Research, University of Michigan. Ann Arbor, Michigan: ISR Social Science Archive.

Sweezy, Paul. 1942. *The Theory of Capitalist Development*. New York: Monthly Review Press.

----------. 1953. *The Present as History*. New York: Monthly Review Press.

Szelenyi, Ivan, and William Martin. 1988. "The Waves of the New Class Theories." *Theory and Society* 175:645-68.

Szymanski, Albert. 1972. "Trends in the American Working Class." *Socialist Revolution* 2(4): 101-121.

Taylor, D. Garth. 1980. "Procedures for Evaluating Trends in Public Opinion." *Public Opinion Quarterly* 44: 86-100.

Thompson, E. P. 1963. *The Making of the English Working Class.* New York: Vintage.

Touraine, Alain. 1971. *The Post-Industrial Society.* New York: Random House.

Traugott, Michael, and John Katosh. 1981. "The Consequences of Validation and Self-Reported Voting Measures." *Public Opinion Quarterly* 45(4): 519ff.

Urry, John. 1973. "Towards a Structural Theory of the Middle Class." *Acta Sociological* 16(3): 175-187.

U. S. Bureau of the Census. 1970. *Census of Population: General Social and Economic Characteristics.* Washington, D.C.: U. S. Government Printing Office.

----------. 1971. *Subject Reports: Occupational Characteristics,* Volume II, PC(2)-7A. Washington, D.C.: U. S. Government Printing Office.

----------. 1980. *Census of Population: General Social and Economic Characteristics.* Washington, D.C.: U. S. Government Printing Office.

---------. 1984. "Household Wealth and Asset Ownership: 1984." *Current Population Reports,* Series R-70, No. 7. Washington, D.C.: Government Printing Office.

U. S. Department of Labor. 1949. *Dictionary of Occupational Titles,* 2d ed. Washington, D.C.: U. S. Government Printing Office.

----------. 1965. *Dictionary of Occupational Titles,* Third Edition. Washington, D.C.: U. S. Government Printing Office.

----------. 1972. *Wages and Hours of Work of Nonsupervisory Employees in All Private, Non-Farm Industries by Coverage Status under the Fair Labor Standards Act.* Washington, D.C.: U. S. Government Printing Office.

----------. 1977a. *Dictionary of Occupational Titles,* Fourth Edition. Washington, D.C.: U. S. Government Printing Office.

----------. 1977b. *Maximum Wage and Minimum Hour Standards Under the Fair Employment Standards Act.* Washington, D.C.: U. S. Government Printing Office.

----------. 1977c. *Employment and Training Report of the President.* Washington, D.C.: U. S. Goverment Printing Office.

----------. Bureau of Labor Statistics. 1983. "Monthly Labor Review." 60:(April):4.

User Guide to the Panel Study of Income Dynamics. 1985. Ann Arbor, Michigan: Inter-university Consortium for Political and Social Research.

Vallas, Steven P. 1987. "The Labor Process as a Source of Class Consciousness: A Critical Examination." *Sociological Forum* 2(2): 237-256.

Vanneman Reeve, and Lynn Weber Cannon. 1987. *The American Perception of Class.* Philadelphia: Temple University Press.

Veblen, Thorstein. 1965. "The Technicians and Revolution." In *The Portable Veblen,* edited by Max Lerner. New York: Viking.

Verba, Sidney, Norman Nie, and Jae-on Kim. 1978. *Participation and Political Equality.* Cambridge: Cambridge University Press.

Veroff, Joseph, Elizabeth Douvan, and Richard Kulka. 1976. *Americans View Their Mental Health.* Ann Arbor, Michigan: Institute for Social Research.

----------. 1980. *Americans View Their Mental Health.* Ann Arbor, Michigan: Institute for Social Research.

Weber, Max. [1922]. 1968. *Economy and Society.* New York: Bedminster.

Witte, John. 1980. *Democracy, Authority, and Alienation in Work: Worker's Participation in an American Corporation.* Chicago: University of Chicago Press.

Wolfinger, Raymond E. and Steven Rosenstone. 1980. *Who Votes?* New Haven: Yale University Press.

Wright, Erik Olin. 1976. "Class Structure and Income Inequality." Unpublished Dissertation. University of California, Berkeley.

----------. 1977. "Class Structure and Occupation: A Research Note." Madison, Wisconsin: Institute for Research on Poverty.

----------. 1978. *Class, Crisis and the State.* London: Verso.

----------. 1979. *Class Structure and Income Determination.* New York: Academic Press.

----------. 1980. "Class and Occupation." *Theory and Society* 9: 177-214.

----------. 1982. "The Status of the Political in the Concept of Class Structure." *Politics and Society* 11(3): 321-341.

----------. 1985. *Classes.* London: New Left Books.

----------. 1986. "What is Middle About the Middle Class?" in John Roemer, *Analytical Marxism: Studies in Marxism and Social Theory.* New York: Cambridge.

----------, and Joachim Singlemann. 1982. "Proletarianization in the Changing American Class Structure." In *Marxist Inquiries,* edited by Michael Burawoy and Theda Skocpol. Supplement to the *American Journal of Sociology.* 88:S176-S209.

----------, Cynthia Costello, David Hachen, and Joey Sprague. 1982. "The American Class Structure." *American Sociological Review* 47: 709-26.

----------, and Bill Martin. 1987. "The Transformation of the American Class Structure, 1960-1980." *American Journal of Sociology* 93(1): 1-29.

Zimbalist, Andrew, ed. 1979. *Case Studies in the Labor Process.* New York: Monthly Review Press.

Index

About the Author

RICHARD SOBEL is an Assistant Professor of Political Science and a Research Associate of the Roper Center for Public Opinion Research at the University of Connecticut in Storrs. His research involves work and politics, and public opinion and public policy. He is a graduate of Princeton University and the University of Massachusetts in Amherst, and has previously taught at Princeton and Smith College.